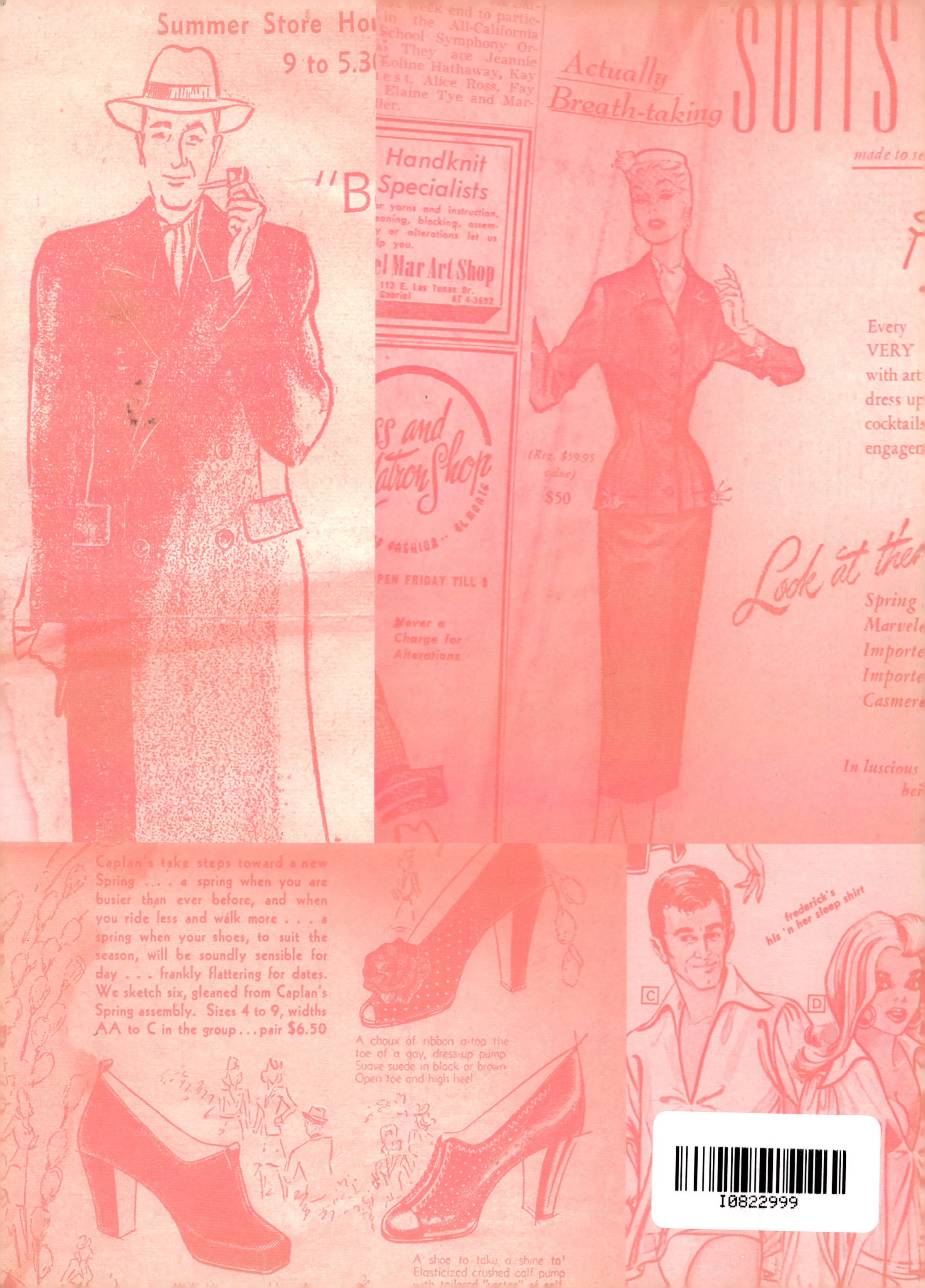
Summer Store Hou
9 to 5.30
"B
week end to partic-
in the All-California
School Symphony Or-
They are Jeannie
Eoline Hathaway, Kay
est, Alice Ross, Fay
Elaine Tye and Mar-
ller.
Handknit
Specialists
yarns and instruction,
blocking, assem-
or alterations let us
you.
Mar Art Shop
113 E. Las Tunas Dr.
Gabriel AT 4-3692
OPEN FRIDAY TILL 9
Never a
Charge for
Alterations
Actually
Breath-taking
SUITS
made to se
(Reg. $59.95
value)
$50
Every
VERY
with art
dress up
cocktails
engagem
Look at the
Spring
Marvele
Importe
Importe
Casmere
In luscious
Caplan's take steps toward a new Spring . . . a spring when you are busier than ever before, and when you ride less and walk more . . . a spring when your shoes, to suit the season, will be soundly sensible for day . . . frankly flattering for dates. We sketch six, gleaned from Caplan's Spring assembly. Sizes 4 to 9, widths AA to C in the group . . . pair $6.50
A choux of ribbon a-top the toe of a gay, dress-up pump Suave suede in black or brown Open toe and high heel!
A shoe to take a shine to! Elasticized crushed calf pump
frederick's
his 'n her sleep shirt
C
D
I0822999

Dorothy's GIRLS

Dorothy's GIRLS

THE PIN-UP ART OF *Dorothy Kahn* FOR FREDERICK'S OF HOLLYWOOD

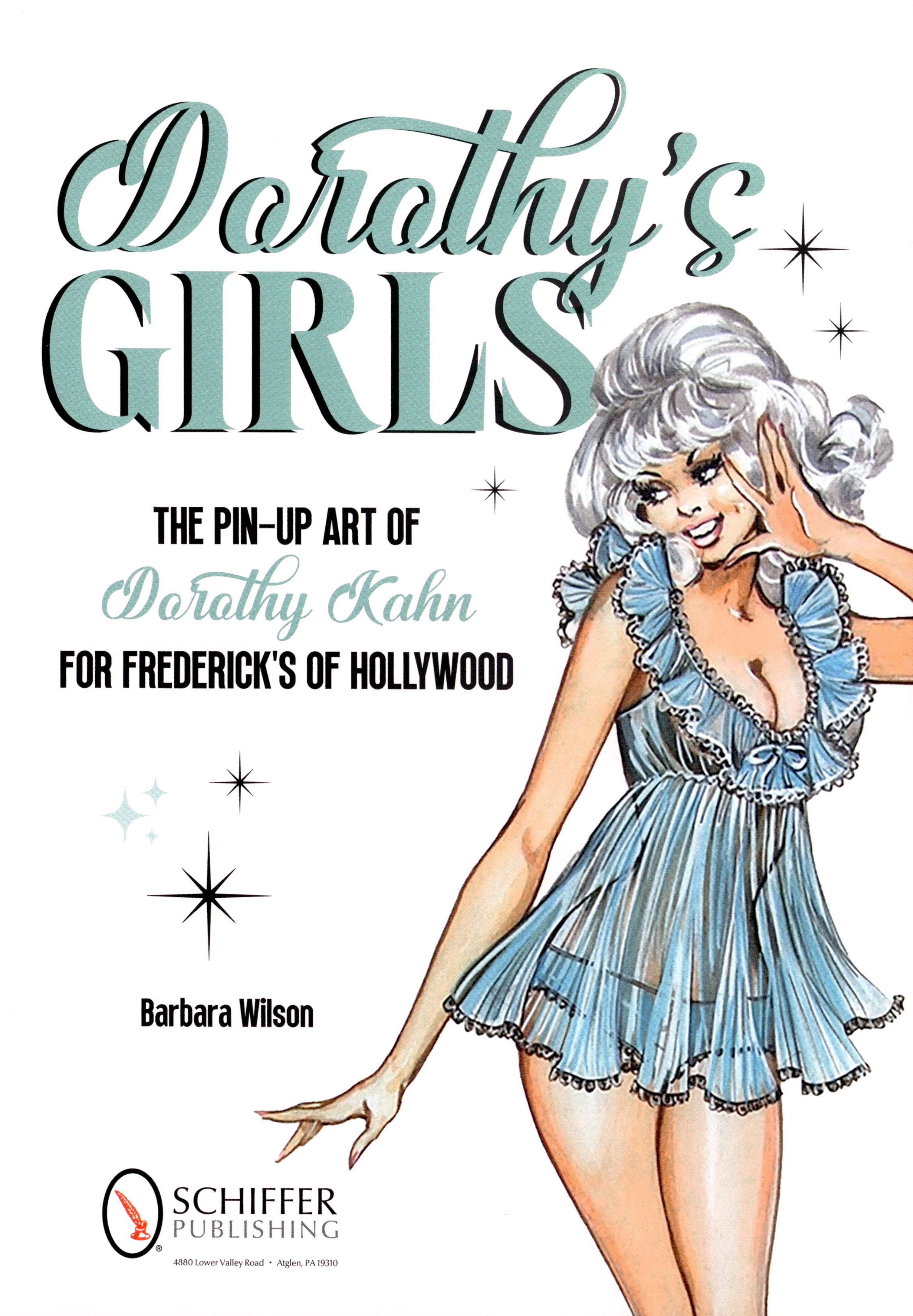

Barbara Wilson

SCHIFFER PUBLISHING
4880 Lower Valley Road • Atglen, PA 19310

Other Schiffer Books on Related Subjects:
Bunny Yeager's Pin-Up Girls of the 1950s, Bunny Yeager, ISBN 978-0-7643-1473-5
Calendar Girls, Sex Goddesses, and Pin-Up Queens of the '40s, '50s, and '60s, Jon Ortner, ISBN 978-0-7643-5788-6

Library of Congress Control Number: 2026932956

Designed by Barbara Wilson
Production design by Molly Shields

Type set in Florida/Warbler Text

ISBN: 978-0-7643-7210-0
ePub: 978-1-5073-0733-5

Printed in China

10 9 8 7 6 5 4 3 2 1

Published by Schiffer Publishing, Ltd.
4880 Lower Valley Road
Atglen, PA 19310
Phone: (610) 593-1777; Fax: (610) 593-2002
Email: info@schifferbooks.com
Web: www.schifferbooks.com

For our complete selection of fine books on this and related subjects, please visit our website at www.schifferbooks.com. You may also write for a free catalog.

Schiffer Publishing's titles are available at special discounts for bulk purchases for sales promotions or premiums. Special editions, including personalized covers, corporate imprints, and excerpts, can be created in large quantities for special needs. For more information, contact the publisher.

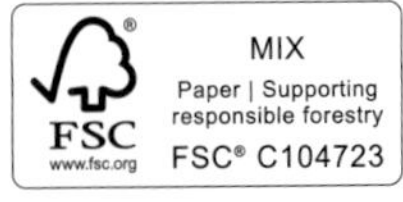

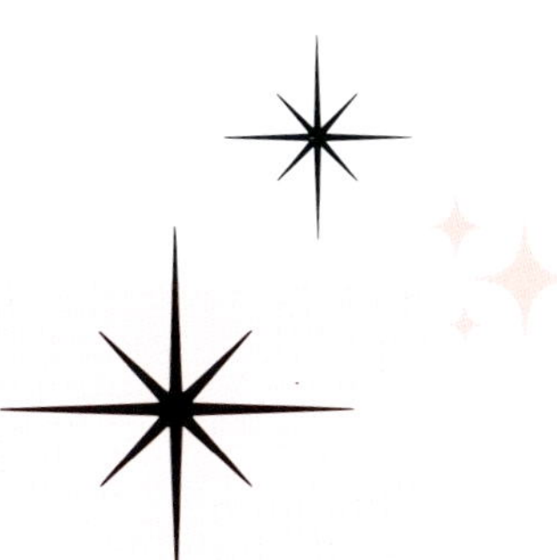

CONTENTS

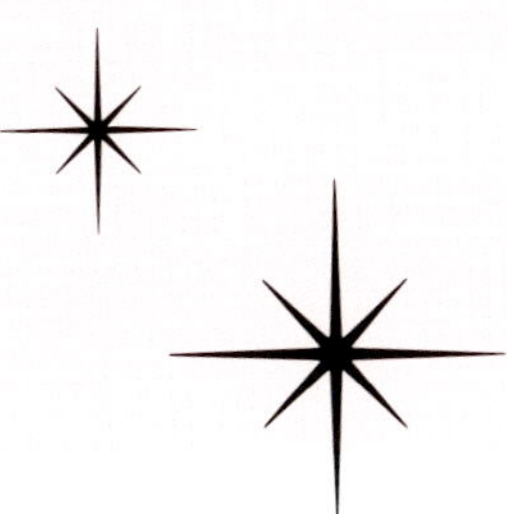

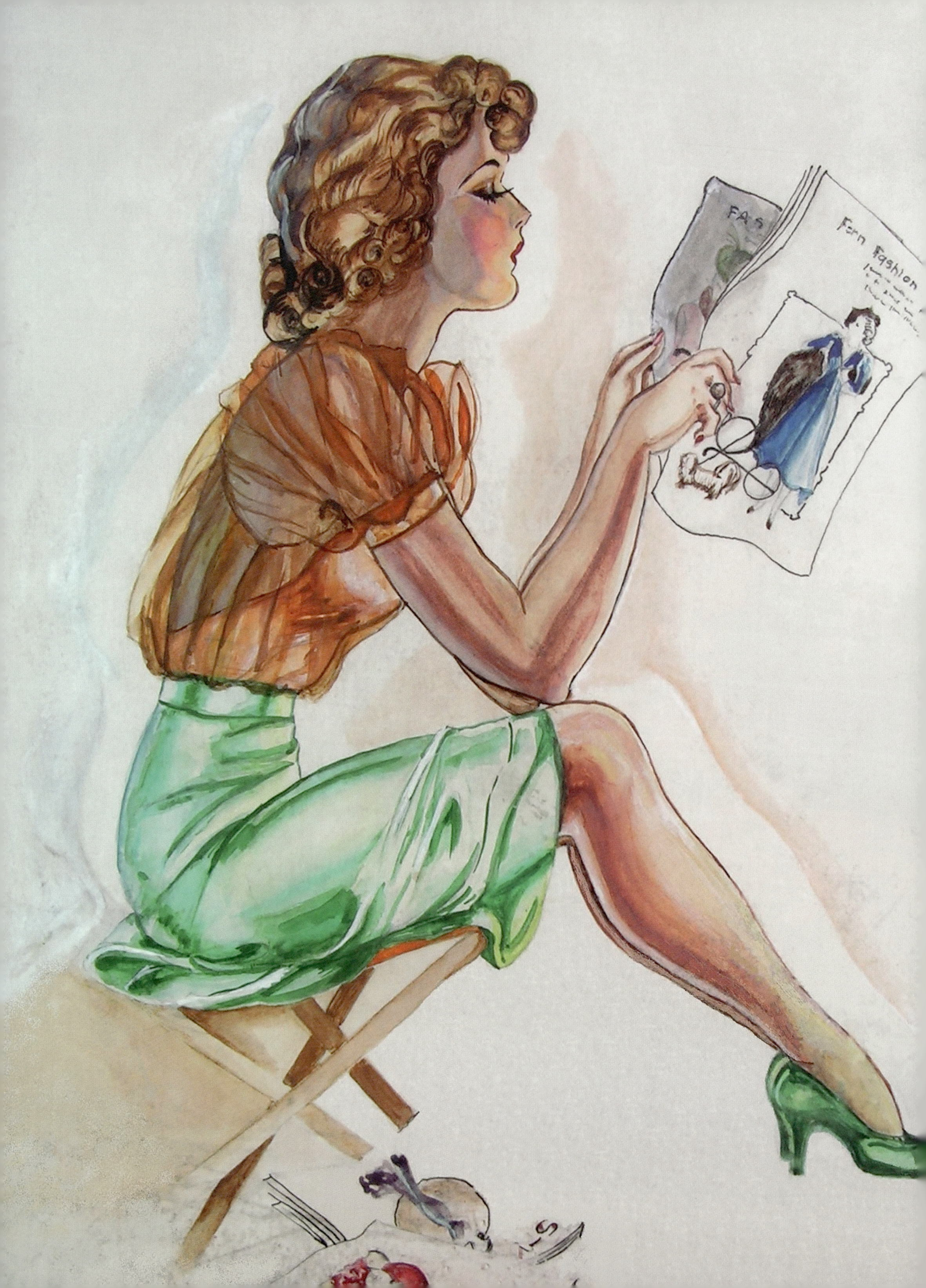
FAS
Fern Fashion

Preface

Welcome to *Dorothy's Girls*, a collection of original pin-up illustrations and artwork by Dorothy Kahn. As her granddaughter, it has been an honor to organize and bring this collection to life, so that her artistry can be shared and appreciated by others.

Dorothy's pin-up illustrations were created in the 1960s and '70s, during a time when the pin-up style was a significant cultural phenomenon. Commissioned by the renowned brand Frederick's of Hollywood, her work captures the essence of the era while showcasing her unique artistic style and undeniable talent.

This project is deeply personal, not just for me but for our entire family. It was a dream of my grandmother's to see her artwork shared with the world and one that she and my beloved mother, Shannon Bacha, worked toward together. In the 1990s, my mother devotedly cared for my grandmother in her late years, while also helping her take the first steps toward preserving her work. Though they are no longer with us, it is a privilege to fulfill this vision and finally share Dorothy's legacy in the way they had always hoped.

Each illustration in this book has been given a name and includes a brief description. In my research, I discovered a handful of vintage Frederick's of Hollywood catalogs featuring Dorothy's artwork. Where possible, I have included images of the catalog pages, along with the original descriptions and prices. This additional context offers a glimpse into how her work was presented and appreciated during its time.

As you flip through the pages of this book, I hope you will gain a deeper appreciation for Dorothy's work, her attention to detail, and her ability to capture the beauty, allure, and personality of her subjects. Her illustrations are not only reflections of the past but are also timeless expressions of art that are sure to continue to inspire and captivate.

This book stands as a tribute to my grandmother, a keepsake for our family, and a treasure for a new generation of art lovers, collectors, and those who appreciate the history of pin-up culture. May it serve as a lasting celebration of Dorothy's life and artistry, cherished and shared for generations to come.

Barbara Wilson
Granddaughter of Dorothy Kahn

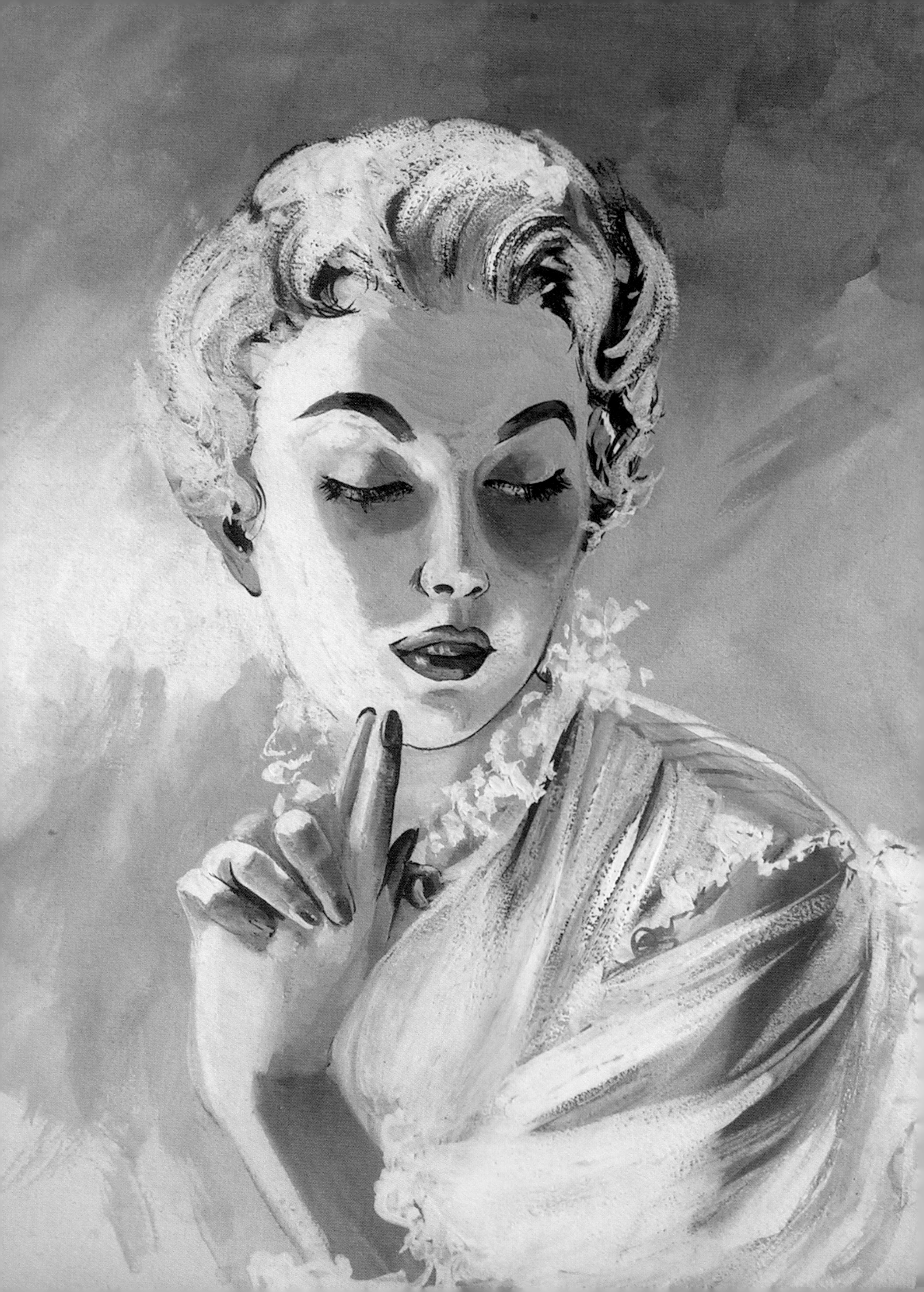

Remembering My Mother

My mom, Dorothy Minerva Kahn, was a rising star in Toronto, Canada, in the early 1940s.

As a young woman in her early twenties, she not only designed dresses for women but also styled and maintained a window display at a Toronto department store, changing the dresses every week.

This led to her opening her own dress shop, and she quickly became somewhat of a local celebrity—and even a bit of a socialite, according to her sister Neysa.

"Oh, she even dated a prince," my aunt Neysa once said.

Things were going great. Dorothy married a hat-manufacturing magnate, and in addition to us two boys, she added a daughter, Shannon, to the family in 1951.

Who would have guessed that one day she'd be painting women in the most provocative attire of the 1960s, after moving to Hollywood, California?

But that's exactly what happened after her husband, Donald, passed away from a stroke in 1952.

Looking for a fresh start, she set her sights on costume design for film and moved to Hollywood—with three children in tow.

Ron Kahn
Son of Dorothy Kahn

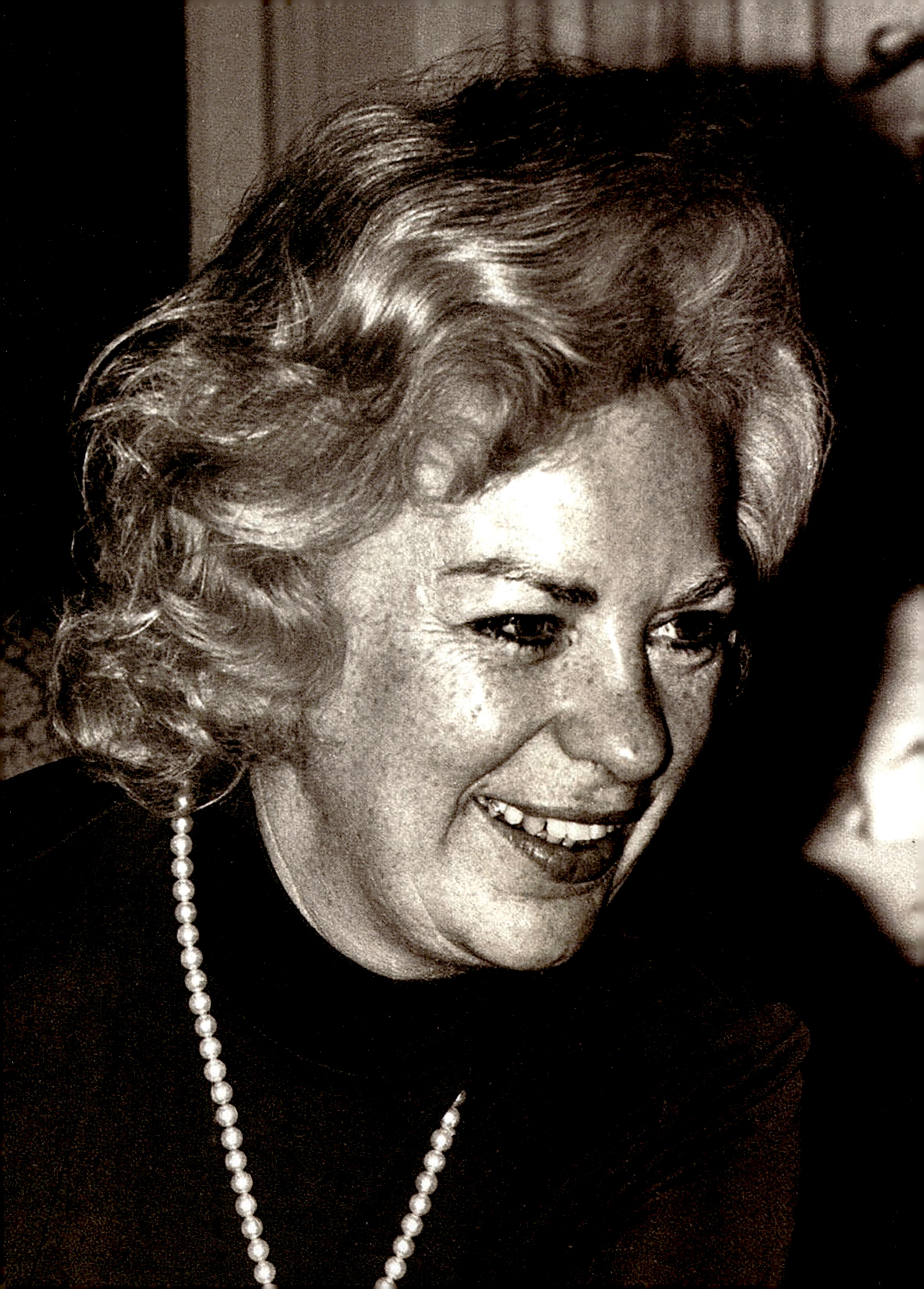

The Artist

DOROTHY KAHN

1922–2000

Canadian-born Dorothy Kahn developed her multifaceted artistic talents at a young age. She was winning art contests as early as grade school. Born in Ottawa, Ontario, in 1922, Kahn attended Ottawa Technical School, where she was an honors art student. She later studied fine art under renowned Canadian artist and teacher Ernest George Fosberg. Her work was commissioned by the Canadian government to illustrate educational books for grade-school students.

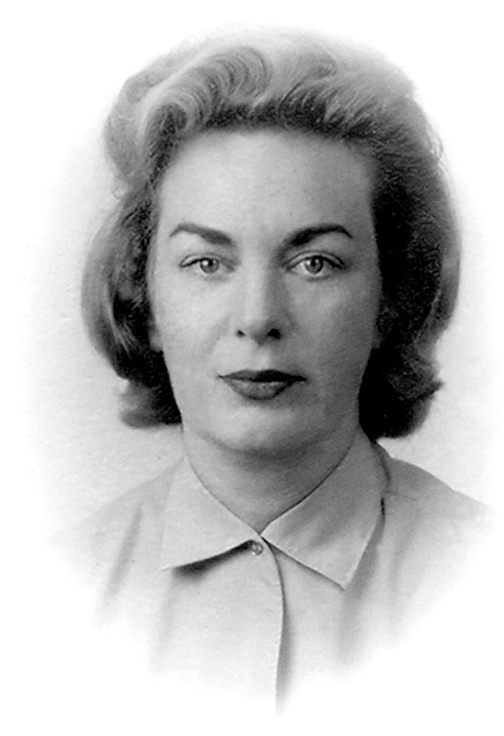

In the late 1930s, Kahn's impressive portraits of King George VI, Queen Elizabeth, Princess Elizabeth, and Princess Margaret were used on Canadian commemorative postage stamps honoring a royal visit to Canada. Kahn became noted for her accomplishments in this field and was often commissioned to paint portraits. Kahn served with the Royal Canadian Navy in World War II as a draftsperson, making technical illustrations for Canadian Corvette jets. Following the war, she became a noted illustrator for newspapers.

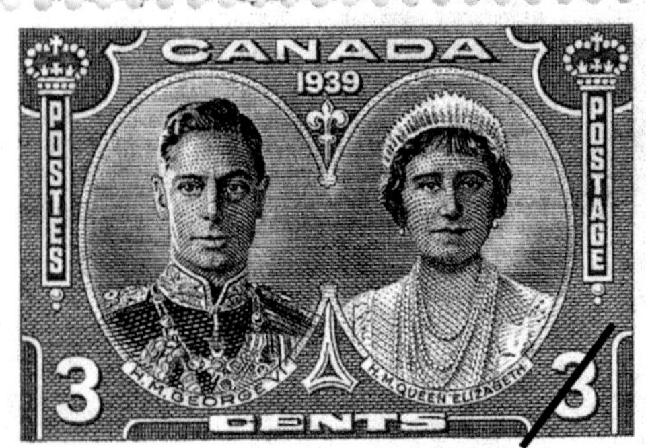

1939 Canadian postage stamp featuring King George VI and Queen Elizabeth, illustrated by Dorothy Kahn

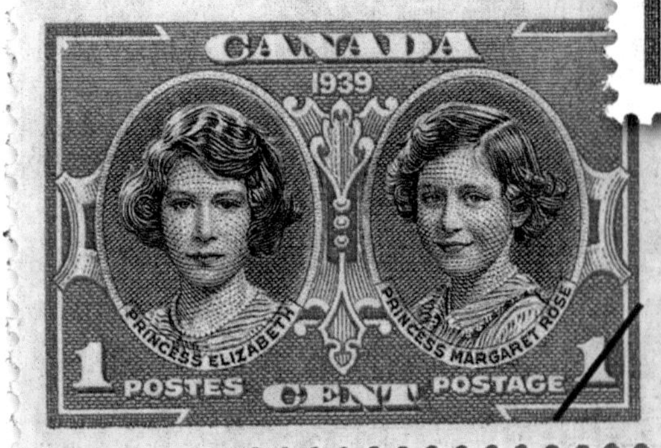

1939 Canadian postage stamp featuring Princess Elizabeth and Princess Margaret Rose

Moving to Toronto in 1948, Kahn started a career as a couturier, opening her own shop where she designed and customized furs, evening wear, lingerie, and entire wardrobes. Kahn's work gained international renown when she moved to California in the 1950s and launched a fifteen-year career with Frederick's of Hollywood. She was the top artist at Frederick's from 1958 to 1973 and created the look and style of the models depicted in the firm's popular catalog. While the women shown in the catalog became known as "Frederick's Girls," they were, thanks to Kahn's crucial contributions, truly "Dorothy's Girls" too.

While raising three children in Hollywood, Kahn worked in her home studio for Frederick's and was active in the selection of fashions she would illustrate for the catalog. She adorned her familiar Frederick's Girl creations with everything from slinky evening wear to swimsuits and sexy lingerie. Her illustrations included every accessory, from hats and wigs to jewelry, gloves, and shoes.

Kahn's famous pin-up-style illustrations became popular all over the world and gained lasting recognition as an icon of the postwar era and the baby boom generation. While in Los Angeles, Kahn met many of Hollywood's elite, including such stars as Jayne Mansfield, Marilyn Monroe, James Mason, Burt Reynolds, and James Arness.

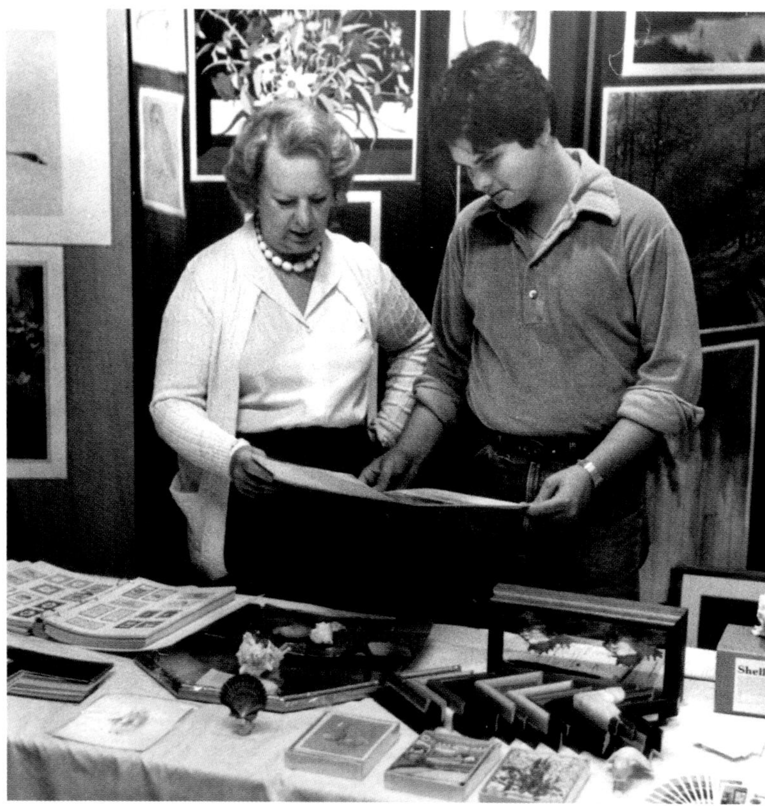

Dorothy in her gallery with nephew Kevin McGrath

In 1964, Frederick's of Hollywood founder Frederick Mellinger wrote to the American consulate in Vancouver to support Dorothy's US residency application. His letter confirms her long-standing freelance role and underscores the value of her contributions to the company.

Mrs. Dorothy Kahn has been working for Frederick's of Hollywood on a free-lance basis as an artist for over seven years. She has done, and will continue to do, a substantial amount of our artwork, but does this on her own premises. We find her work satisfactory and definitely intend to continue our business relationship with her. Her approximate annual earnings have been about $9,000.

—Frederick Mellinger, president of Frederick's of Hollywood (December 7, 1964)

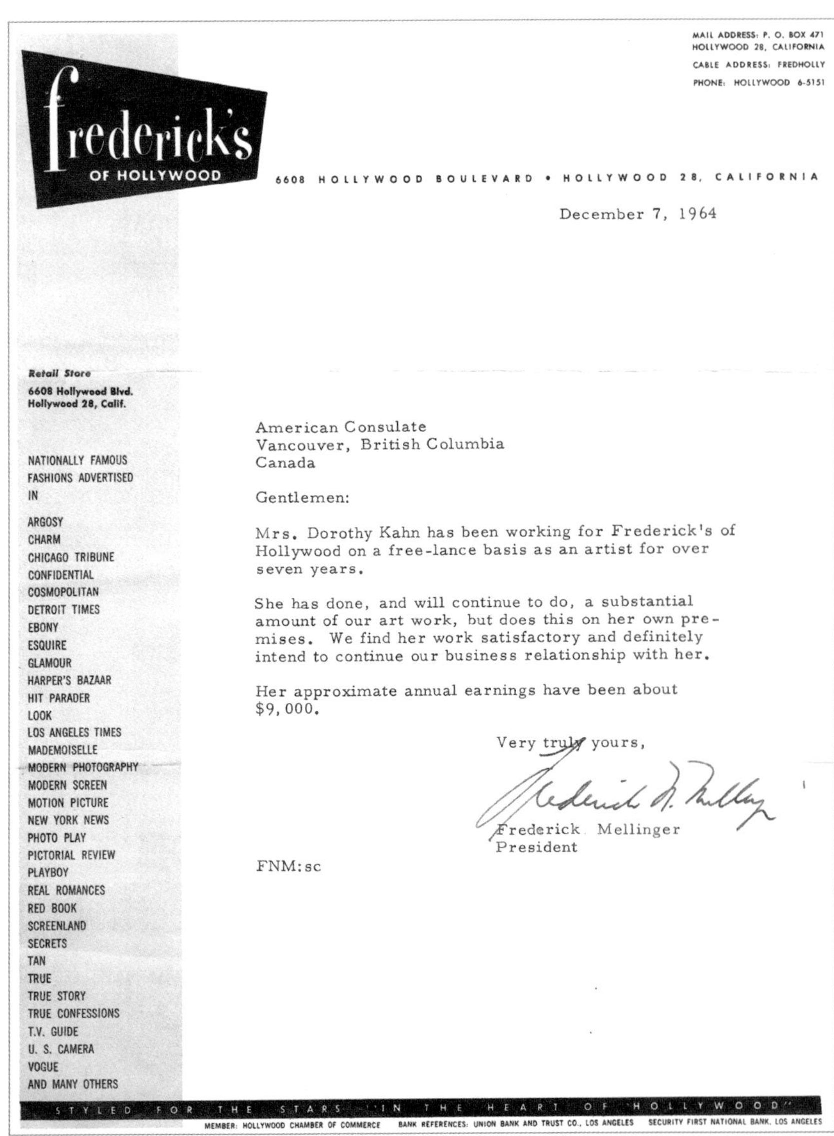

frederick's OF HOLLYWOOD

MAIL ADDRESS: P. O. BOX 471 HOLLYWOOD 28, CALIFORNIA
CABLE ADDRESS: FREDHOLLY
PHONE: HOLLYWOOD 6-5151

6608 HOLLYWOOD BOULEVARD • HOLLYWOOD 28, CALIFORNIA

December 7, 1964

Retail Store
6608 Hollywood Blvd.
Hollywood 28, Calif.

NATIONALLY FAMOUS FASHIONS ADVERTISED IN
ARGOSY
CHARM
CHICAGO TRIBUNE
CONFIDENTIAL
COSMOPOLITAN
DETROIT TIMES
EBONY
ESQUIRE
GLAMOUR
HARPER'S BAZAAR
HIT PARADER
LOOK
LOS ANGELES TIMES
MADEMOISELLE
MODERN PHOTOGRAPHY
MODERN SCREEN
MOTION PICTURE
NEW YORK NEWS
PHOTO PLAY
PICTORIAL REVIEW
PLAYBOY
REAL ROMANCES
RED BOOK
SCREENLAND
SECRETS
TAN
TRUE
TRUE STORY
TRUE CONFESSIONS
T.V. GUIDE
U. S. CAMERA
VOGUE
AND MANY OTHERS

American Consulate
Vancouver, British Columbia
Canada

Gentlemen:

Mrs. Dorothy Kahn has been working for Frederick's of Hollywood on a free-lance basis as an artist for over seven years.

She has done, and will continue to do, a substantial amount of our art work, but does this on her own premises. We find her work satisfactory and definitely intend to continue our business relationship with her.

Her approximate annual earnings have been about $9,000.

Very truly yours,

Frederick Mellinger
President

FNM:sc

STYLED FOR THE STARS "IN THE HEART OF HOLLYWOOD"

MEMBER: HOLLYWOOD CHAMBER OF COMMERCE BANK REFERENCES: UNION BANK AND TRUST CO., LOS ANGELES SECURITY FIRST NATIONAL BANK, LOS ANGELES

Adjusted for inflation, $9,000 in 1964 is the equivalent of nearly $92,000 today—a remarkable sum for a freelance artist at the time that speaks to Kahn's success.

At home in virtually any media from oils to watercolors, Kahn again expanded her horizons when she moved to Ocean Shores, Washington. There she opened her own art gallery, featuring the works of top artists as well as many of her own originals.

Dorothy had a deep love for gardening and flowers, which often inspired her nature-focused paintings.

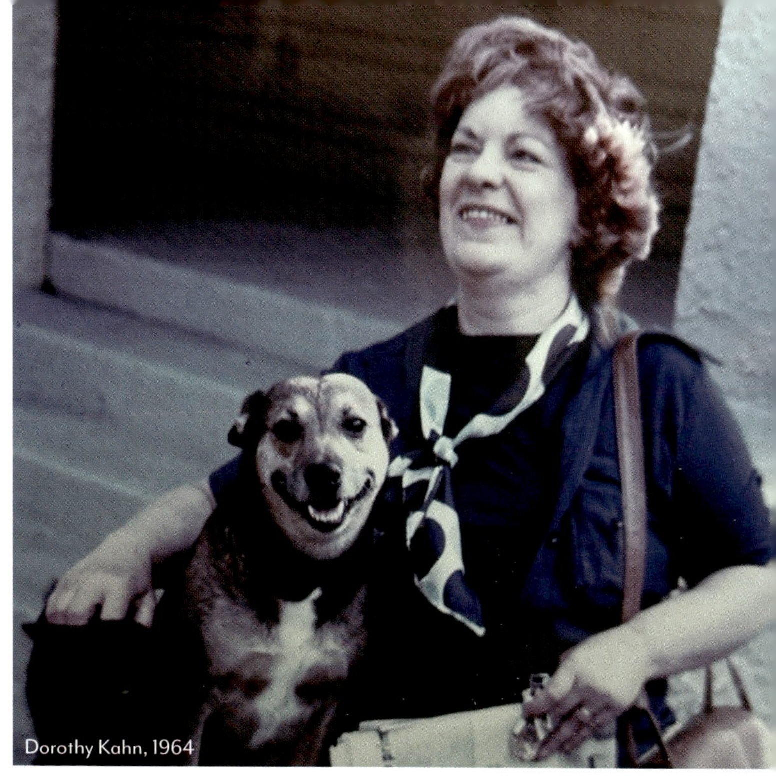
Dorothy Kahn, 1964

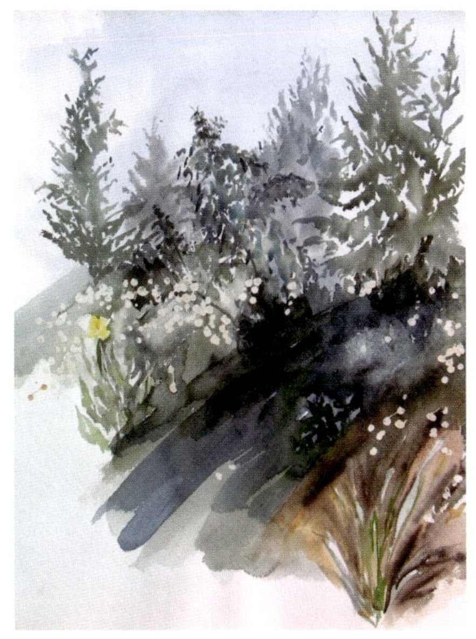

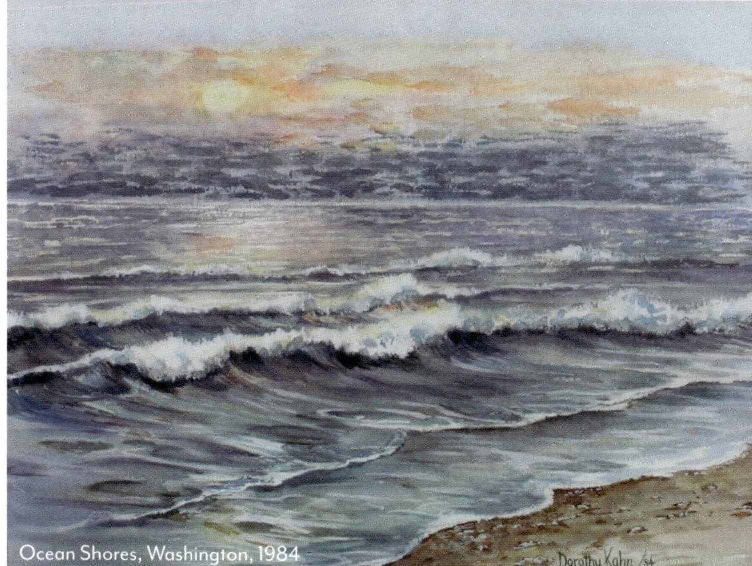

Ocean Shores, Washington, 1984

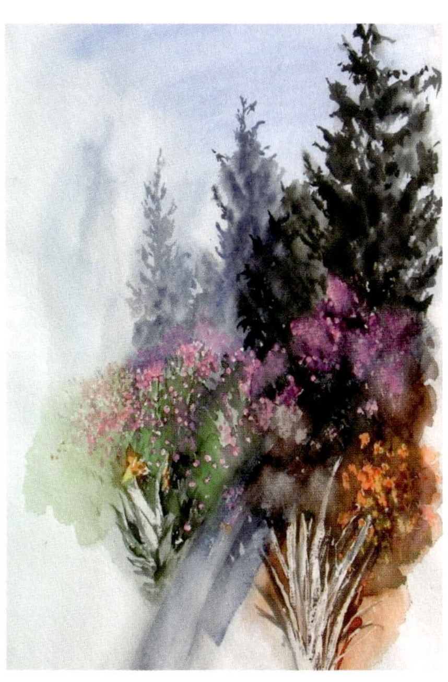

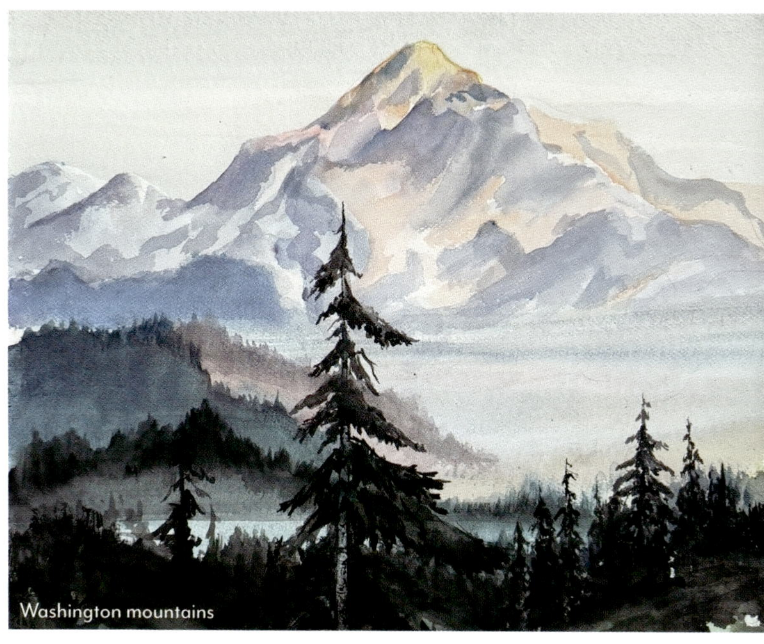
Washington mountains

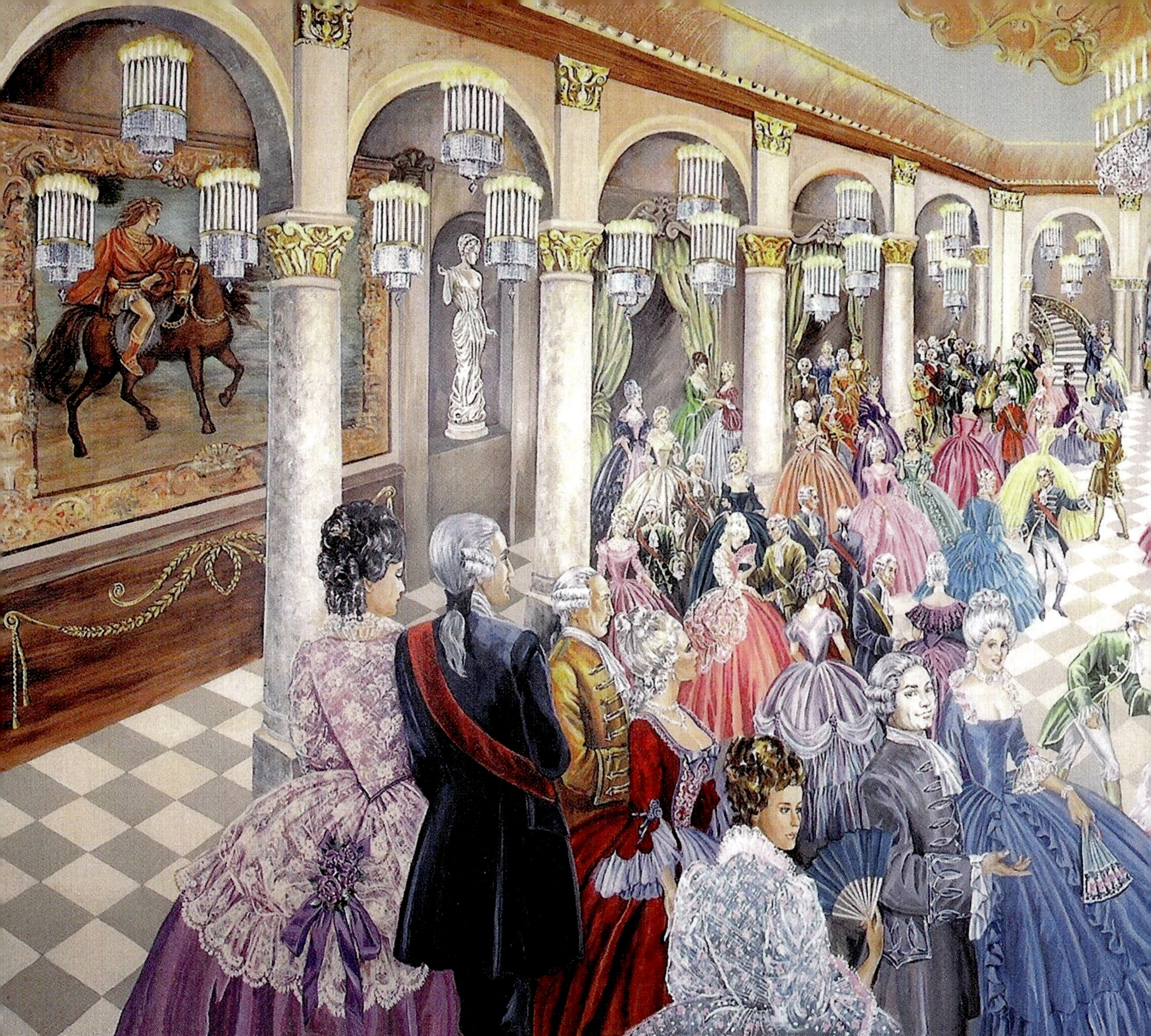

The Royal Ballroom mural by Dorothy Kahn, commissioned by the London Bridge Resort in 1987. This stunning 17-by-7-foot mural captures an elegant palace ball, showcasing Kahn's unparalleled attention to detail and exquisite realism.

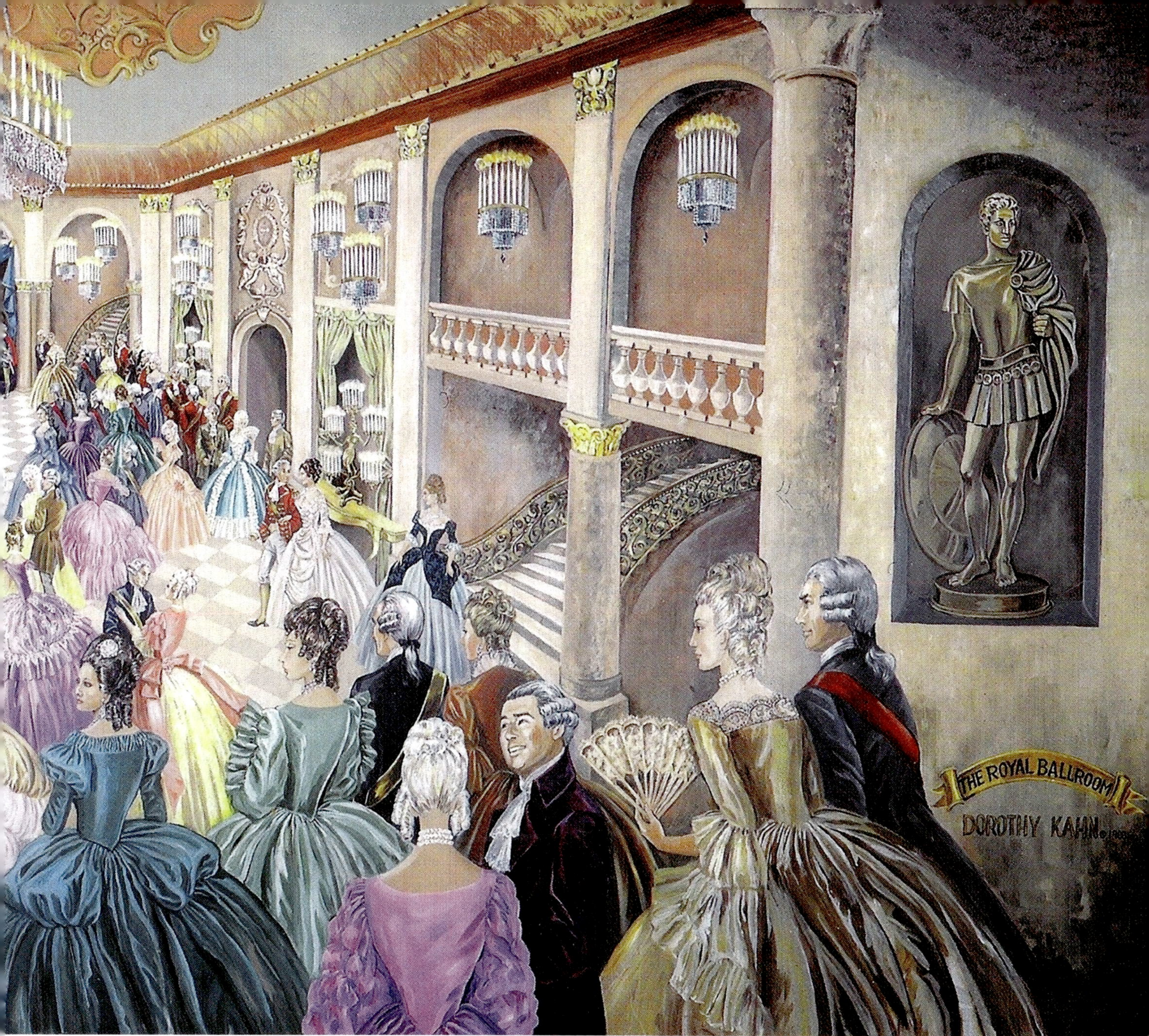

One of Kahn's most famous works has become a major attraction for art aficionados and tourists in Lake Havasu City, Arizona. In 1987, Kahn was commissioned by the London Bridge Resort to paint a large mural for permanent display in its castle-like main building. The result was a magnificent work titled *The Royal Ballroom*. The massive mural, some 17 feet long and 7 feet high, depicts a sweeping panoramic view of an elegant palace ball presided over by royalty. The three-dimensional effect of this exquisitely detailed mural draws viewers right into the scene. The project required untold hours of research and over six months of actual painting to complete, but the intricate lifelike attention to the smallest detail sets a new standard of realism for major murals in the United States. The artistry of Dorothy Kahn has gained international acclaim for over three generations.

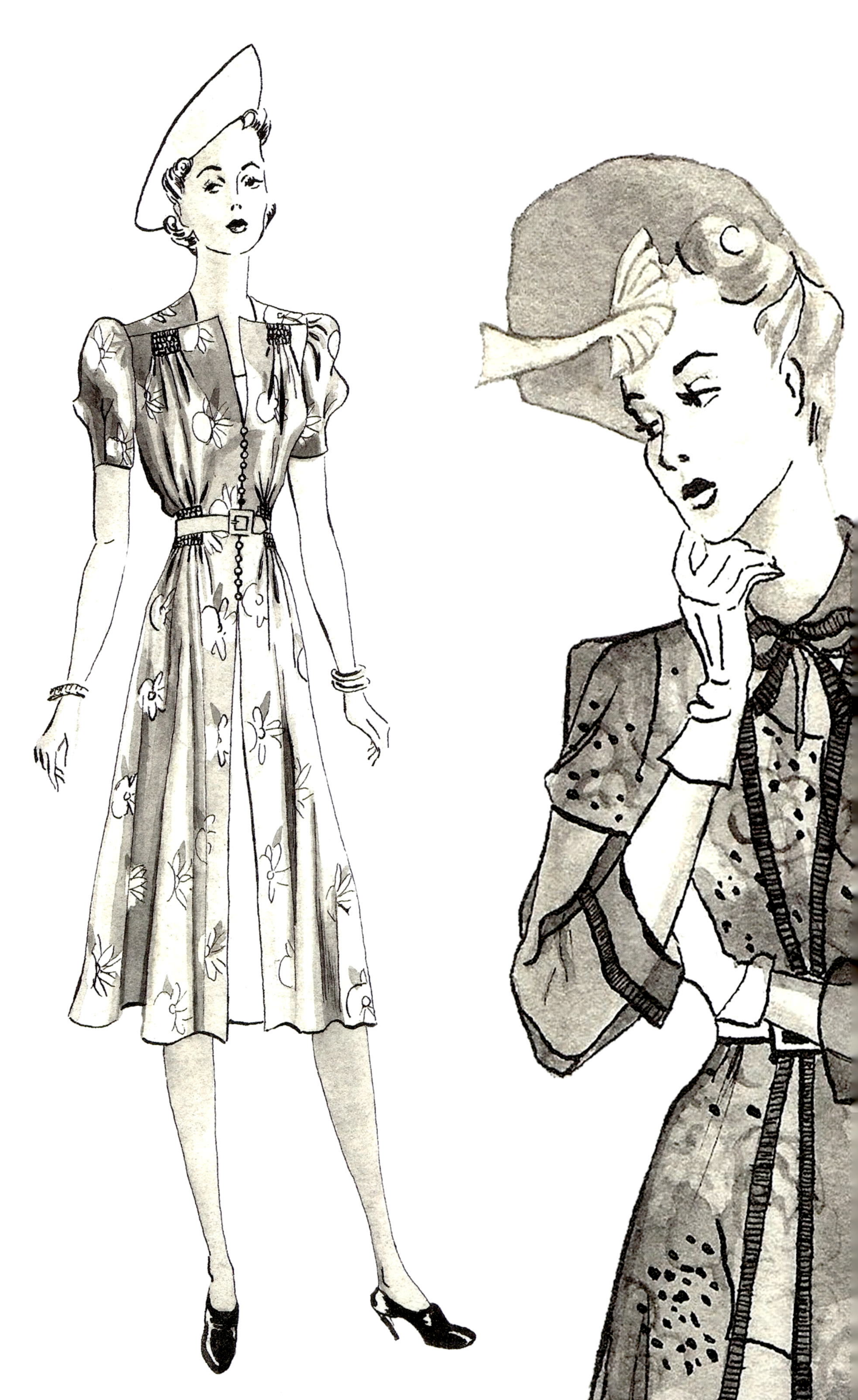

The Illustrations

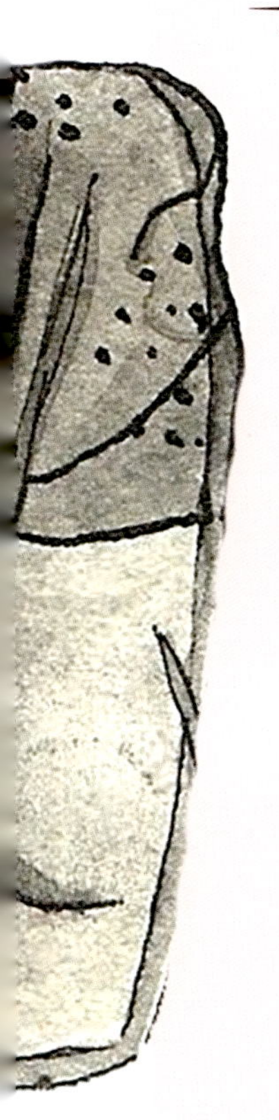

A GLIMPSE INTO THE EARLY YEARS

The following pages feature some of Dorothy's earlier illustrations. These graceful, elegant examples showcase her unmistakable talent. Long before her work became iconic at Frederick's of Hollywood, Dorothy had a natural gift for drawing people. It was something that came so effortlessly to her, and her love for capturing the human form was evident from the very beginning. Whether these pieces were created during her early days with Frederick's or while working as a couturier, they reflect her classic sense of style and ability to bring her subjects to life.

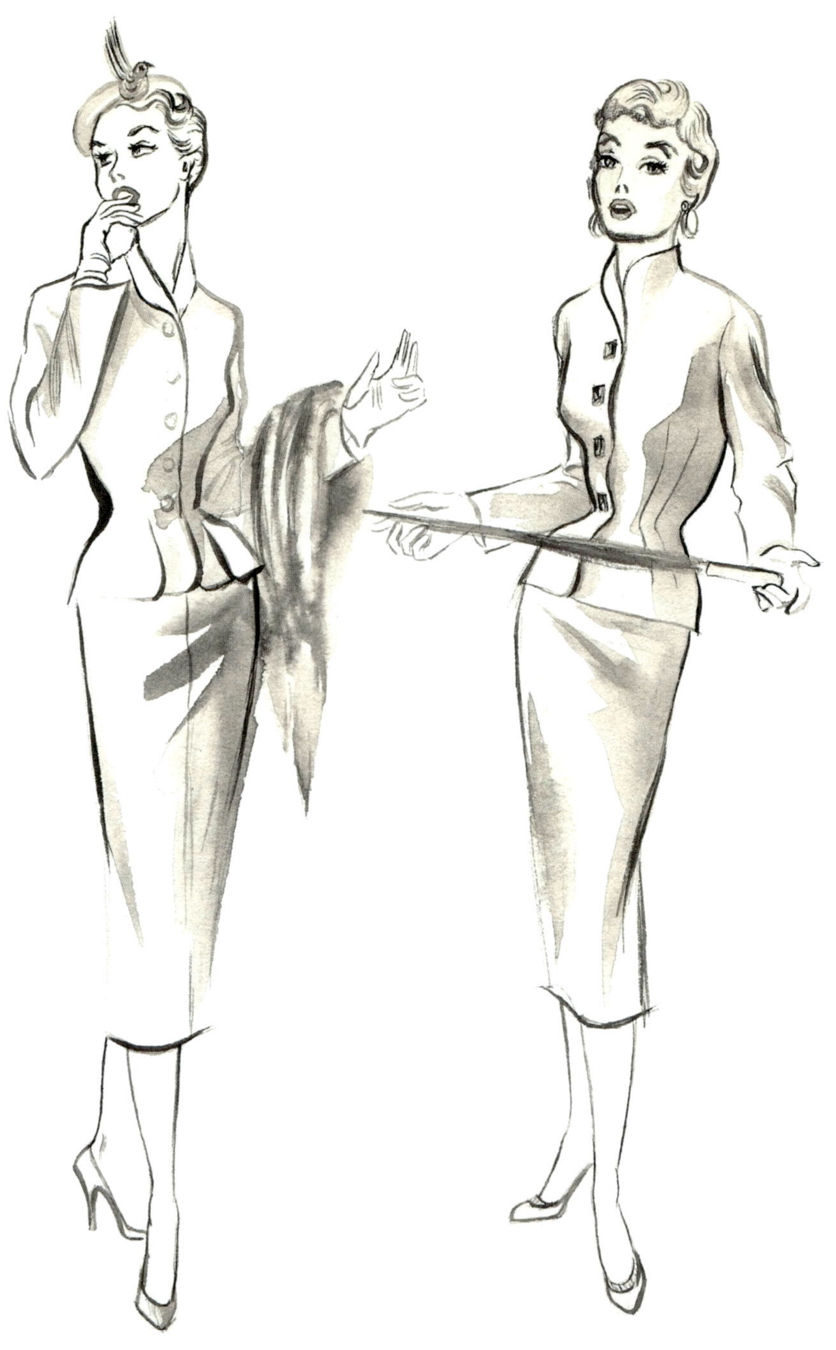

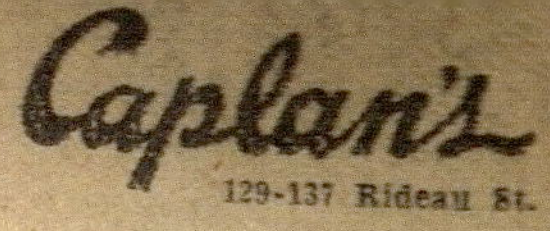

129-137 Rideau St.

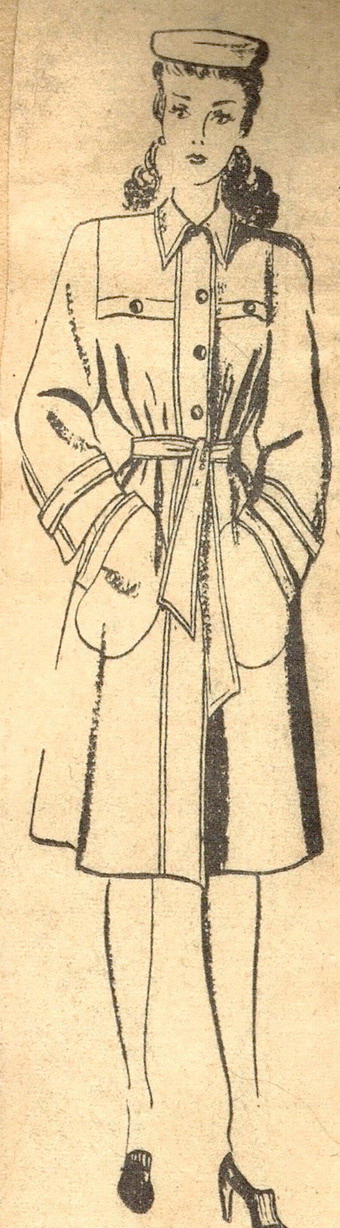

FOR RAINY DAYS AHEAD

Just received! 50 only, Showerproof officer style raincoats. Exactly as illustrated. Hollywood tie-belt. Tabs on sleeves. Gun patch. Deep slash pockets. Eight colors. Sizes 12 to 20. We advise early selection. Exceptional value.

10.95

UMBRELLAS

Handsome rayon umbrellas in pretty prints and plaids. Striking plastic handles.

2.98 to 4.98

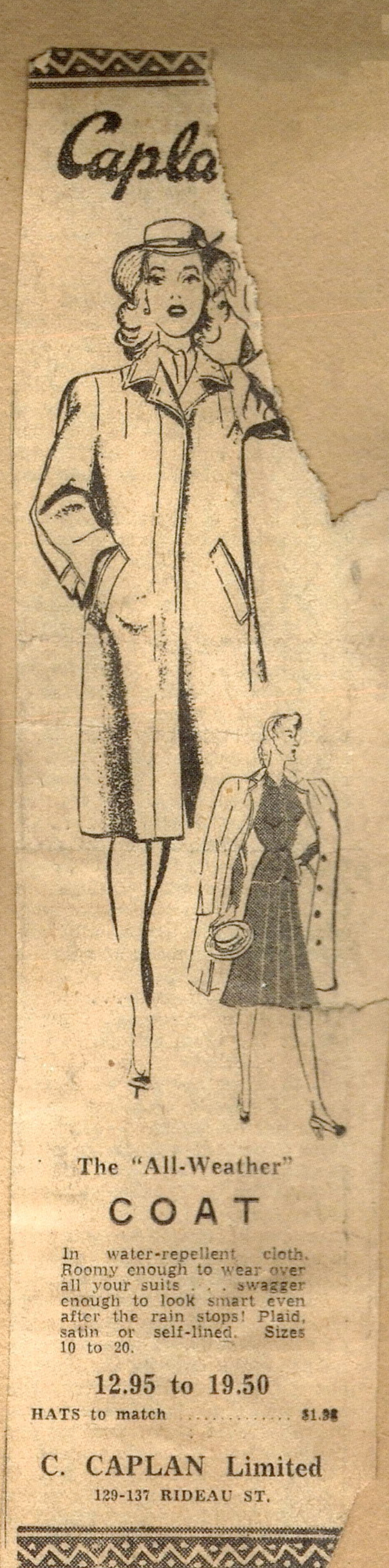

The "All-Weather"

COAT

In water-repellent cloth. Roomy enough to wear over all your suits . . . swagger enough to look smart even after the rain stops! Plaid, satin or self-lined. Sizes 10 to 20.

12.95 to 19.50

HATS to match $1.98

C. CAPLAN Limited

129-137 RIDEAU ST.

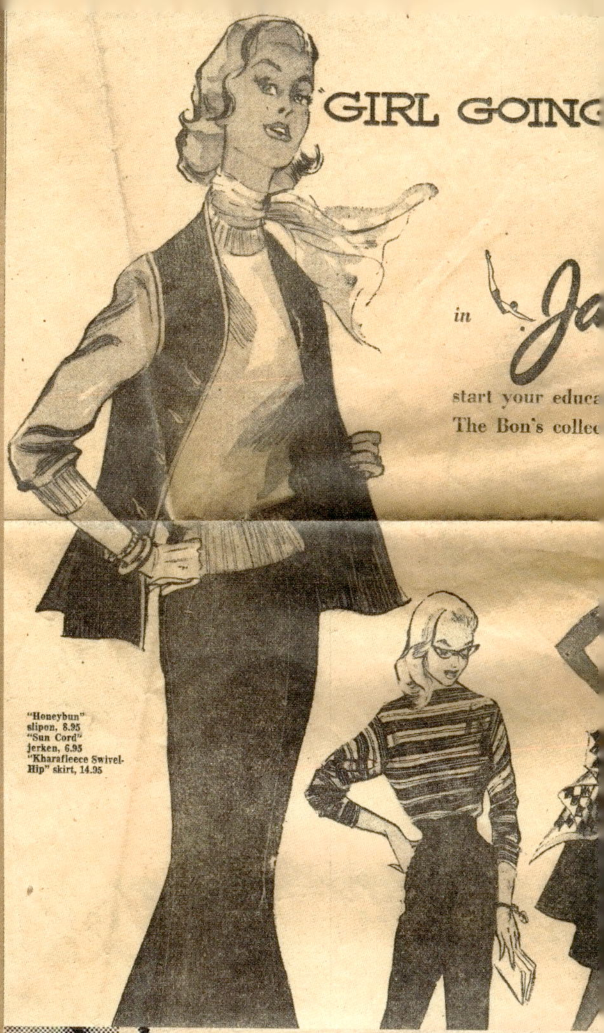

"GIRL GOING

in Ja

start your educa

The Bon's collec

"Honeybun"
slipon, 8.95
"Sun Cord"
jerken, 6.95
"Kharafleece Swivel-
Hip" skirt, 14.95

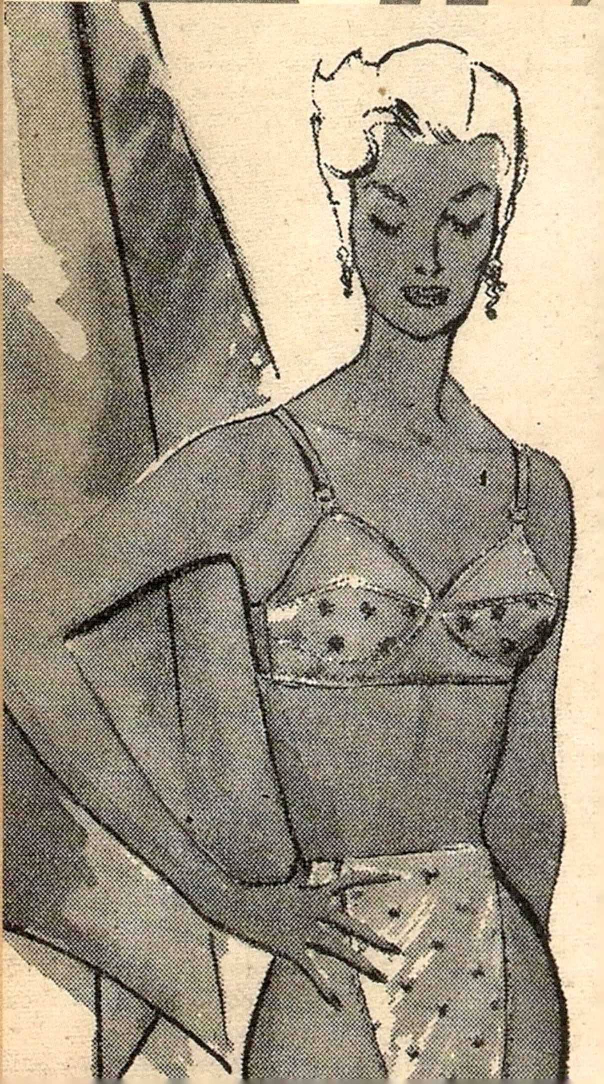

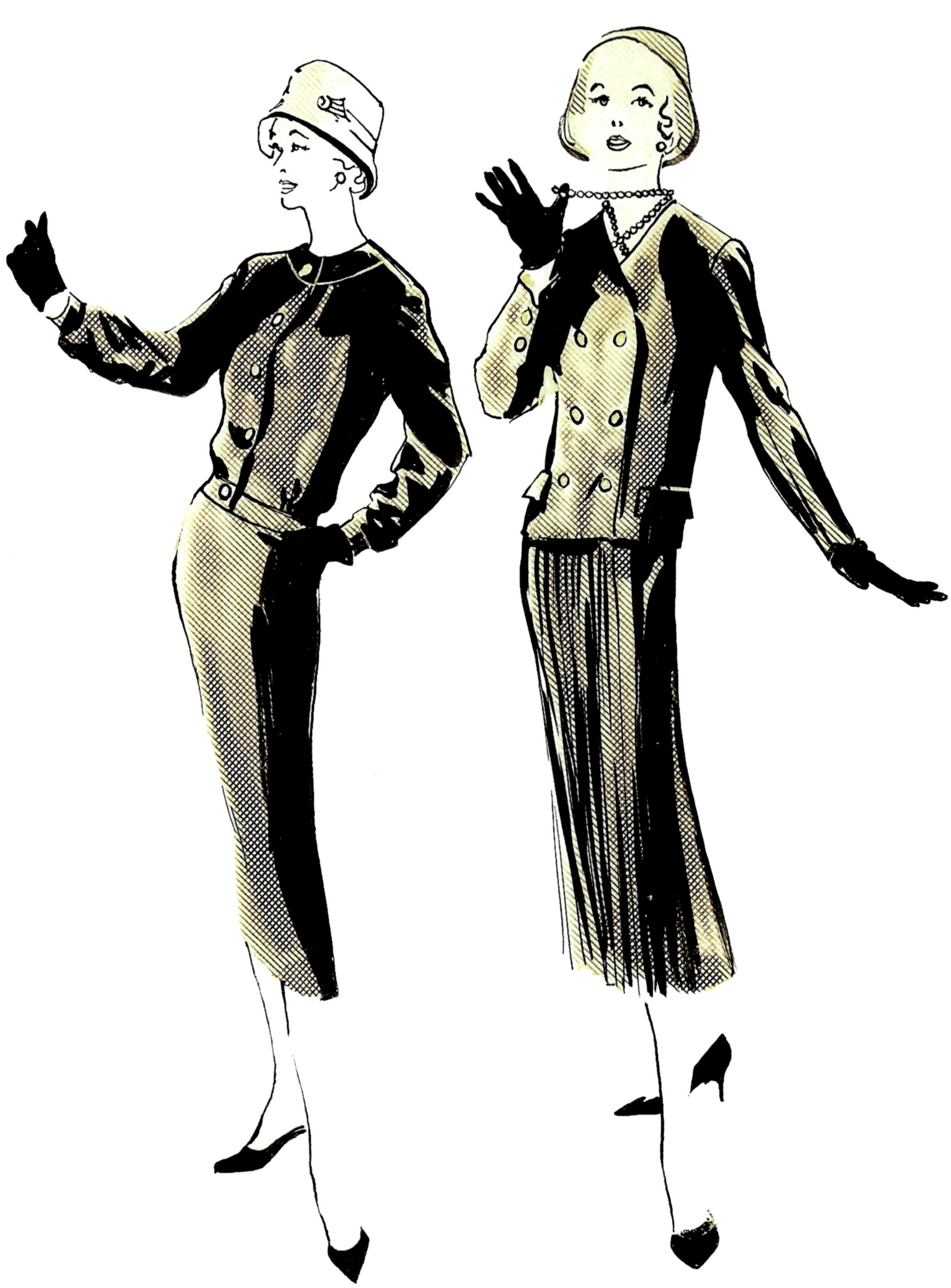

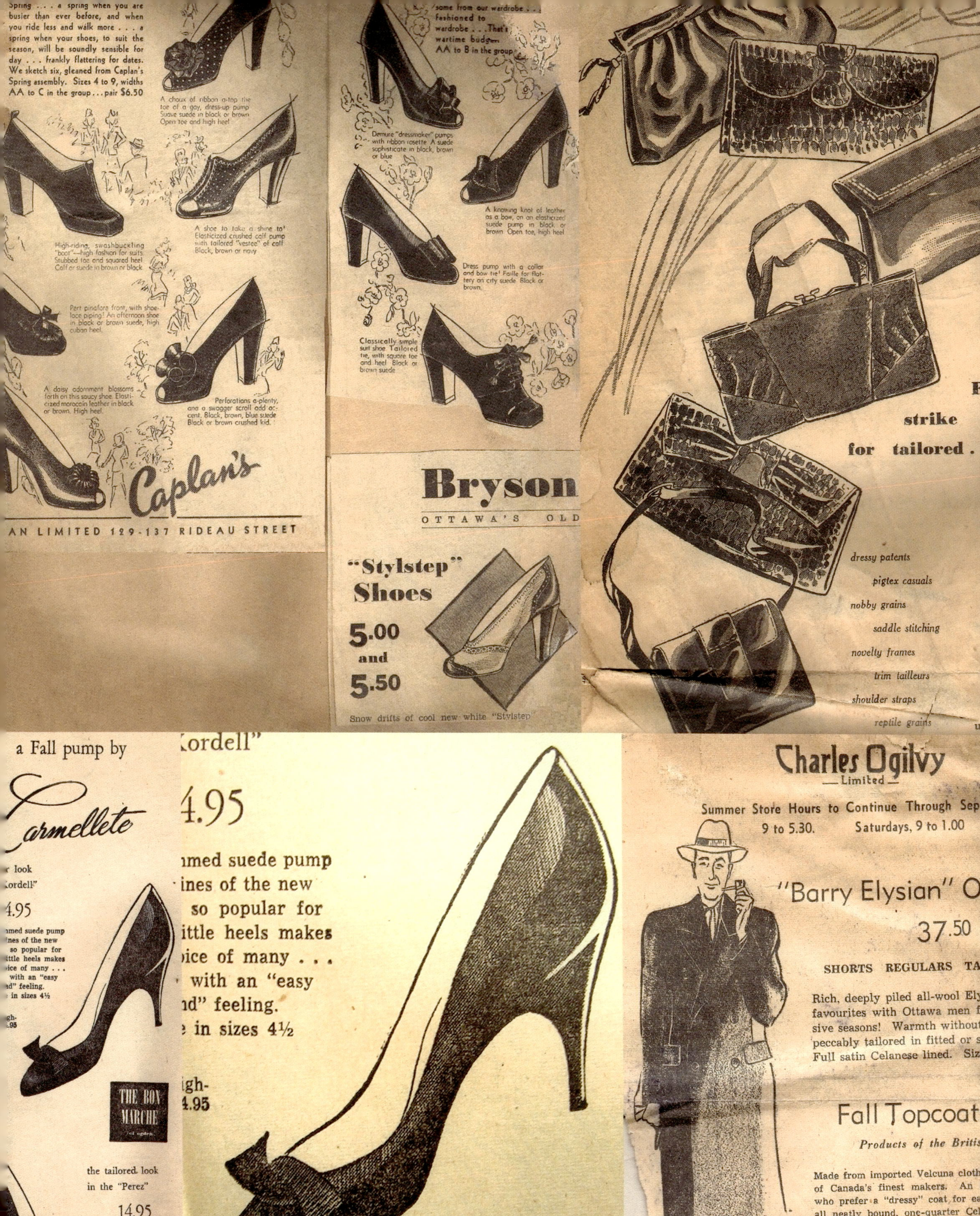

Spring . . . a spring when you are busier than ever before, and when you ride less and walk more . . . a spring when your shoes, to suit the season, will be soundly sensible for day . . . frankly flattering for dates. We sketch six, gleaned from Caplan's Spring assembly. Sizes 4 to 9, widths AA to C in the group . . . pair $6.50
A choux of ribbon a-top the toe of a gay, dress-up pump. Suave suede in black or brown. Open toe and high heel
High-riding, swashbuckling "boot"—high fashion for suits. Stubbed toe and squared heel. Calf or suede in brown or black
A shoe to take a shine to! Elasticized crushed calf pump with tailored "vestee" of calf. Black, brown or navy
Pert pinafore front, with shoe-lace piping! An afternoon shoe in black or brown suede, high cuban heel.
A daisy adornment blossoms forth on this saucy shoe. Elasticized morocco leather in black or brown. High heel.
Perforations a-plenty, and a swagger scroll add accent. Black, brown, blue suede. Black or brown crushed kid.
Caplan's
AN LIMITED 129-137 RIDEAU STREET
same from our wardrobe . . . fashioned to wardrobe . . . That's wartime budget. AA to B in the group
Demure "dressmaker" pumps with ribbon rosette. A suede sophisticate in black, brown or blue
A knowing knot of leather as a bow, on an elasticized suede pump in black or brown. Open toe, high heel
Dress pump with a collar and bow tie! Faille for flattery on city suede. Black or brown.
Classically simple suit shoe. Tailored tie, with square toe and heel. Black or brown suede
Bryson
OTTAWA'S OLD
"Stylstep" Shoes
5.00 and 5.50
Snow drifts of cool new white "Stylstep"
strike
for tailored . . .
dressy patents
pigtex casuals
nobby grains
saddle stitching
novelty frames
trim tailleurs
shoulder straps
reptile grains
a Fall pump by
Carmellete
"Kordell"
4.95
trimmed suede pump lines of the new so popular for little heels makes choice of many . . . with an "easy and" feeling. in sizes 4½
High- 4.95
THE BON MARCHE
the tailored look in the "Perez"
14.95
Black, suede trimmed with faille. And with little buttons on the vamp to provide you with an elegant touch in your new shoe. Sizes 5-9 in AAA to B widths.
Women's Fashion Shoes, Upper Level
THE BON MARCHE
Charles Ogilvy
—Limited—
Summer Store Hours to Continue Through Sep
9 to 5.30. Saturdays, 9 to 1.00
"Barry Elysian" O
37.50
SHORTS REGULARS TA
Rich, deeply piled all-wool Ely favourites with Ottawa men f sive seasons! Warmth without peccably tailored in fitted or s Full satin Celanese lined. Siz
Fall Topcoat
Products of the Britis
Made from imported Velcuna cloth of Canada's finest makers. An who prefer a "dressy" coat for ea all neatly bound, one-quarter Cel raglan, set-in sleeve, slash poc green. 35 to 42.
Men's Suits
35.00

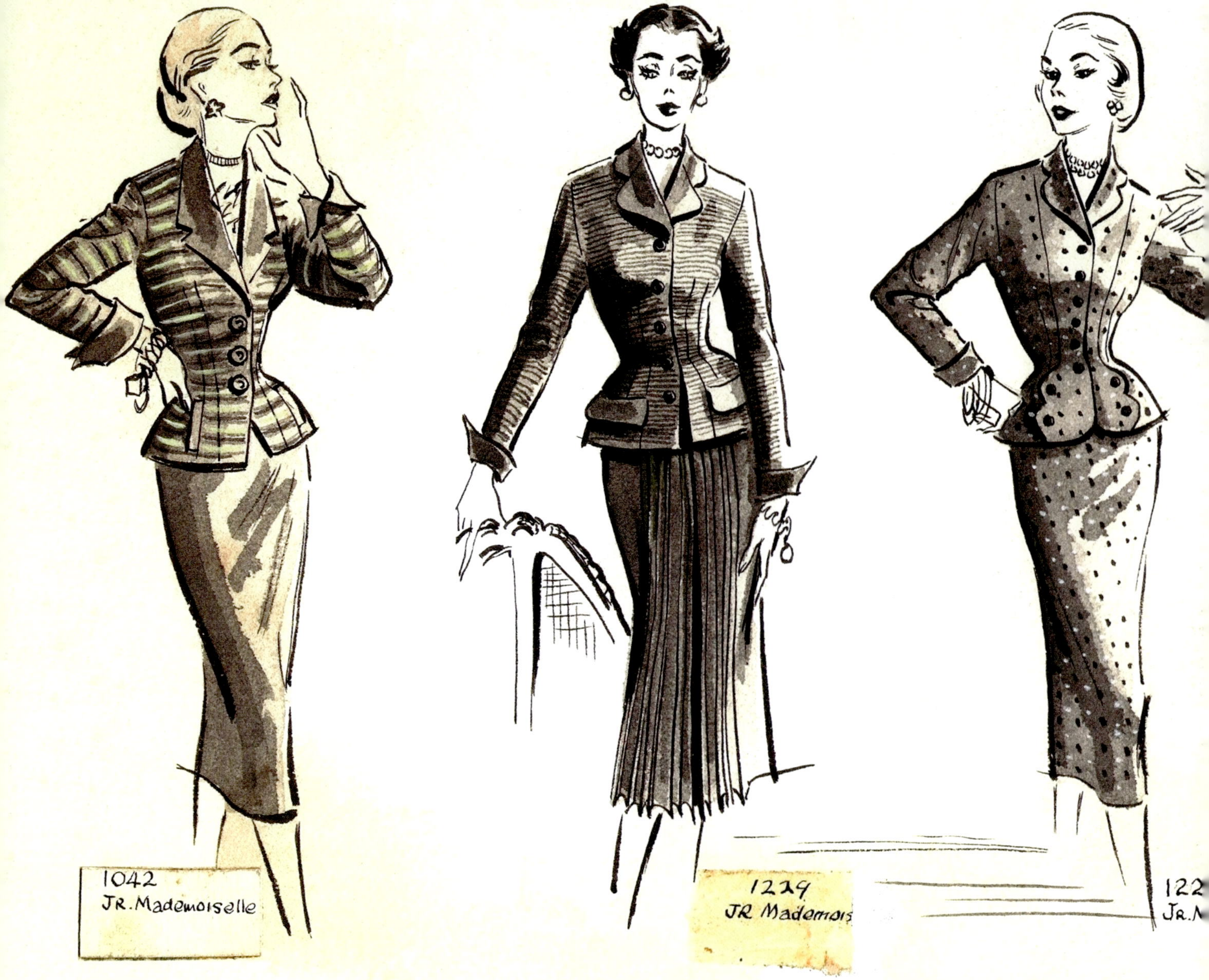

1042
JR. Mademoiselle

1229
JR Mademois

122
JR. M

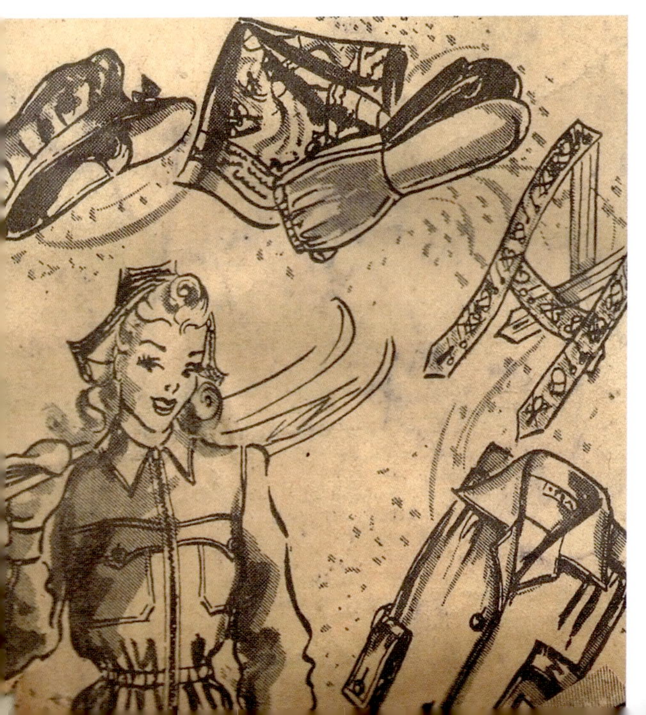

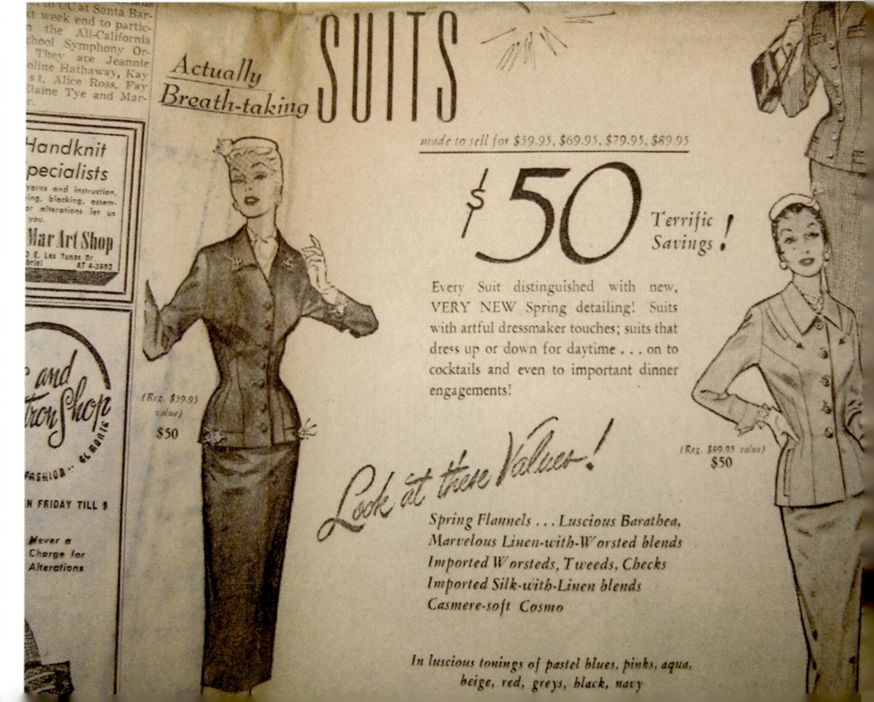

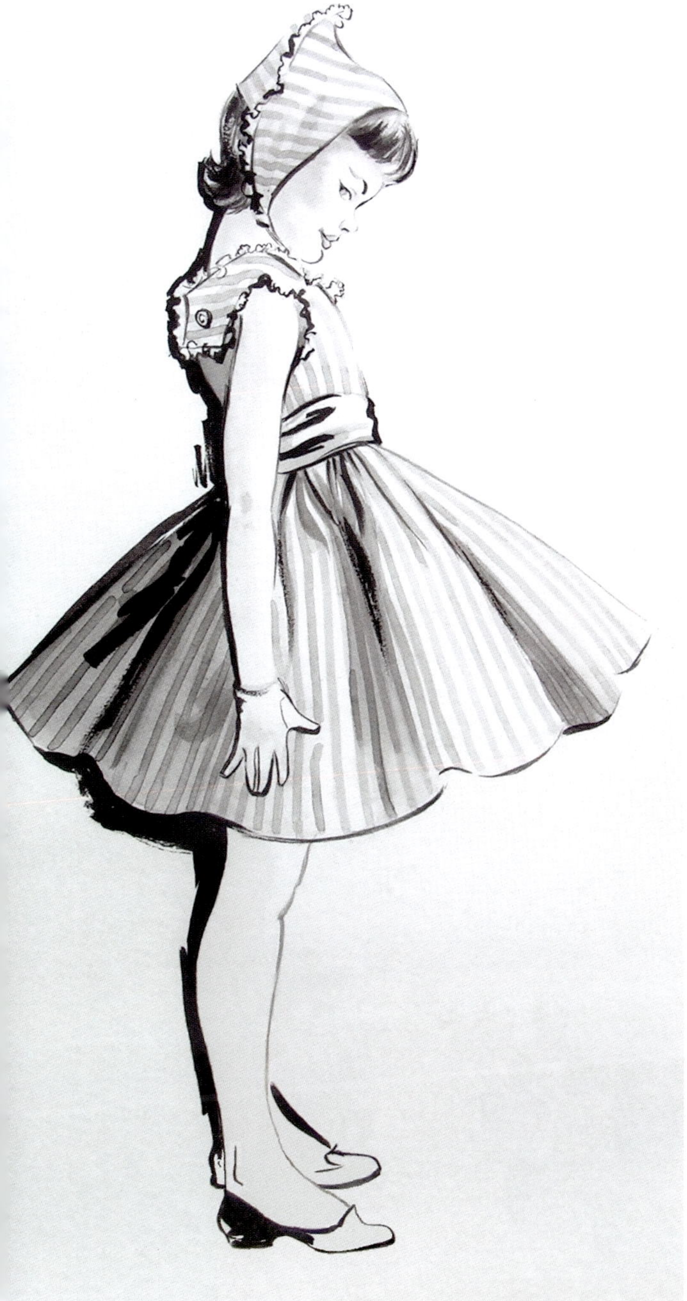

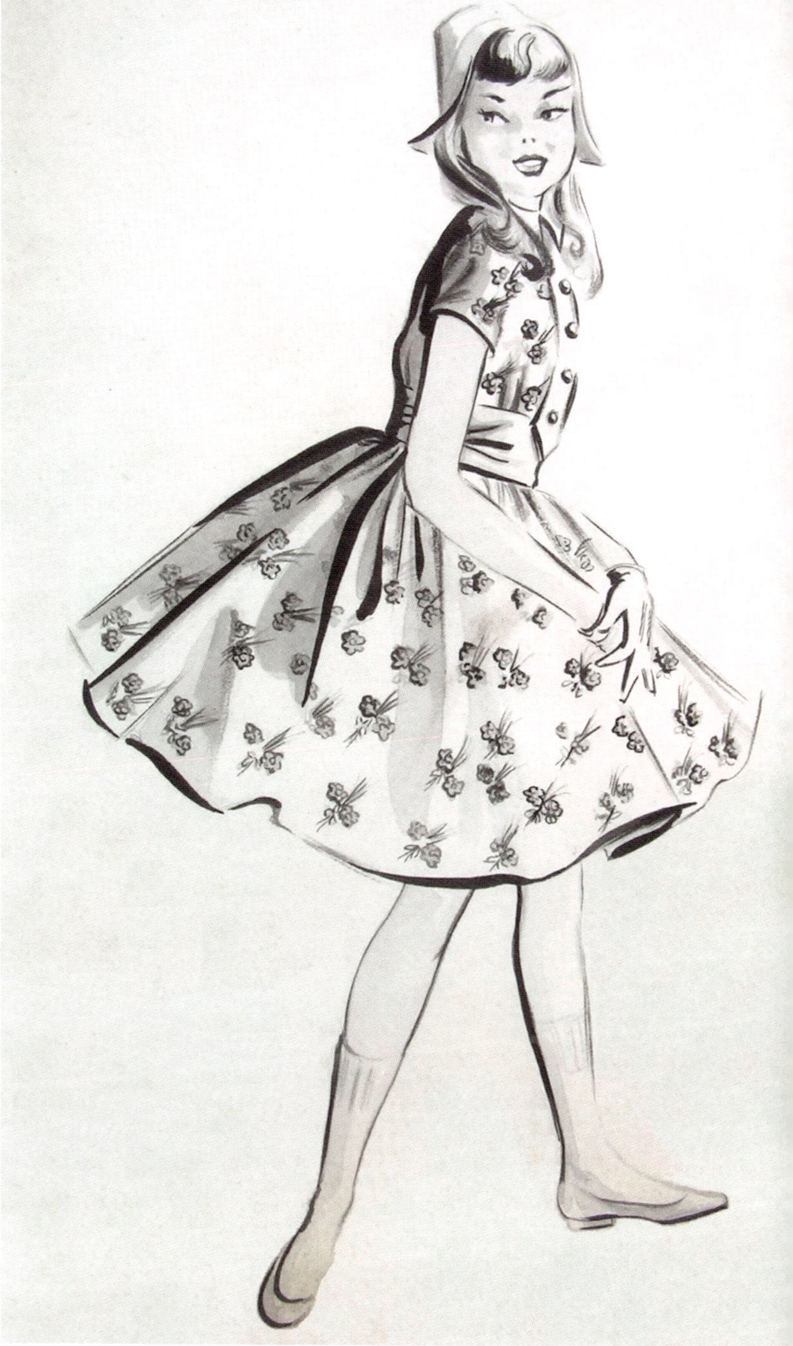

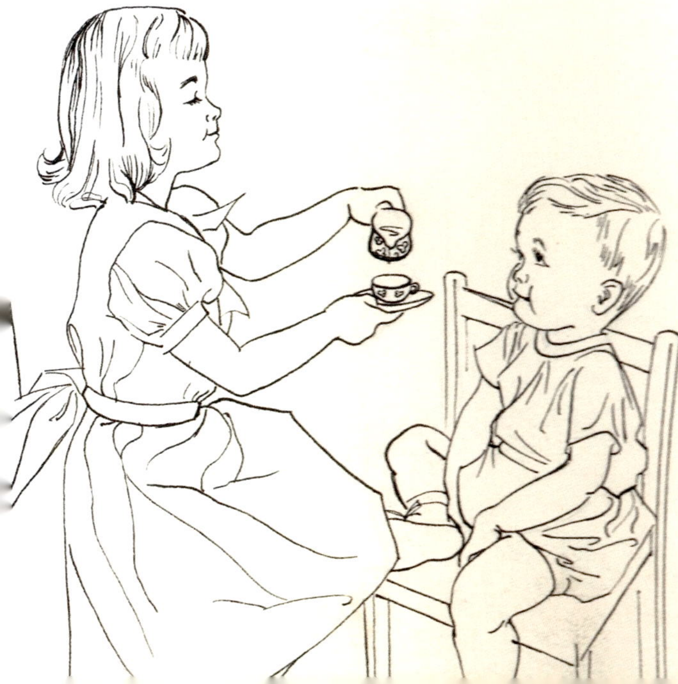

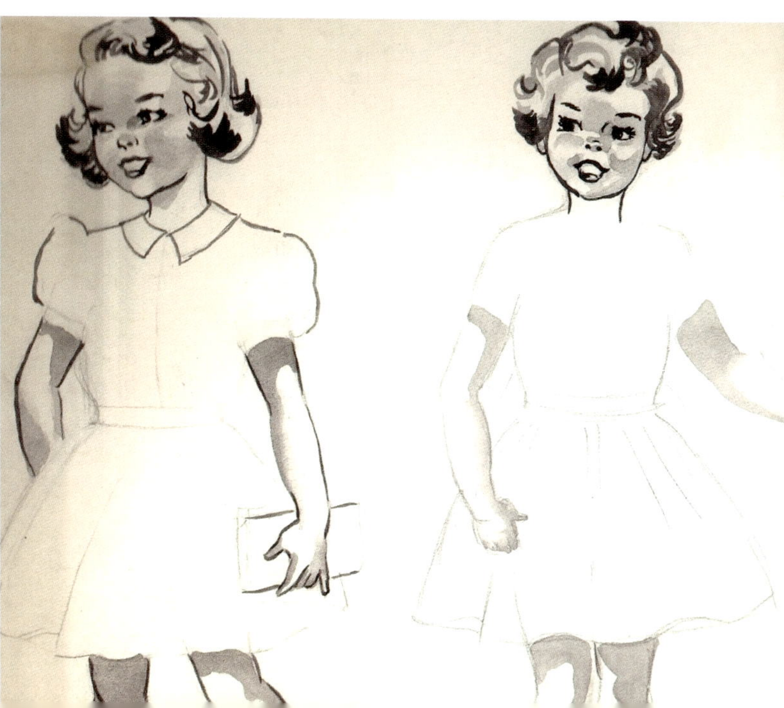

FREDERICK'S OF HOLLYWOOD

The Lingerie Revolution

Frederick Mellinger was a visionary who revolutionized the lingerie industry and shaped the way that American women viewed intimate apparel. Mellinger founded Frederick's of Hollywood in 1946, inspired by the seductive and sophisticated designs he witnessed when he was stationed in Europe during World War II. Unlike the purely functional undergarments that were common in the United States at the time, to Mellinger, lingerie was an expression of confidence, allure, and sophistication.

Originally setting up operations in New York, Mellinger quickly realized that Hollywood, with its dazzling movie sirens and glamour, was a better place to bring his vision to life. In 1947, he relocated to the West Coast, where Hollywood provided the perfect backdrop for his daring and innovative lingerie designs, with starlets and models becoming some of his first customers.

Frederick's of Hollywood quickly rose to fame and dressed some the biggest stars in Hollywood—including Mae West, Marilyn

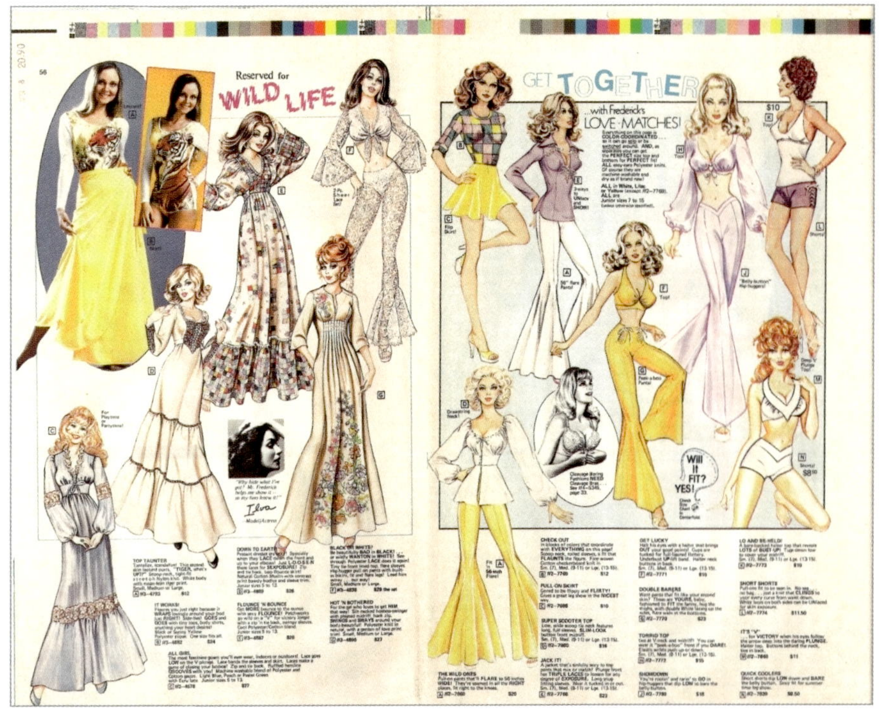

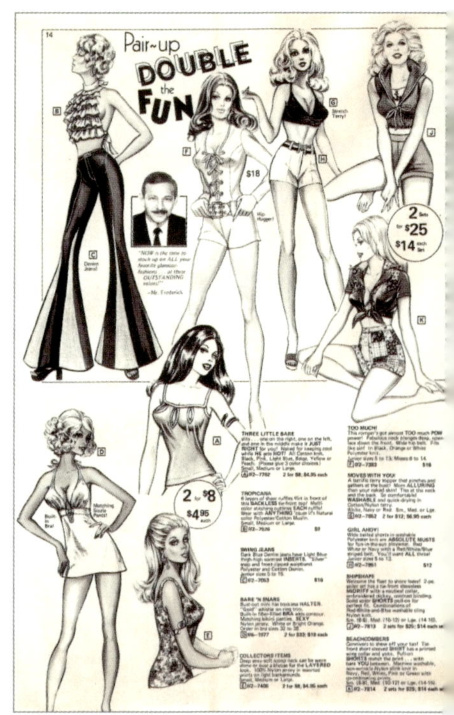

Monroe, and Zsa Zsa Gabor—cementing its brand as a symbol of glamour.

Frederick's of Hollywood was the first to introduce the push-up bra, an innovation that changed women's fashion forever. His "Rising Star" bra gave women the lifted, shapely silhouette that became synonymous with mid-century glamour. He also popularized black lingerie at a time when white and pastel undergarments were the standard. He even introduced the bikini to America after spotting the daring two-piece bathing suit on the beaches of France.

Throughout the 1950s, '60s, and '70s, Frederick's of Hollywood was the ultimate name in lingerie. The store's catalog became an iconic fashion resource, offering not only lingerie but also dresses, stockings, and accessories designed to make women feel beautiful and sexy.

By the 1960s, Frederick's of Hollywood had expanded into mall locations across the country, bringing its signature blend of sultry and sophisticated styles to an even wider audience. Interestingly, the brand found immense popularity in the Midwest, proving that glamour wasn't just for Hollywood actresses. In the late '70s, the company even expanded into men's fashion.

For decades, Frederick's of Hollywood set the standard for lingerie, blending function with fantasy and making bold, sexy fashion accessible to women everywhere. Though the industry has evolved and new brands have emerged, Frederick's of Hollywood remains an industry leader and an iconic name in intimate apparel, continuing its legacy of style, innovation, and confidence for women around the world.

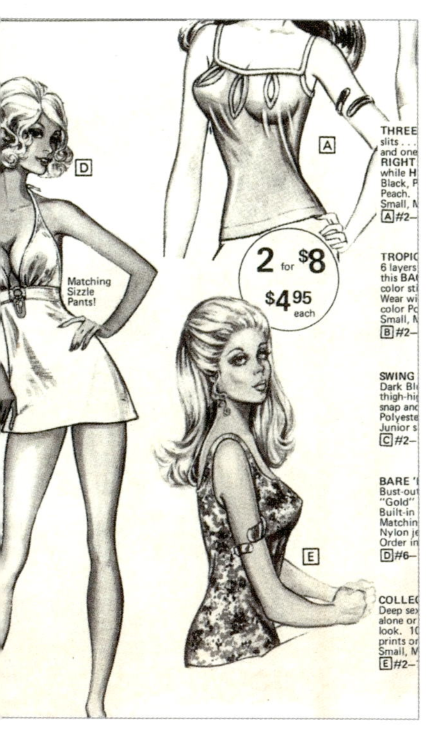

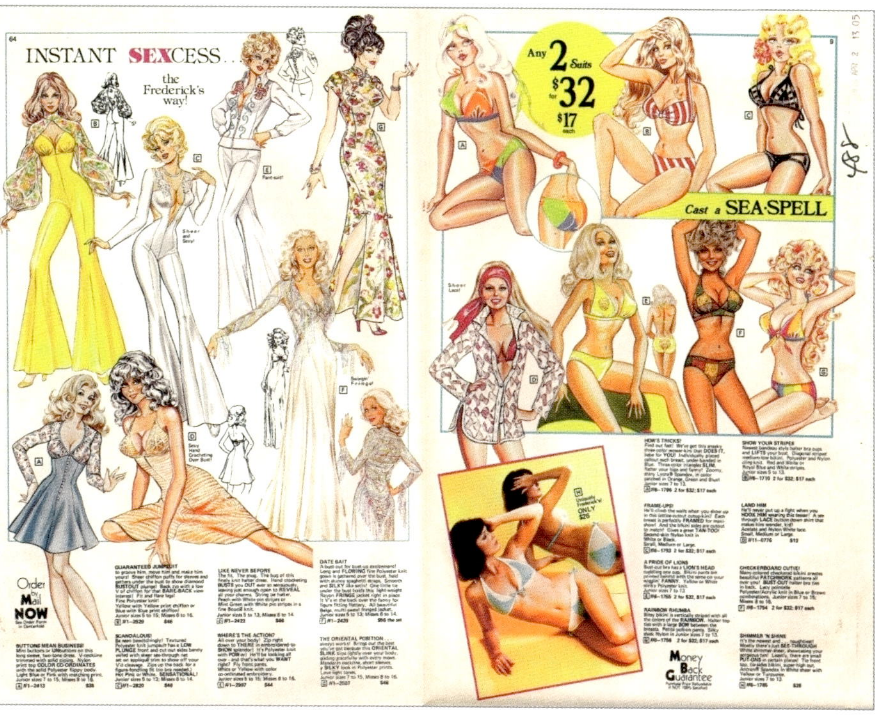

THE ART IN PROGRESS

Sketches & Work Orders

Behind each of Dorothy Kahn's illustrations was a thoughtful and creative process. Shown here are examples that give us a glimpse into Kahn's working world, from early pencil sketches to annotated work orders and reference notes. These materials provide a glimpse into how poses were requested, garments were described, and adjustments were carefully planned to bring each design to life. Much like the final illustrations, even Kahn's rough drafts radiate style and precision.

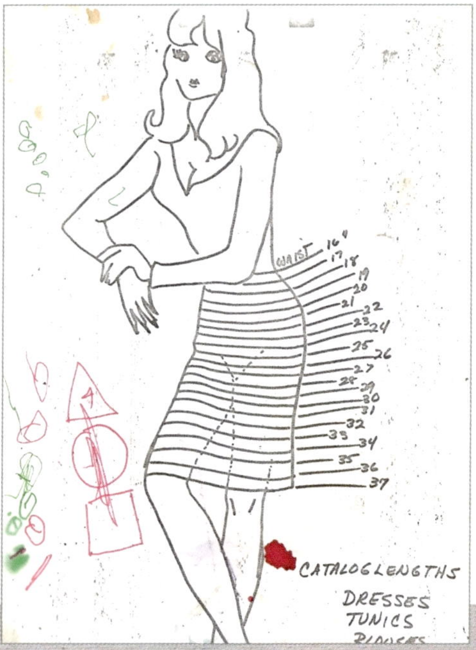

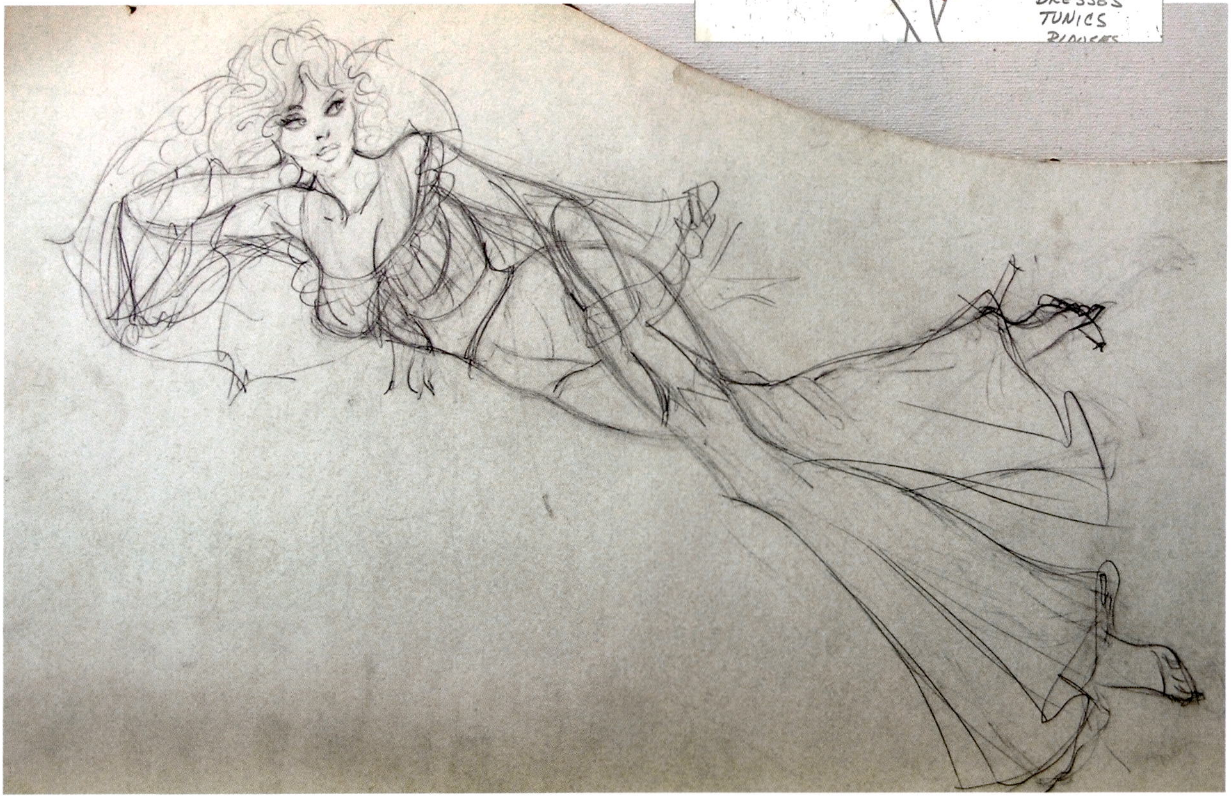

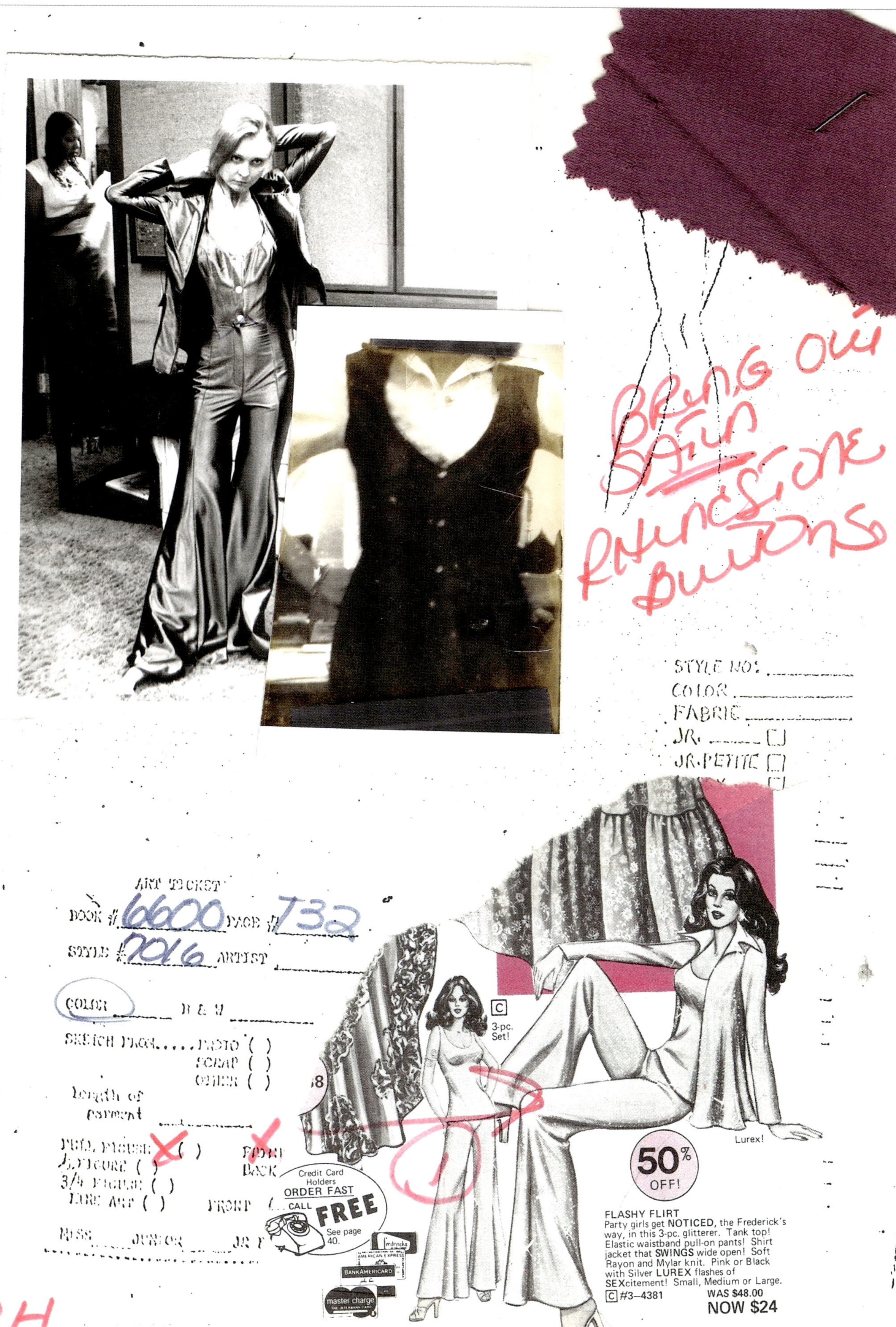
BRING OUT SATIN
RHINESTONE BUTTONS
STYLE NO:
COLOR
FABRIC
JR.
JR. PETITE
ART TICKET
BOOK # 6600 PAGE # T32
STYLE # 7016 ARTIST
COLOR B & W
SKETCH FROM.....PHOTO ( )
SCRAP ( )
OTHER ( )
Length of garment
FULL FIGURE ( )
3/4 FIGURE ( )
LINE ART ( )
FRONT
BACK
MISS JUNIOR
Credit Card Holders
ORDER FAST
CALL FREE
See page 40.
BankAmericard
master charge
3-pc. Set!
Lurex!
50% OFF!
FLASHY FLIRT
Party girls get NOTICED, the Frederick's way, in this 3-pc. glitterer. Tank top! Elastic waistband pull-on pants! Shirt jacket that SWINGS wide open! Soft Rayon and Mylar knit. Pink or Black with Silver LUREX flashes of SEXcitement! Small, Medium or Large.
C #3–4381
WAS $48.00
NOW $24

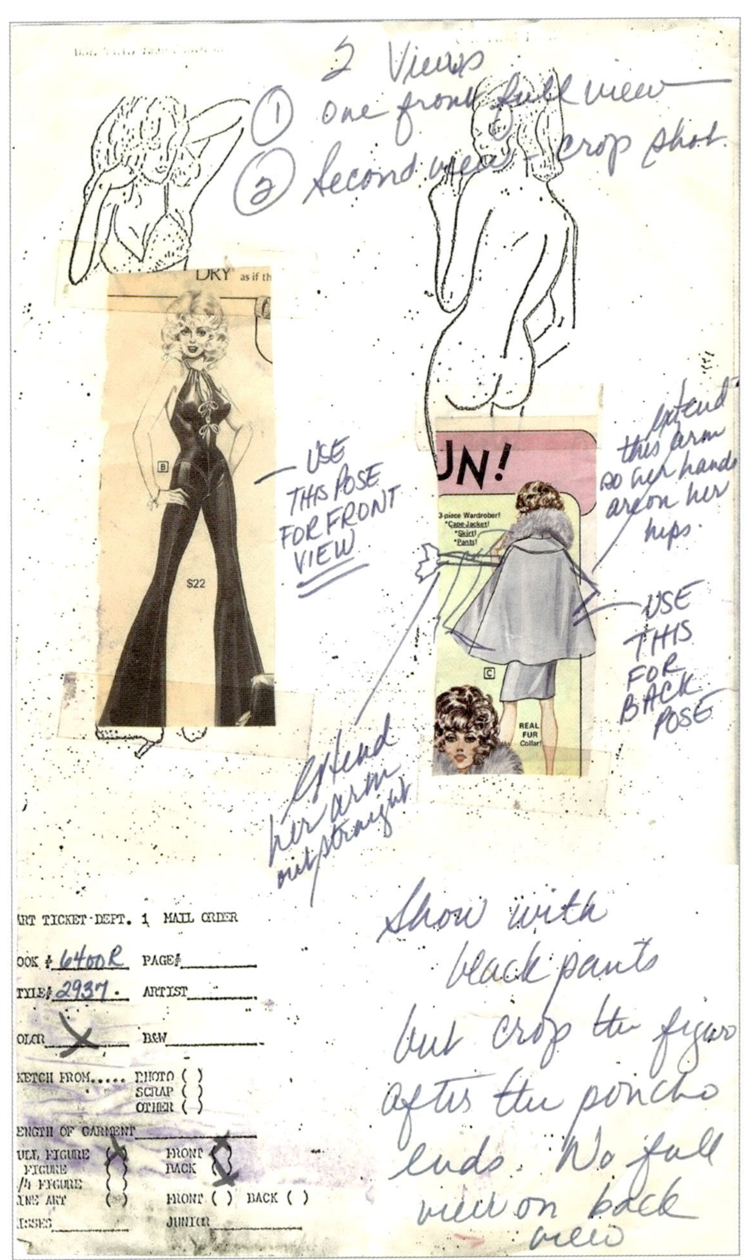
2 Views
① one front full view
② second view crop shot
USE THIS POSE FOR FRONT VIEW
extend this arm so her hands are on her hips
USE THIS FOR BACK POSE
extend her arm out straight
ART TICKET-DEPT. 1 MAIL ORDER
BOOK # 6400R PAGE#
STYLE# 2937 ARTIST
COLOR X B&W
SKETCH FROM..... PHOTO ( ) SCRAP ( ) OTHER ( )
LENGTH OF GARMENT
FULL FIGURE FRONT
BACK
LINE ART FRONT ( ) BACK ( )
JUNIOR
Show with black pants but crop the figure after the poncho ends. No full view on back view

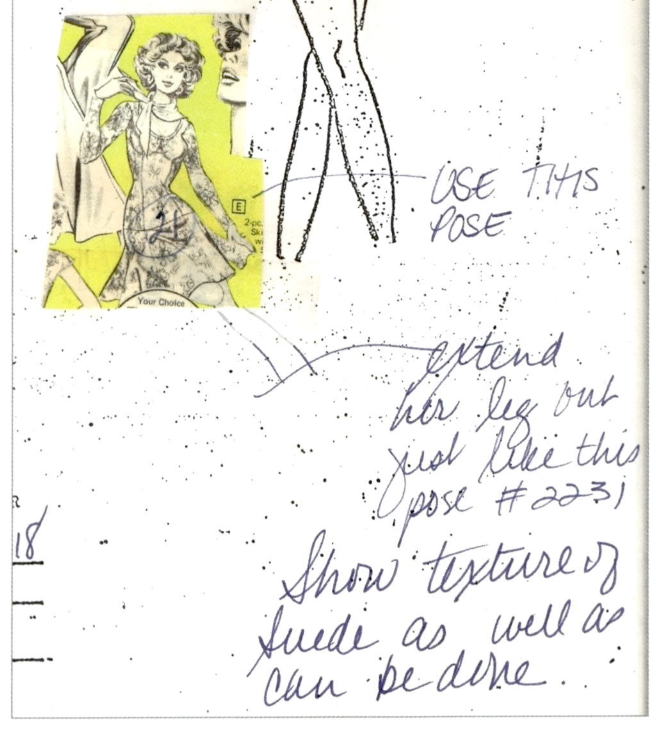
USE THIS POSE
extend her leg out just like this pose #2231
Show texture of suede as well as can be done.

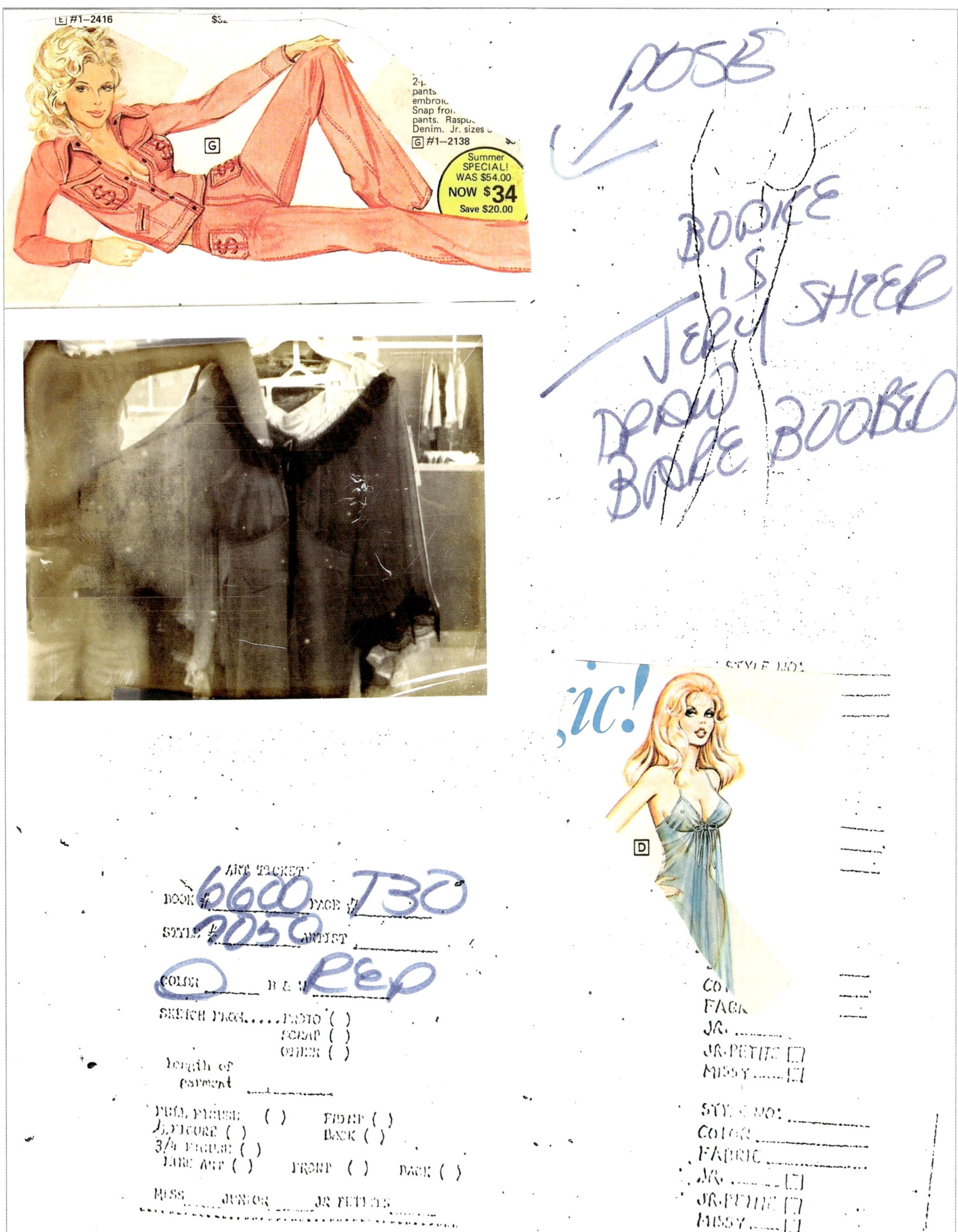
#1-2416
Summer SPECIAL! WAS $54.00 NOW $34 Save $20.00
#1-2138
POSE
BODICE IS VERY SHEER
DRAW BARE BOOBED
ART TICKET
BOOK # 6600 PAGE # T30
STYLE # 7050 ARTIST
COLOR B & W REP
SKETCH FROM.....PHOTO ( )
SCRAP ( )
OTHER ( )
length of garment
FULL FIGURE ( ) FRONT ( )
FIGURE ( ) BACK ( )
3/4 FIGURE ( )
LINE ART ( ) FRONT ( ) BACK ( )
MISS JUNIOR JR PETITE
JR. PETITE
MISSY
STYLE NO:
COLOR
FABRIC
JR.
JR. PETITE
MISSY

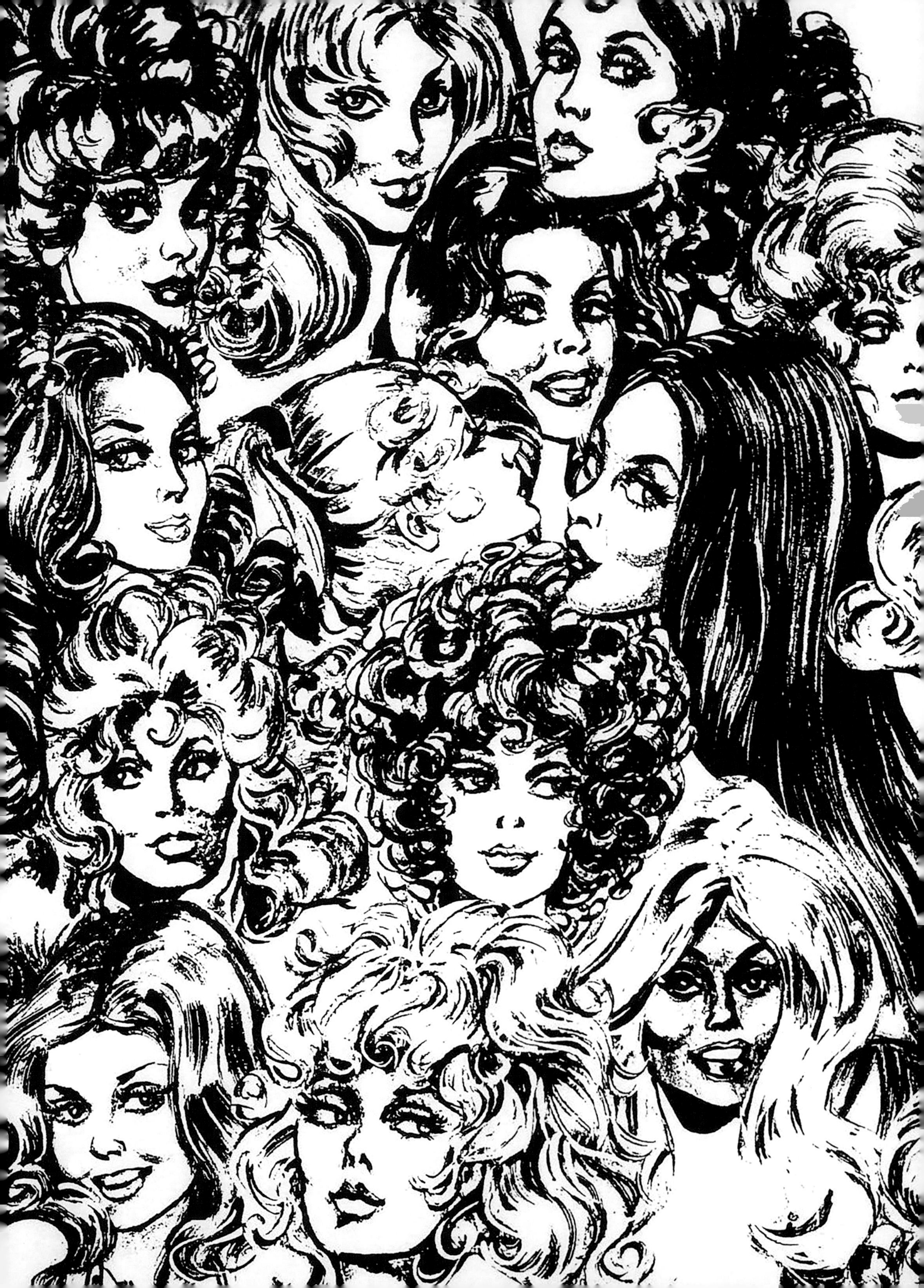

The Collection

CONNIE

A sophisticated woman draped in a luxurious, voluminous coat that falls just above the knee. The coat, with its rich, glossy texture, envelops her in effortless elegance, its wide sleeves billowing gracefully. A plush trim lines the cuffs and collar, adding a touch of opulence, while discreet pockets are seamlessly integrated into the design. She pairs the ensemble with sheer stockings and sleek, pointed heels, elongating her poised stance.

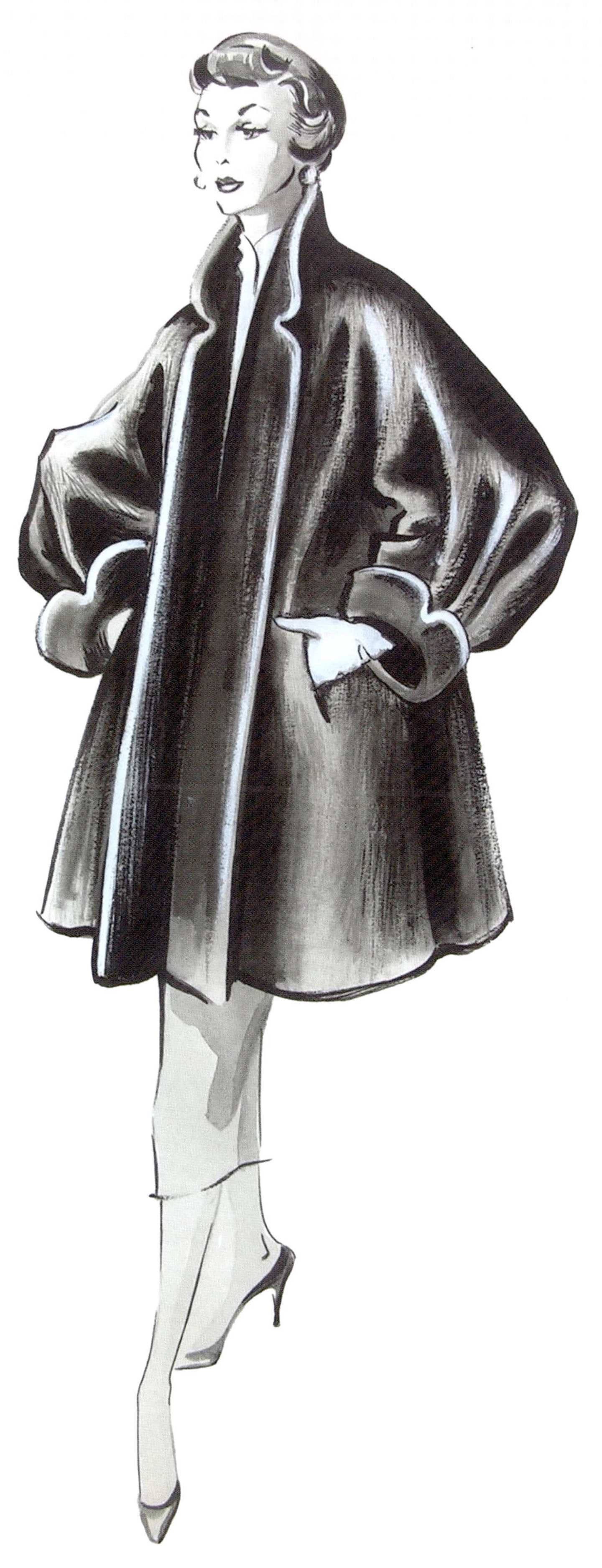

CHRISTINE

A poised woman in a knee-length, sleeveless dress with a sleek, fitted silhouette. The dress is adorned with a delicate chevron pattern, shimmering with a subtle sheen, and is accentuated by a ruffled trim cascading down the neckline. A floral embellishment at the waist adds an extra touch of elegance. This lovely shift dress reflects common fashion trends of the mid- to late 1960s, when mod and streamlined designs were popular. Completing the look are her classic Mary Jane–style shoes, fastened with a bold buckle, reinforcing the timeless elegance of this fashion-forward moment.

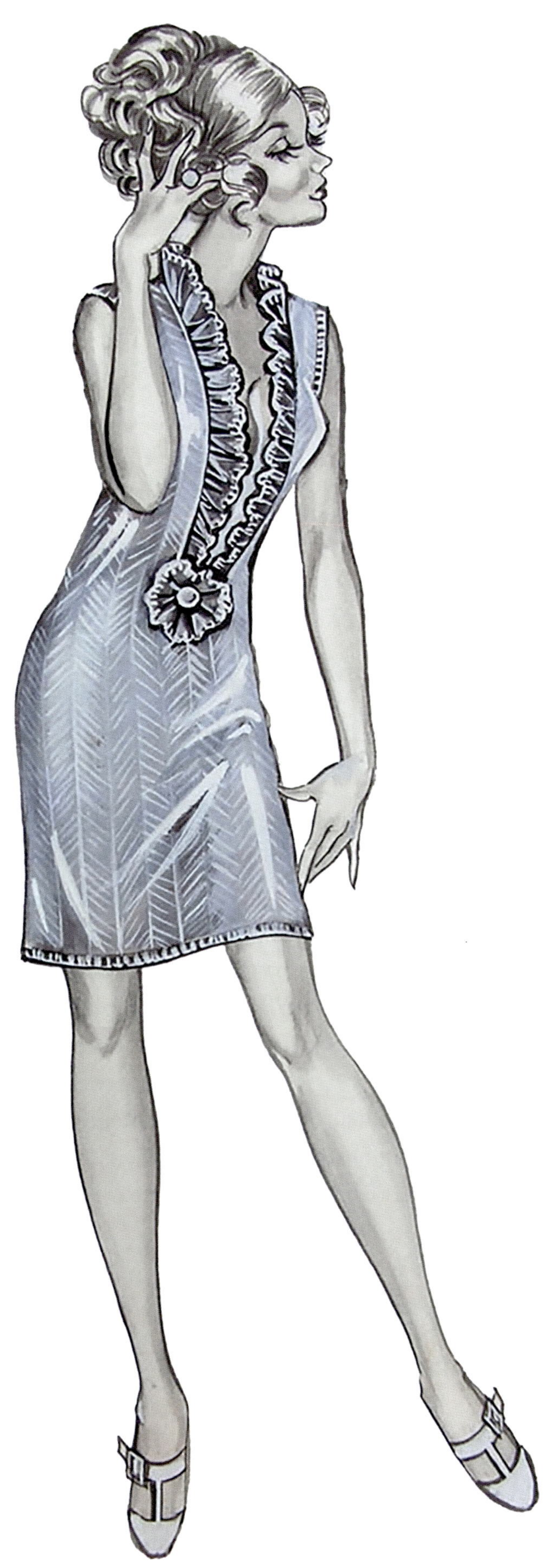

DONNA

A bold, knee-length dress with a sharply tailored silhouette, accentuated by a dramatic wide-collared neckline in contrasting white, adding a touch of sophistication. Long, voluminous sleeves taper into crisp cuffs, while a cinched waist, emphasized by a statement belt with a bold buckle, enhances the structured elegance of the look. Her ensemble is completed with chic, low-heeled shoes adorned with a matching square buckle. A pair of striking purple drop earrings frame her face, adding a pop of color and a hint of playful allure to her sophisticated ensemble. This mid-century design bridges the structured elegance of the 1950s with the bold, modern style of the 1960s.

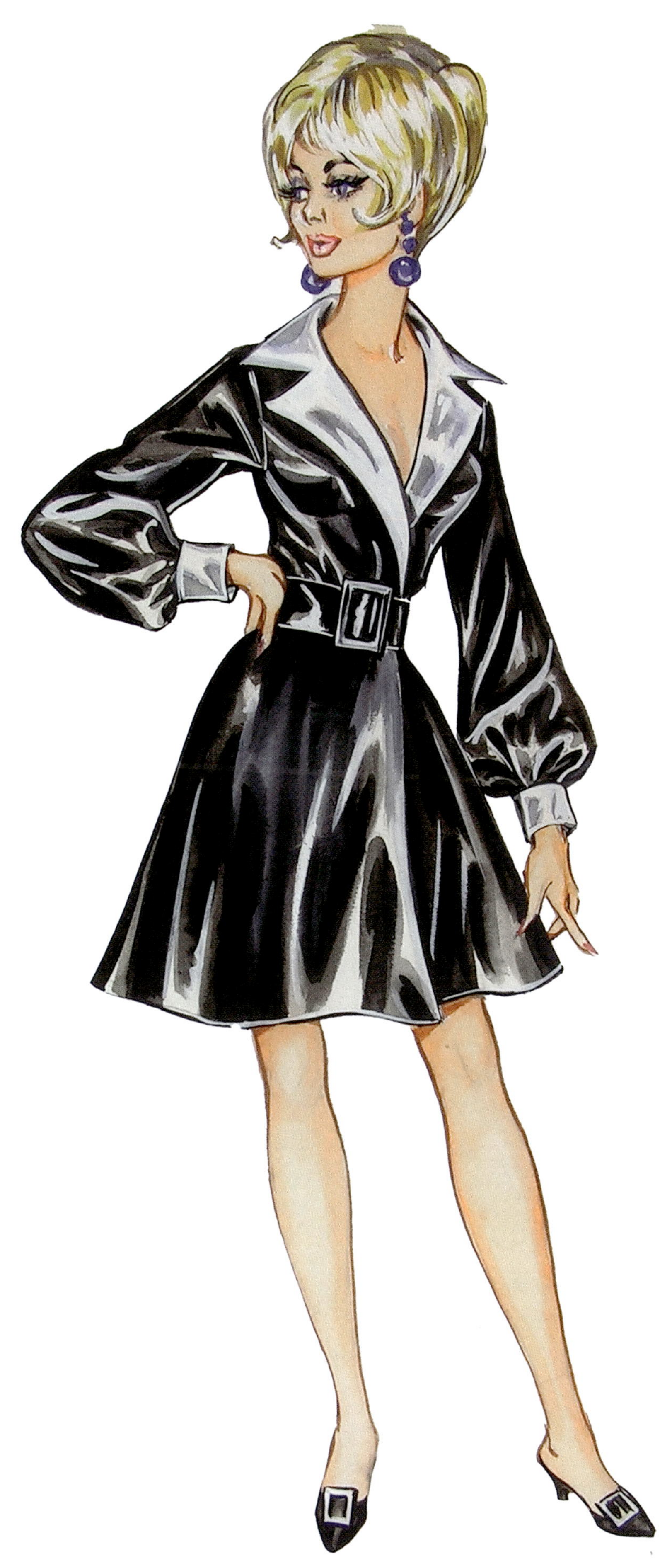

AVA

This stylish '70s ensemble captures the era's signature bohemian-glam aesthetic. A fitted, short-sleeved top with delicate lace trim and subtle pleating accentuates the figure, while high-waisted, flared trousers elongate the legs with effortless elegance. Her voluminous, cascading waves frame her face, adding to the sultry, free-spirited vibe, while platform heels complete the ensemble with a bold, retro touch.

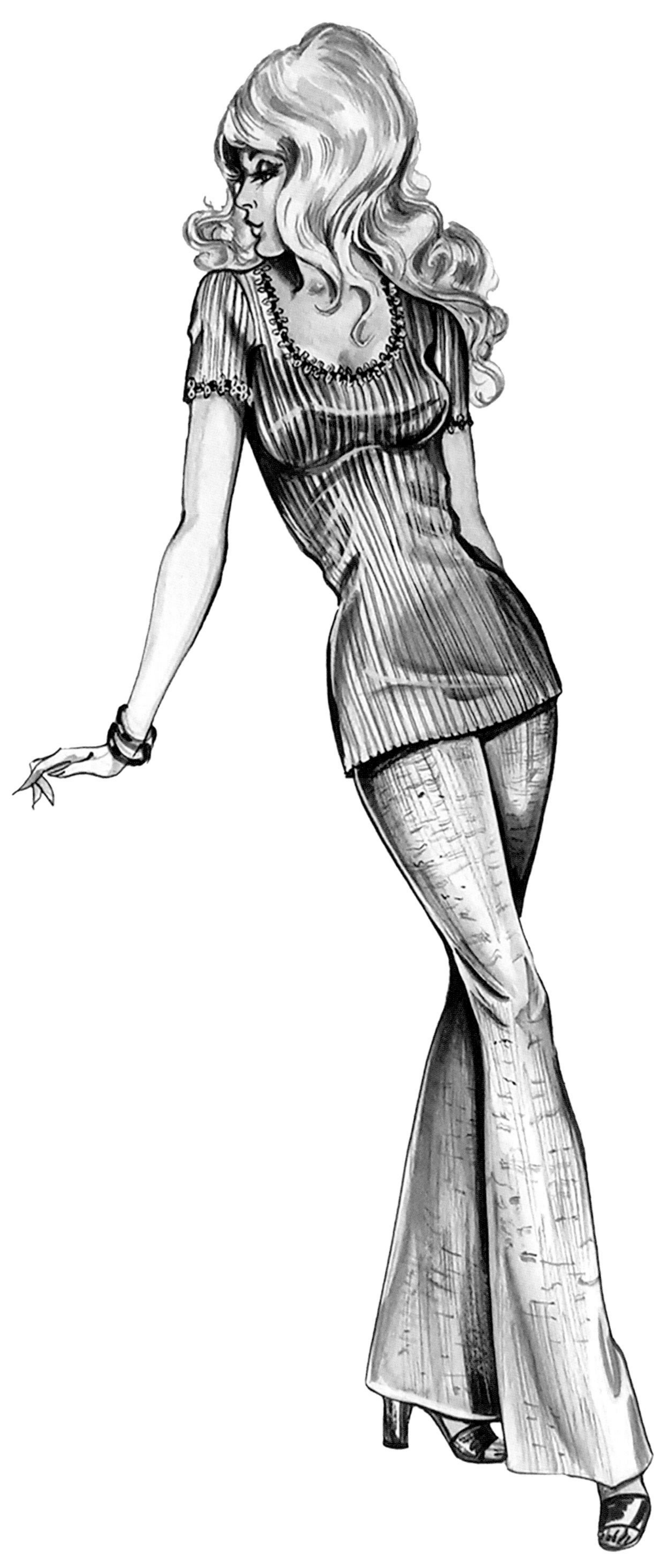

CLAIRE

Step into the bold fashion of the 1970s with vintage sophistication in a silky lavender blouse with dramatic sleeves and gemstone details, paired with a luxe faux-fur miniskirt. High-shine knee-high boots complete the ensemble, channeling disco-era glamour with a modern edge.

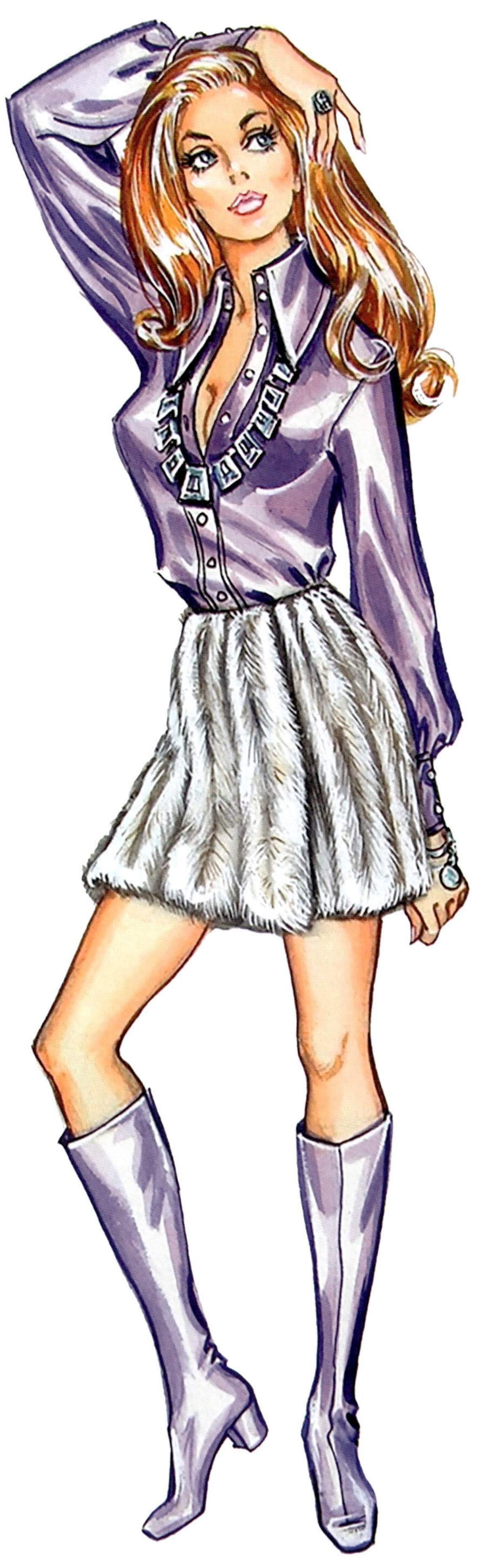

ALICE

Refined sophistication featuring a tailored blazer with a cinched waist and single-button closure, enhancing an hourglass silhouette. The matching pencil skirt, a timeless mid-century staple, falls gracefully below the knee. A structured hat and delicate earrings add a touch of polished charm, while classic pumps complete the ensemble.

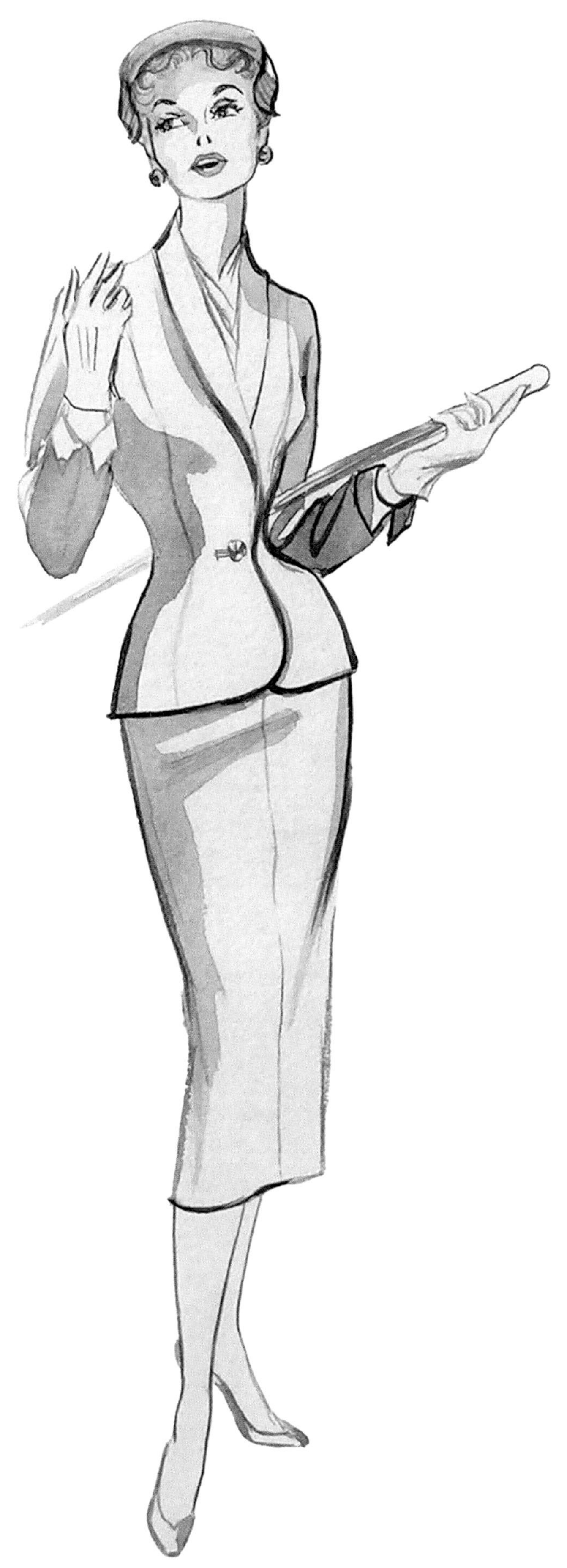

GLORIA

Effortlessly chic, this ensemble features a tailored button-up dress with a structured high collar and elegant bishop sleeves. A statement belt cinches the waist, accentuating an hourglass silhouette, while the soft pleats of the skirt add movement and charm. The look is completed with coordinating kitten heels and delicate accessories, embodying refined mid-century sophistication.

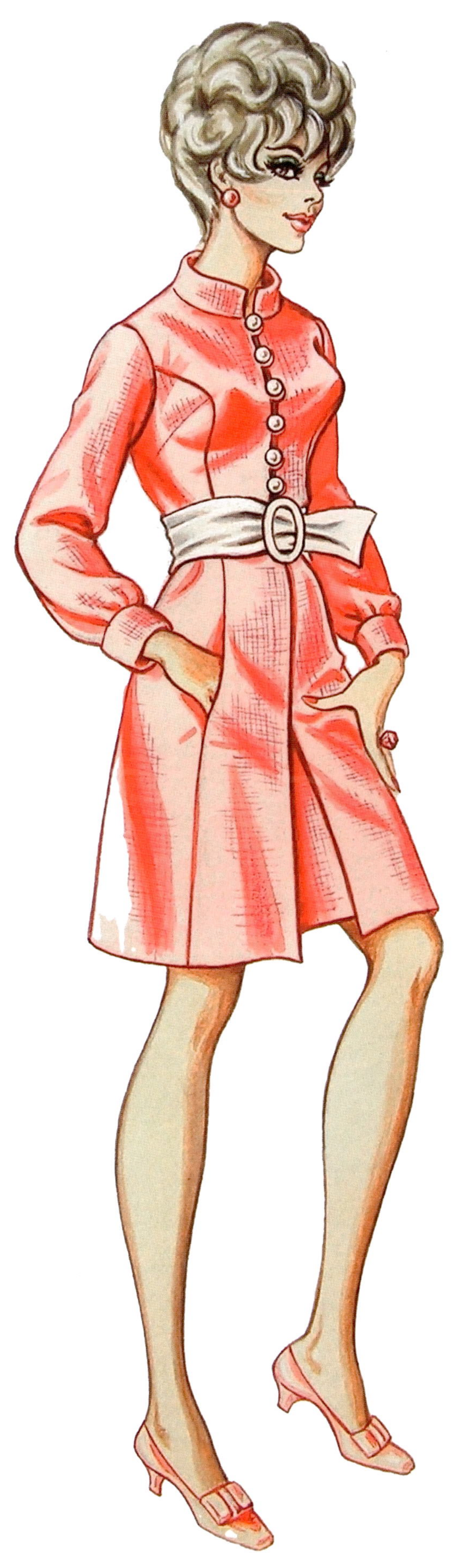

JUDITH

This model is stunning with timeless glamour in a luxurious fur coat draped effortlessly over a chic red sheath dress. Her ensemble is completed with classic black buckle heels, pearl accessories, and elegant white gloves. Her voluminous silver curls and poised stance add a touch of old-Hollywood allure.

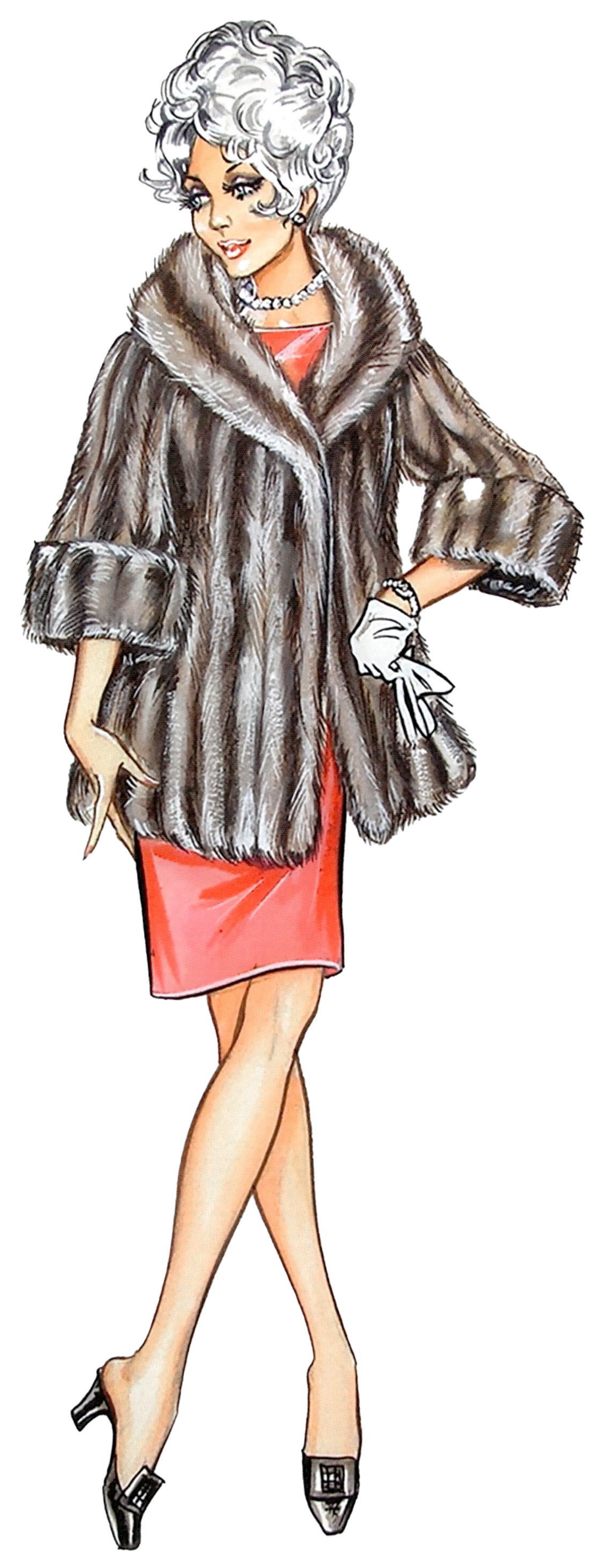

KIMBERLY

This illustration radiates vintage charm with a fun and feminine 1970s look. The high-waisted, wide-leg trousers elongate the silhouette, while the pink blouse with delicate lace detailing and sheer embroidered sleeves adds a romantic touch. The voluminous half-up hairstyle complements the era's aesthetic, and the matching pink heels tie the whole ensemble together in a polished, retro-chic way.

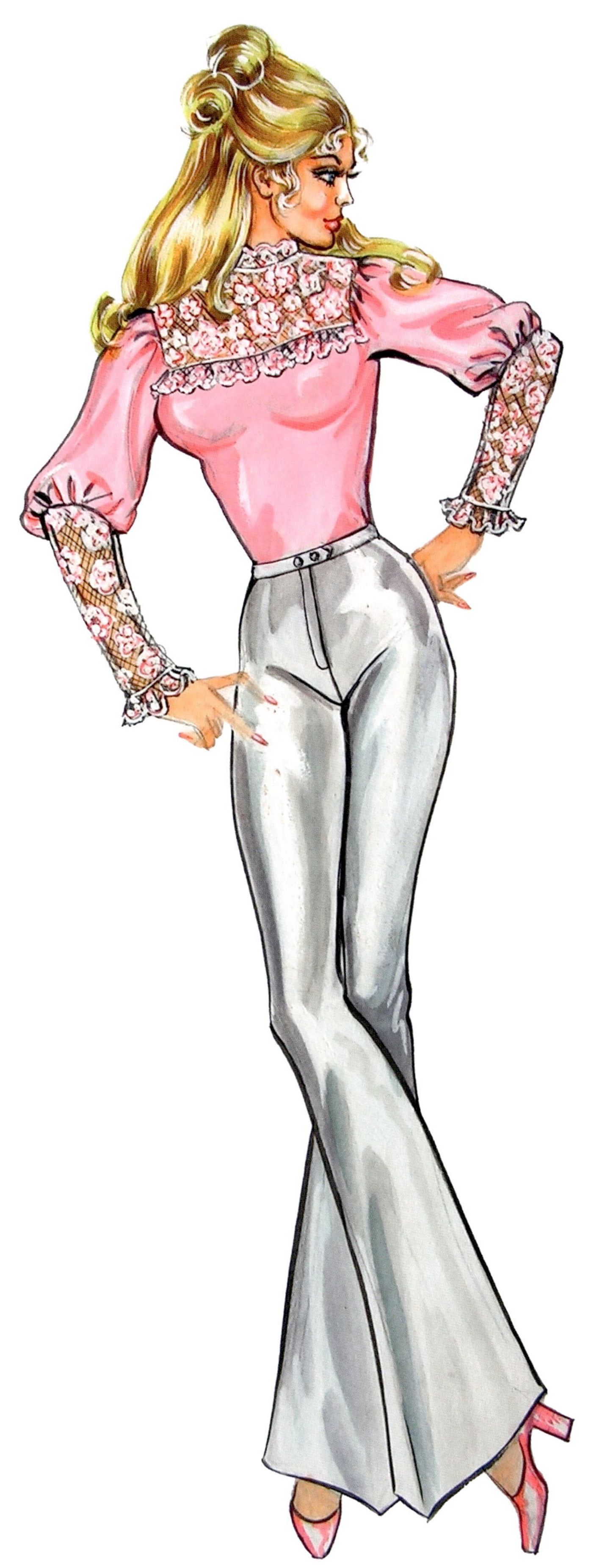

CAROLYN

Classic mid-century glamour, reminiscent of the late 1950s to early 1960s fashion. The sleek trench coat, cinched at the waist with a tied belt, creates an elegant and structured silhouette. The glossy fabric suggests sophistication, while the bold polka-dot blouse peeking from underneath adds a playful contrast. The voluminous, wavy hairstyle, statement earrings, and gloves complete the look, embodying the timeless elegance of vintage high fashion.

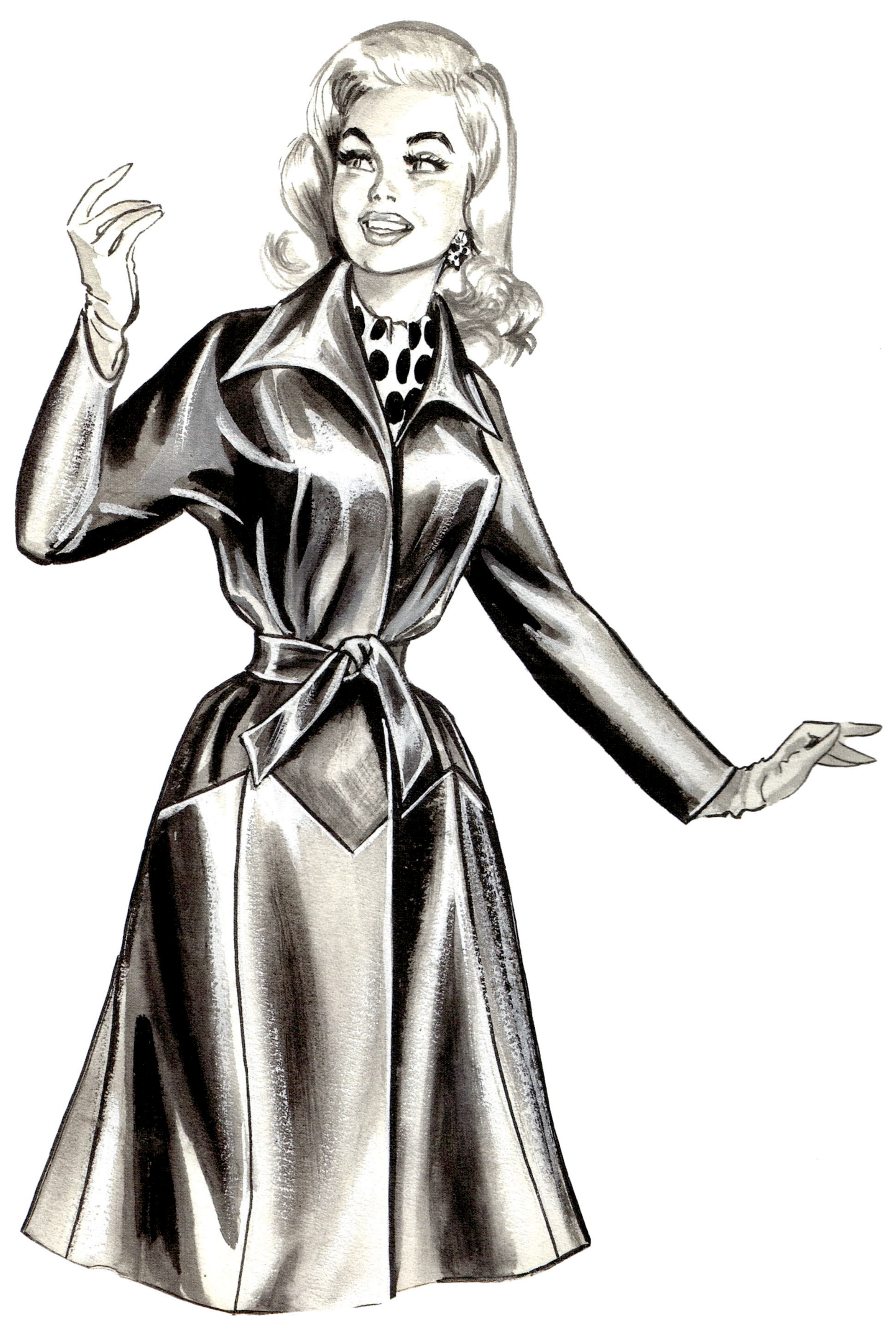

HEATHER

Dreamy, romantic, and ultrafeminine! This flowing pastel dress with its empire waist, puffed sleeves, and delicate ribbon tie at the bust gives a soft, ethereal feel. The choker with a floral detail adds a touch of vintage charm, while her relaxed yet sultry pose enhances the overall elegance and allure of this composition.

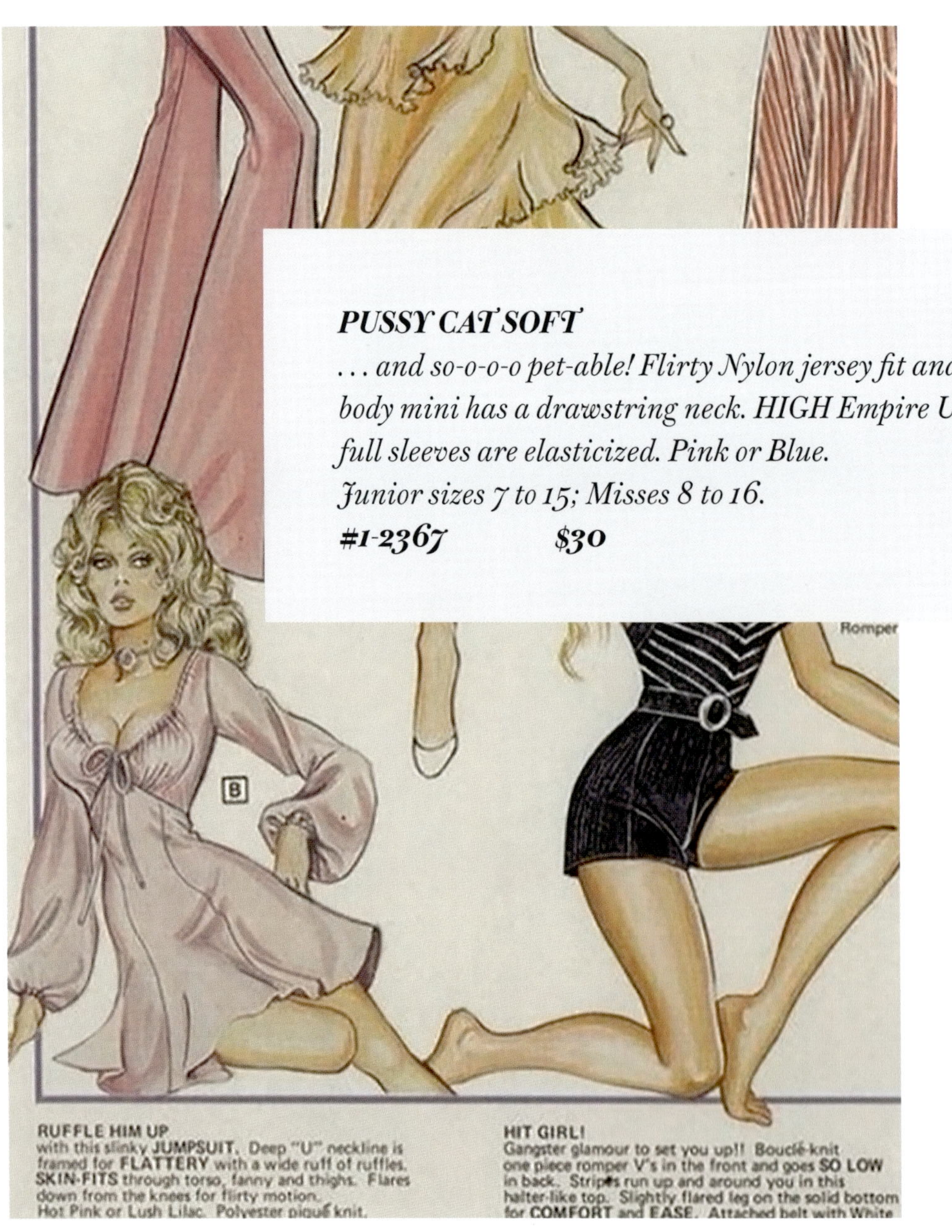

PUSSY CAT SOFT
. . . and so-o-o-o pet-able! Flirty Nylon jersey fit and fit 'n flare body mini has a drawstring neck. HIGH Empire UPlift. Long, full sleeves are elasticized. Pink or Blue.
Junior sizes 7 to 15; Misses 8 to 16.
#1-2367 ***$30***

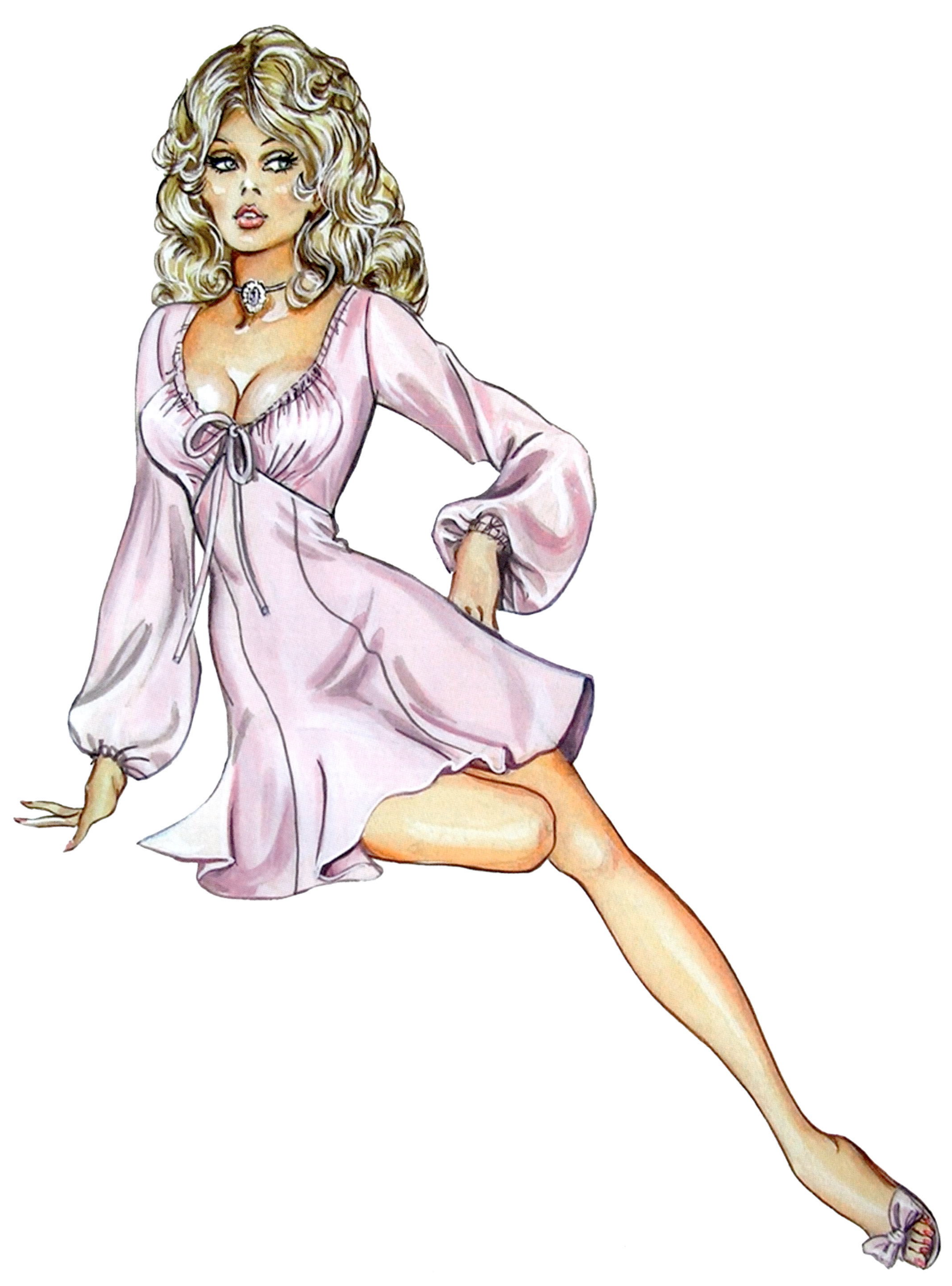

ARIELLE

This sexy '70s-era jumpsuit is a showstopper, radiating disco-queen energy with a touch of showgirl glam. The bold red hue, sheer cutouts, and wide, flowing bell-bottoms create a head-turning silhouette that's equal parts daring and dazzling. Perfect for commanding the dance floor or making a dramatic entrance, this jumpsuit guarantees jaw-dropping reactions.

Frederick's of Hollywood catalog description:

SHEER DELIGHT
A jumpsuit to show him how good you really look! Sheer Nylon inserts reveal front and arms. Body is clingin' Acetate knit . . . very sexy! Red with Nude sheer; Black with Black.
Junior sizes 5 to 13.
#2-7954 $44

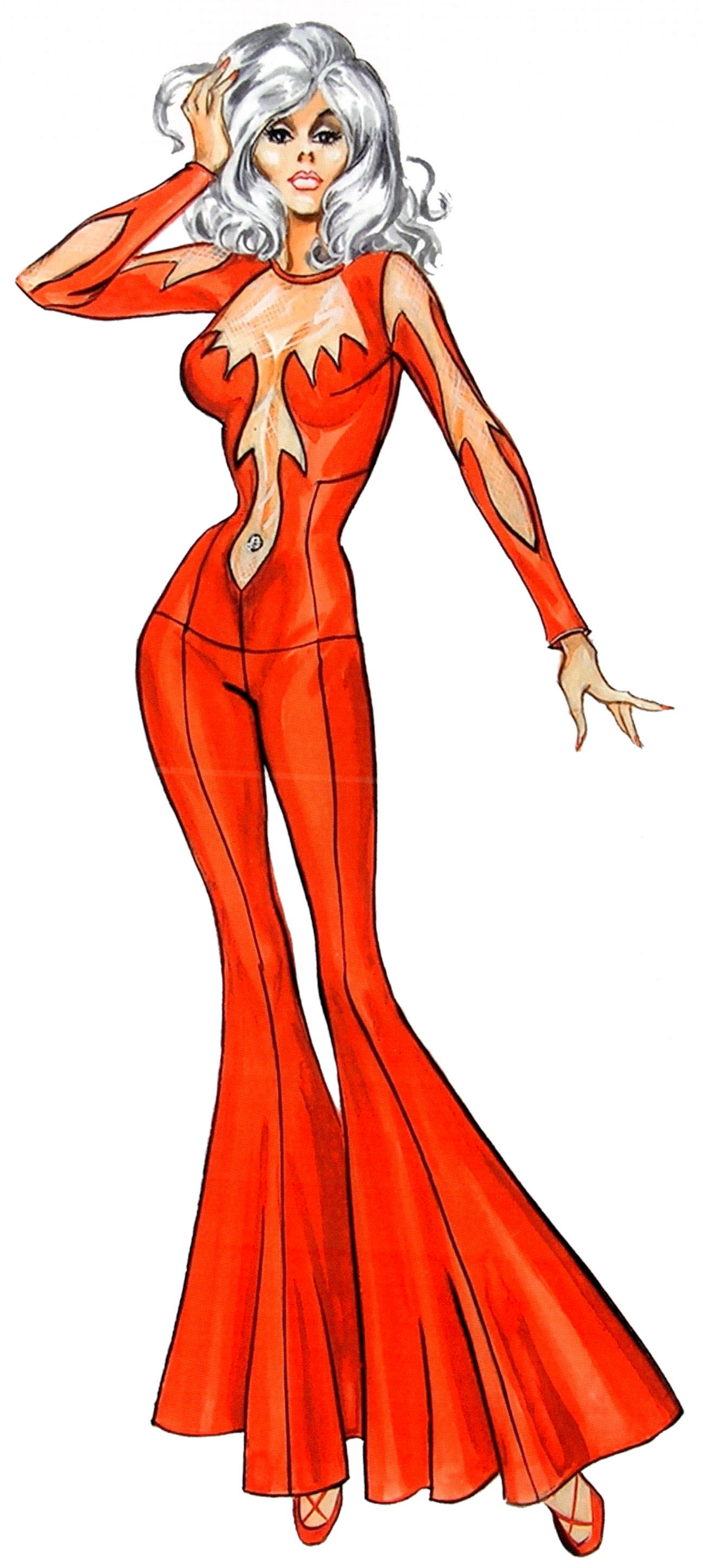

CARMEN

This elegant, floor-length gown stuns in a vibrant, spicy orange, exuding confidence and allure. Lace-up arm cutouts and a daring plunging neckline add a sultry edge, making it the epitome of high-fashion seduction. Pairing the gown with glossy lips and smoldering smoky eyes, she embodies the timeless glamour of Hollywood's most iconic starlets.

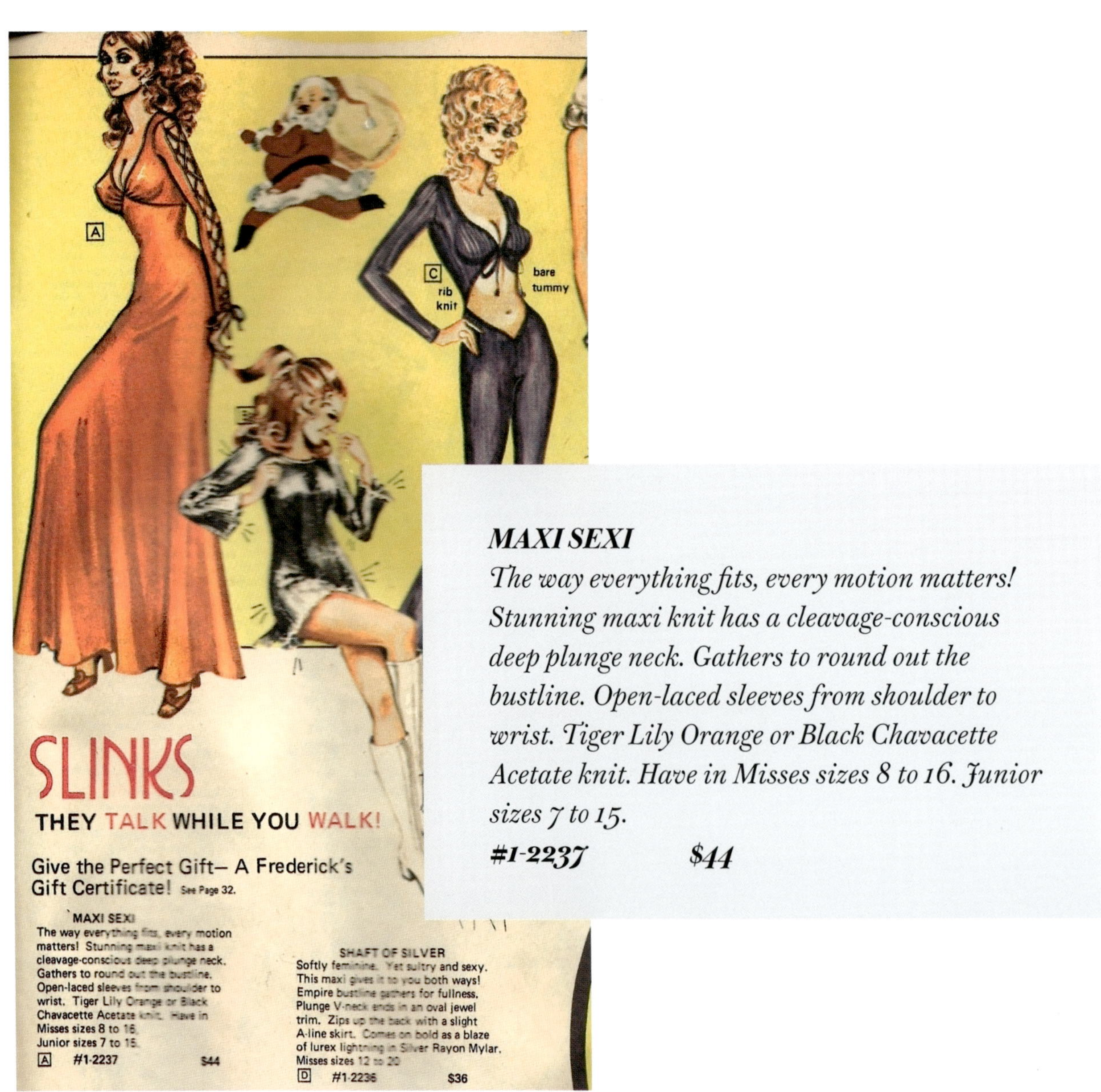

MAXI SEXI

The way everything fits, every motion matters! Stunning maxi knit has a cleavage-conscious deep plunge neck. Gathers to round out the bustline. Open-laced sleeves from shoulder to wrist. Tiger Lily Orange or Black Chavacette Acetate knit. Have in Misses sizes 8 to 16. Junior sizes 7 to 15.

#1-2237 ***$44***

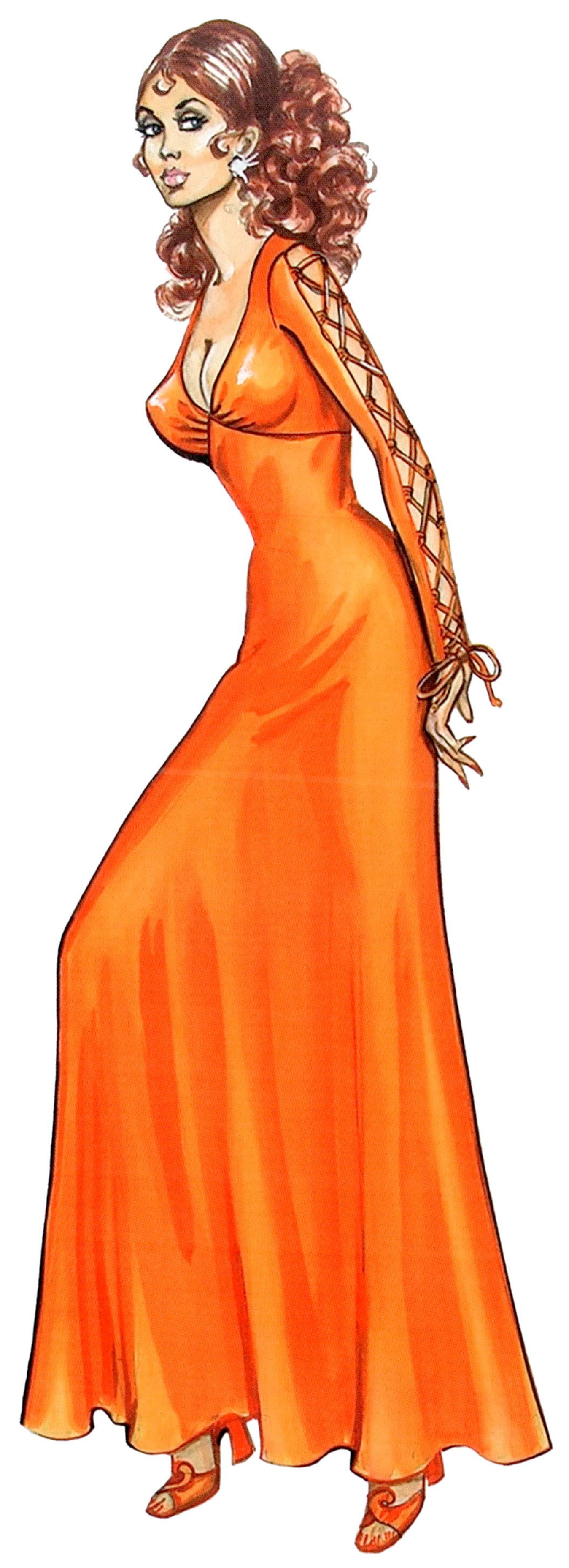

MURIEL

This dazzling '70s jumpsuit radiates disco glamour with its shimmering fabric and curve-hugging silhouette. A plunging neckline, bold buttons, and draped chain detail add sophistication, while billowy sleeves and wide-leg bell-bottoms bring vintage drama.

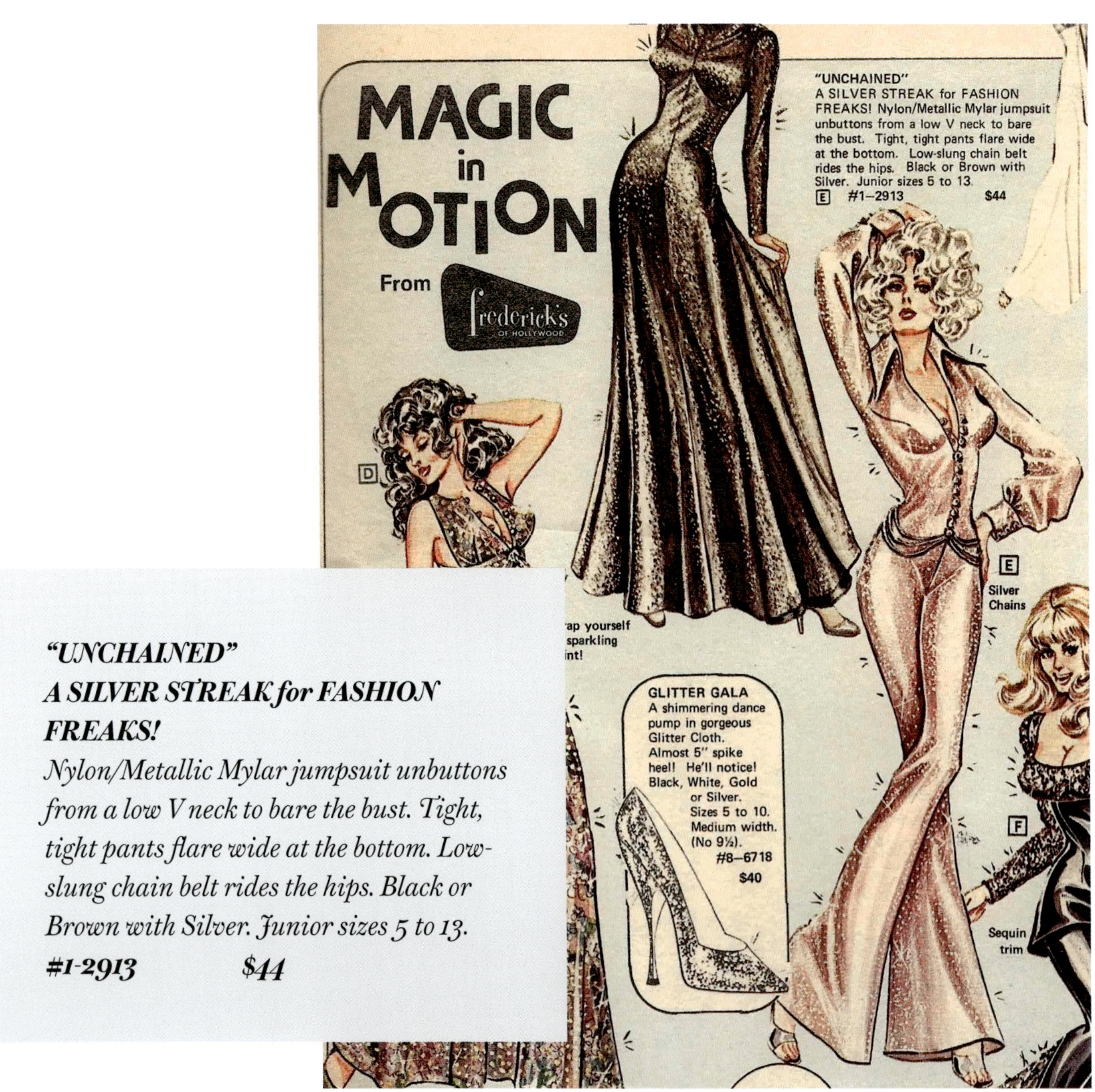

"UNCHAINED"
A SILVER STREAK for FASHION FREAKS!
Nylon/Metallic Mylar jumpsuit unbuttons from a low V neck to bare the bust. Tight, tight pants flare wide at the bottom. Low-slung chain belt rides the hips. Black or Brown with Silver. Junior sizes 5 to 13.
#1-2913 $44

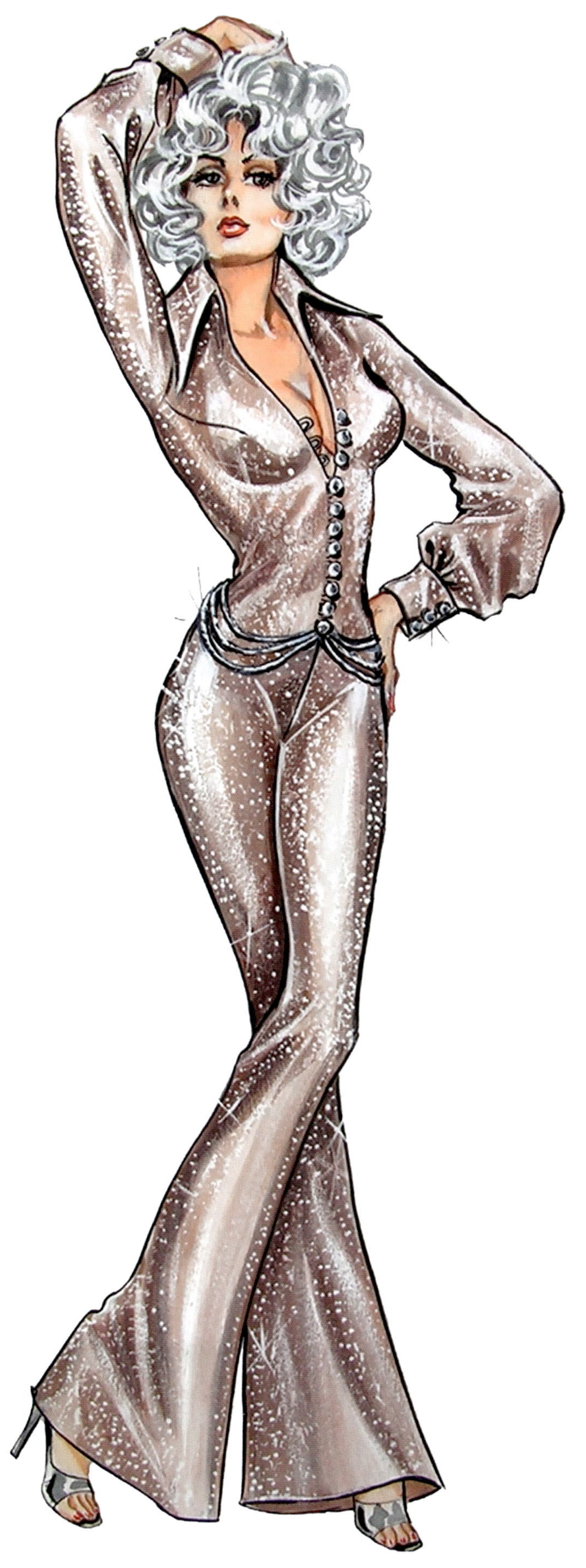

CARLY

A seductive two-piece suit perfect for the dance floor. Sparkling jacket and short shorts are complemented by a plunging neckline. Illustrated with and without the jacket, this model exudes '70s sex appeal.

Frederick's of Hollywood catalog description:

SHORT, SEXY, SHINEY
LUREX ROMPER for a gal who dares to wear the shortest pants in town! Zips in back. Matches short Lurex battle jacket. Joins bare-plunged bare-backed Acetate knit top. Rayon and Metallic in Silver with White, or All Black. Juniors 5 to 13.
#2-7020 2-pcs. $42

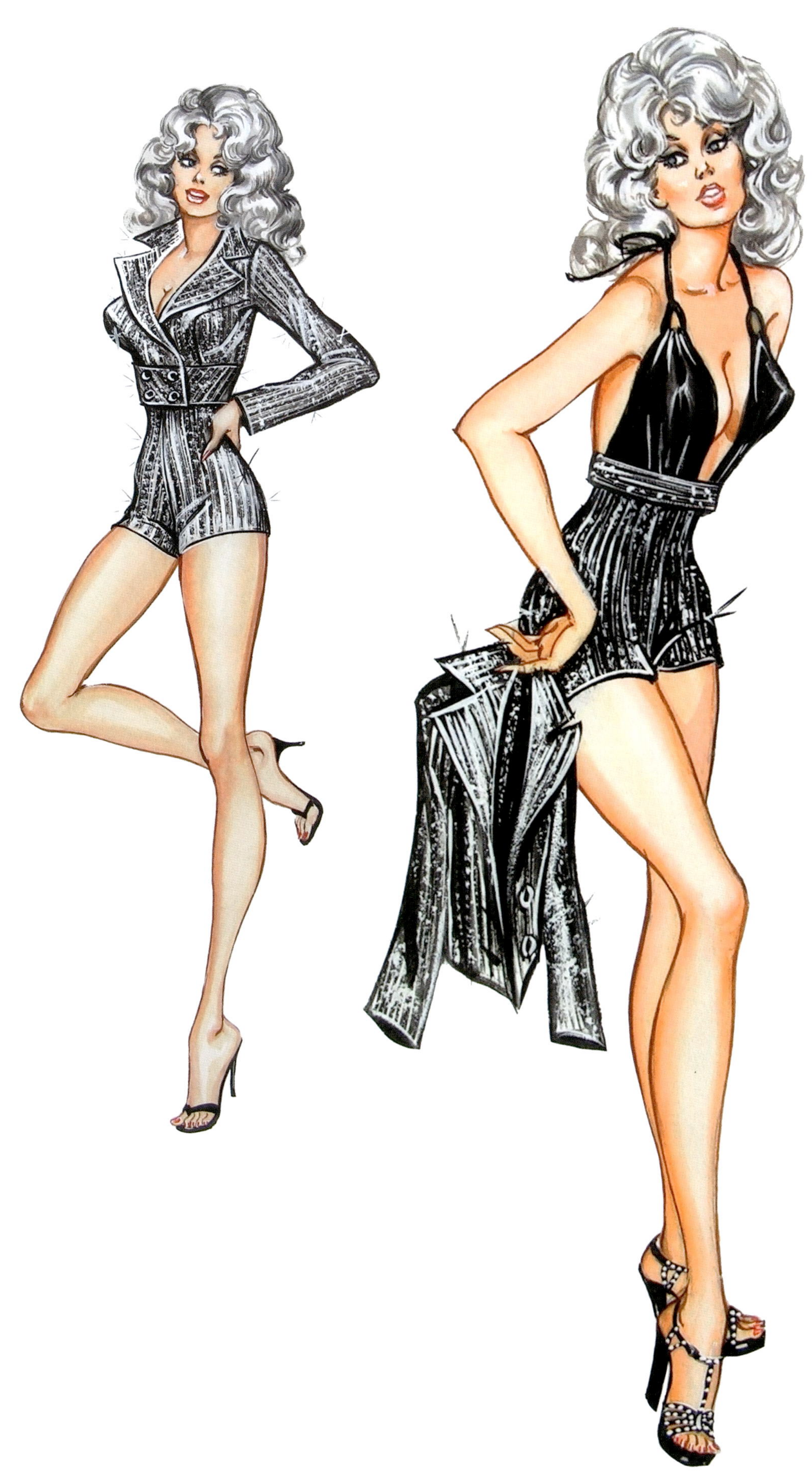

BEVERLY

This striking red gown channels retro sophistication with its figure-flattering silhouette and bold floral bolero with a tied front. The low neckline adds allure, while the long, flowing skirt drapes elegantly, creating an effortlessly glamorous look. Her windswept hair and confident pose complete the scene, evoking a timeless, vintage allure.

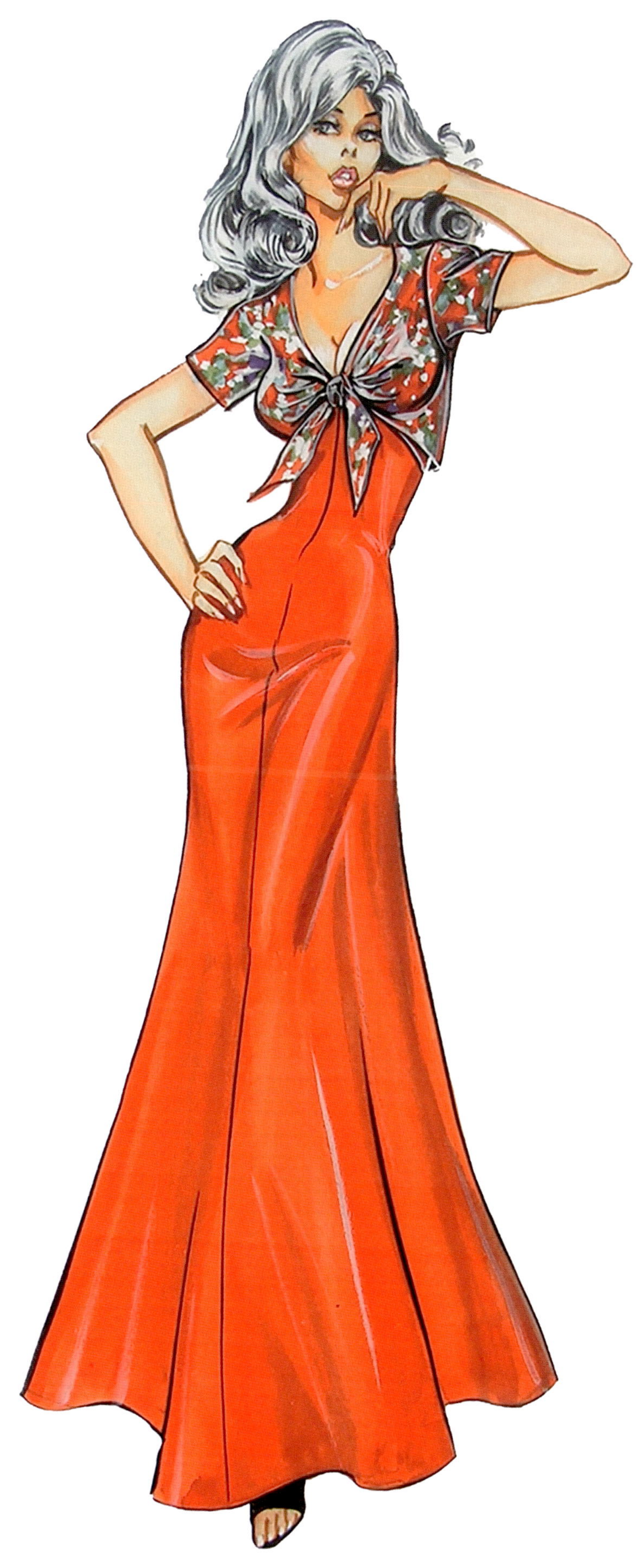

NICOLETTE

This full-length gown drapes effortlessly in a silky, flowing fabric, creating head-turning silhouette. A daring waist cutout adds just the right touch of allure, elevating her '70s glam.

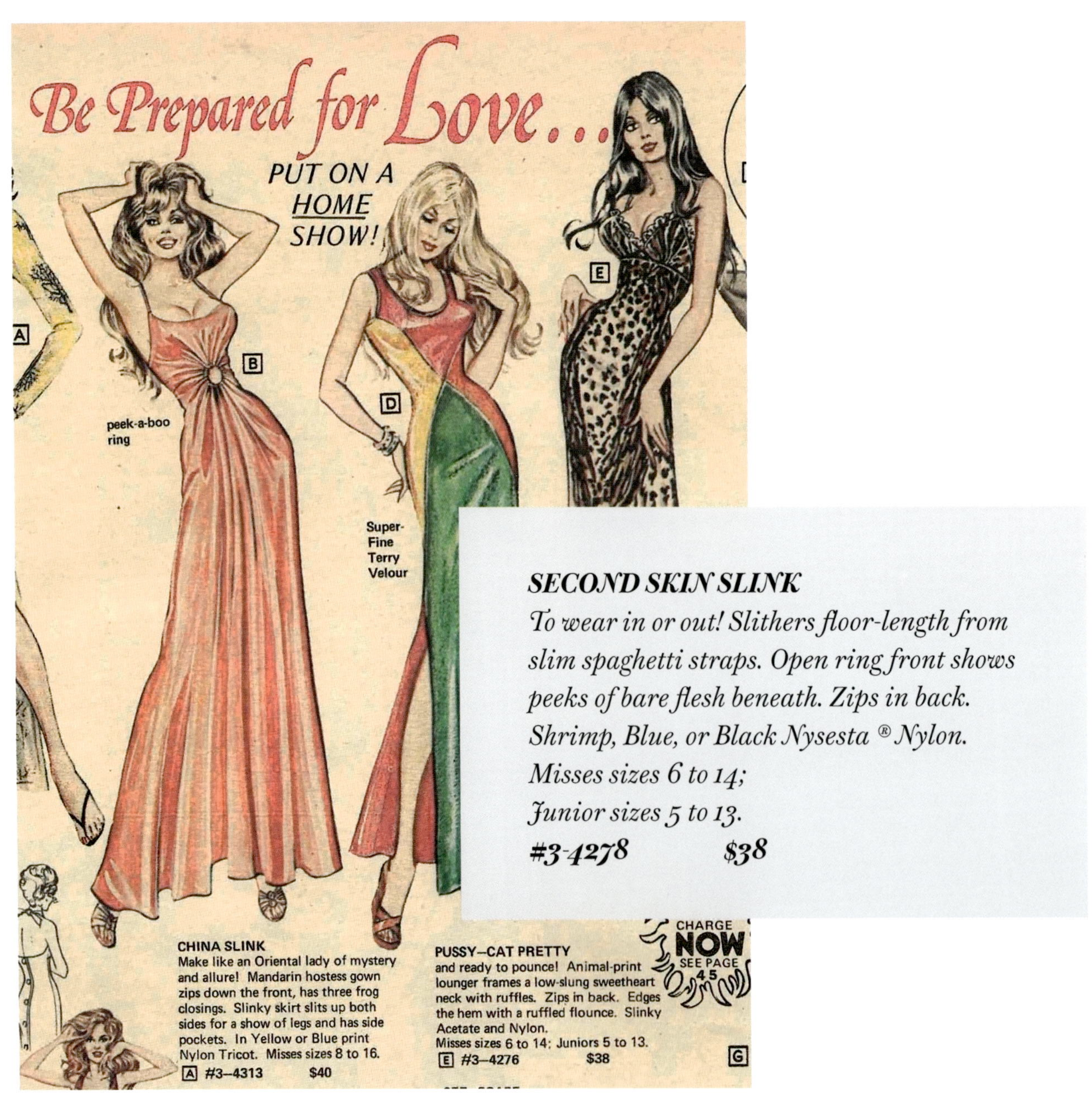

SECOND SKIN SLINK

To wear in or out! Slithers floor-length from slim spaghetti straps. Open ring front shows peeks of bare flesh beneath. Zips in back. Shrimp, Blue, or Black Nysesta ® Nylon. Misses sizes 6 to 14; Junior sizes 5 to 13.

#3-4278 $38

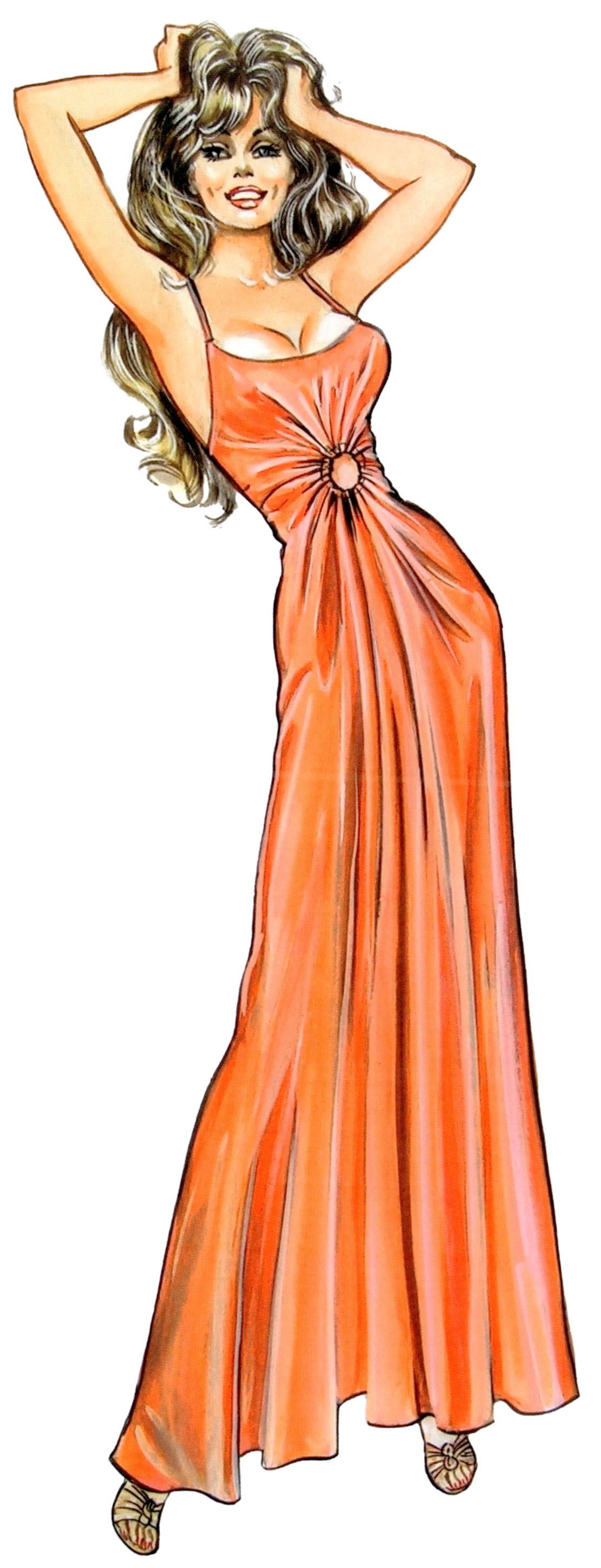

VANESSA

This stylish retro ensemble radiates bold 1970s glamour with a modern edge. The sleek, lavender-colored fabric hugs the body, highlighting the figure, while the crop top with button details and long sleeves adds a touch of sophistication. The high-waisted, flared pants with dramatic slits and button accents create movement and flair, making this look both edgy and elegant. The model's voluminous, wavy red hair and sultry expression complete the look.

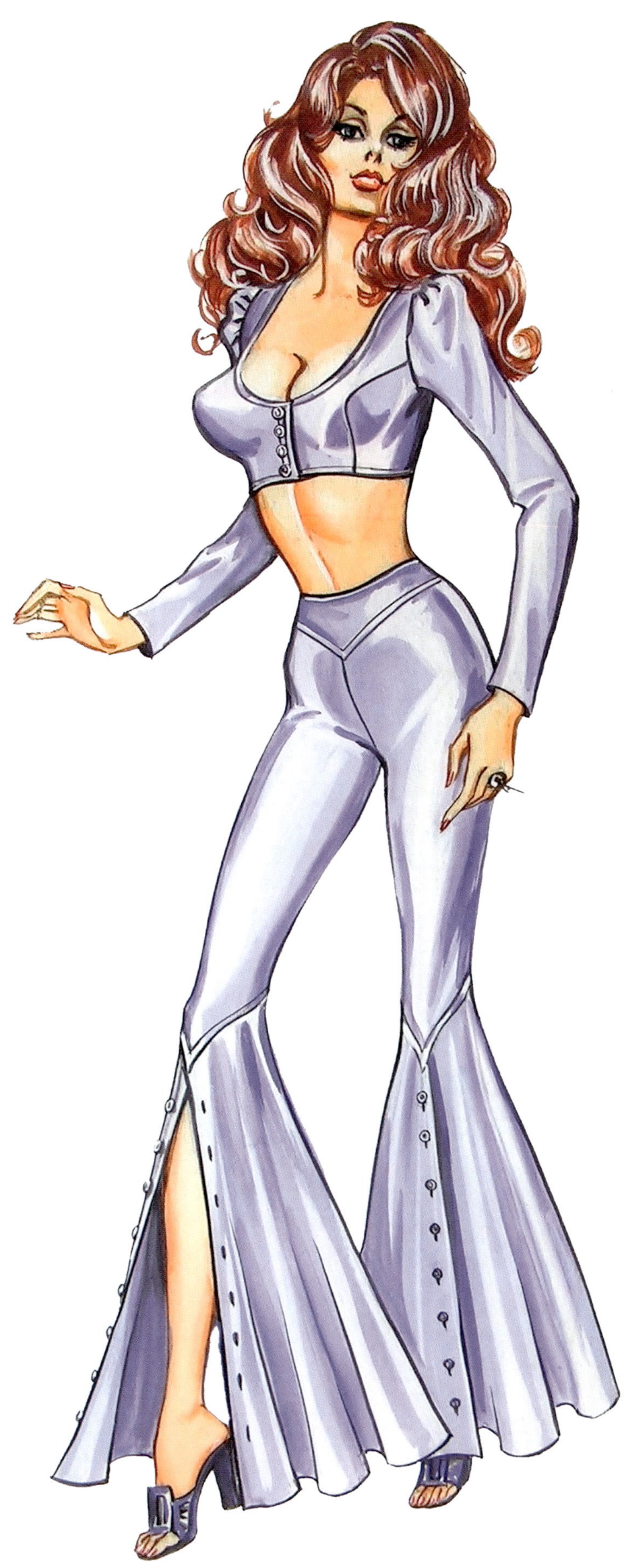

RHONDA

Wow! This model commands attention in a bold and sexy ensemble. Its catalog listing presents the outfit as a swimsuit and cover-up, but it would be equally suitable as club wear. The sleek lines and cropped top highlight her stunning figure, making it impossible to miss this gorgeous redhead—a true 1970s diva—whether she's at the pool or on the dance floor.

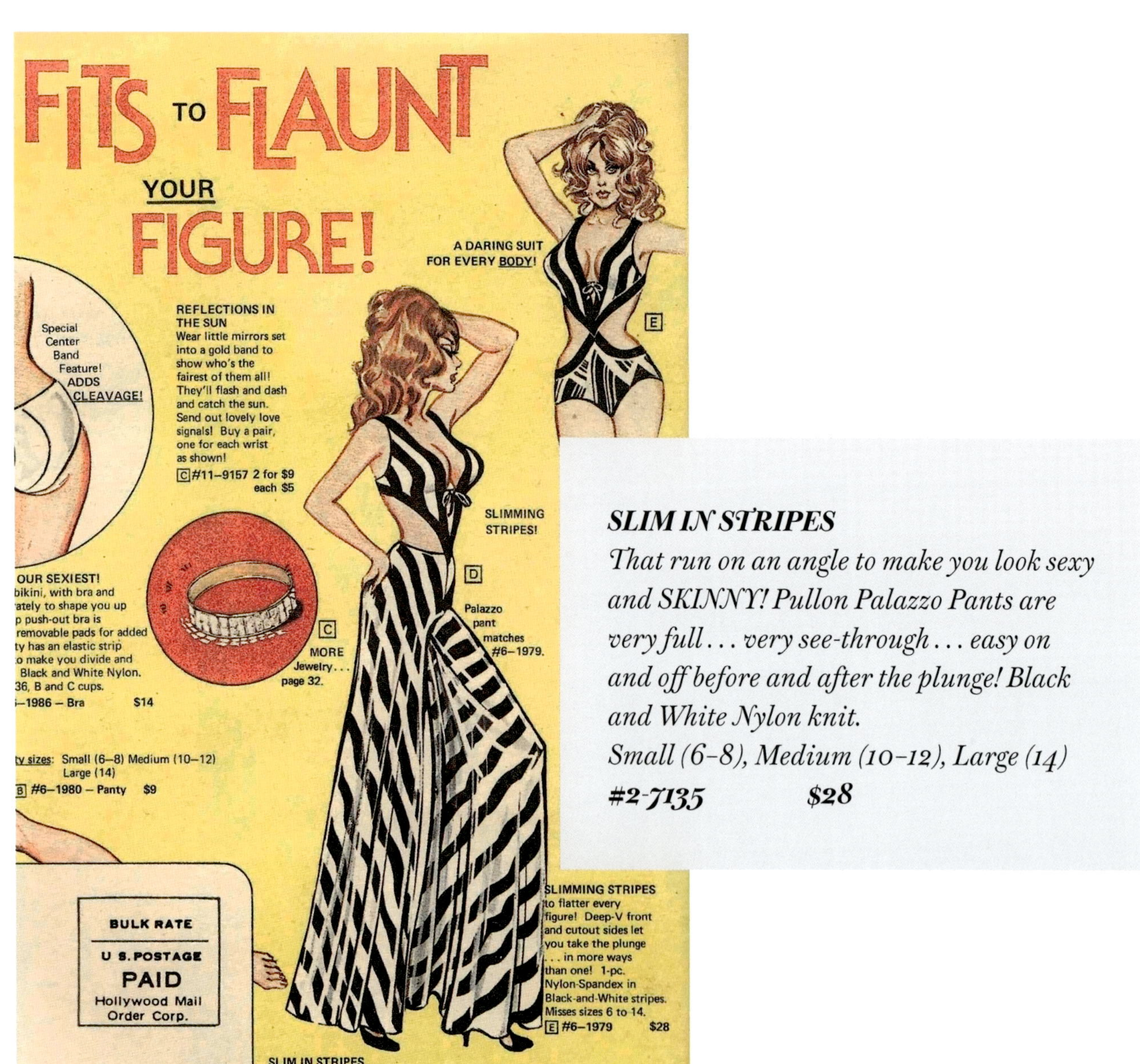

SLIM IN STRIPES
That run on an angle to make you look sexy and SKINNY! Pullon Palazzo Pants are very full . . . very see-through . . . easy on and off before and after the plunge! Black and White Nylon knit.
Small (6–8), Medium (10–12), Large (14)
#2-7135 $28

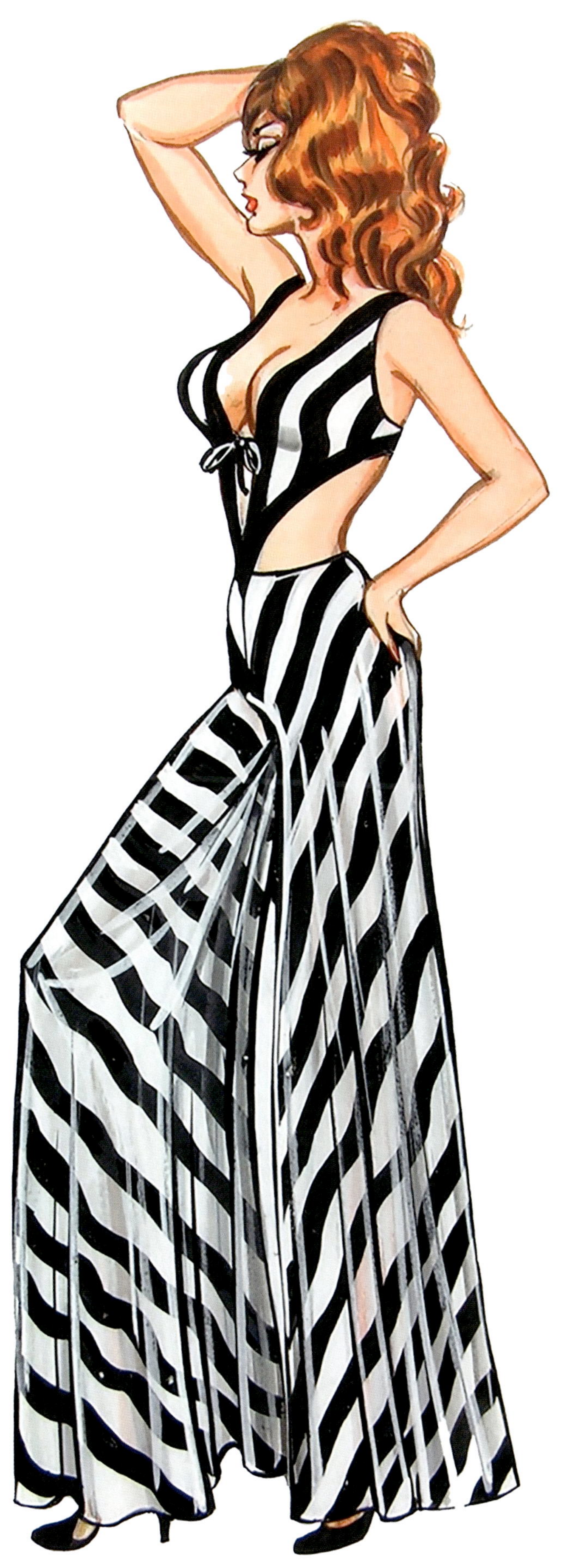

RITA

Another stunner in a showstopping jumpsuit, featuring daring side cutouts, a plunging neckline, and wide, flowing flared pants. The metal ring at the bust adds an extra edgy touch, revealing even more skin, while the curve-hugging fabric makes a bold and unforgettable statement.

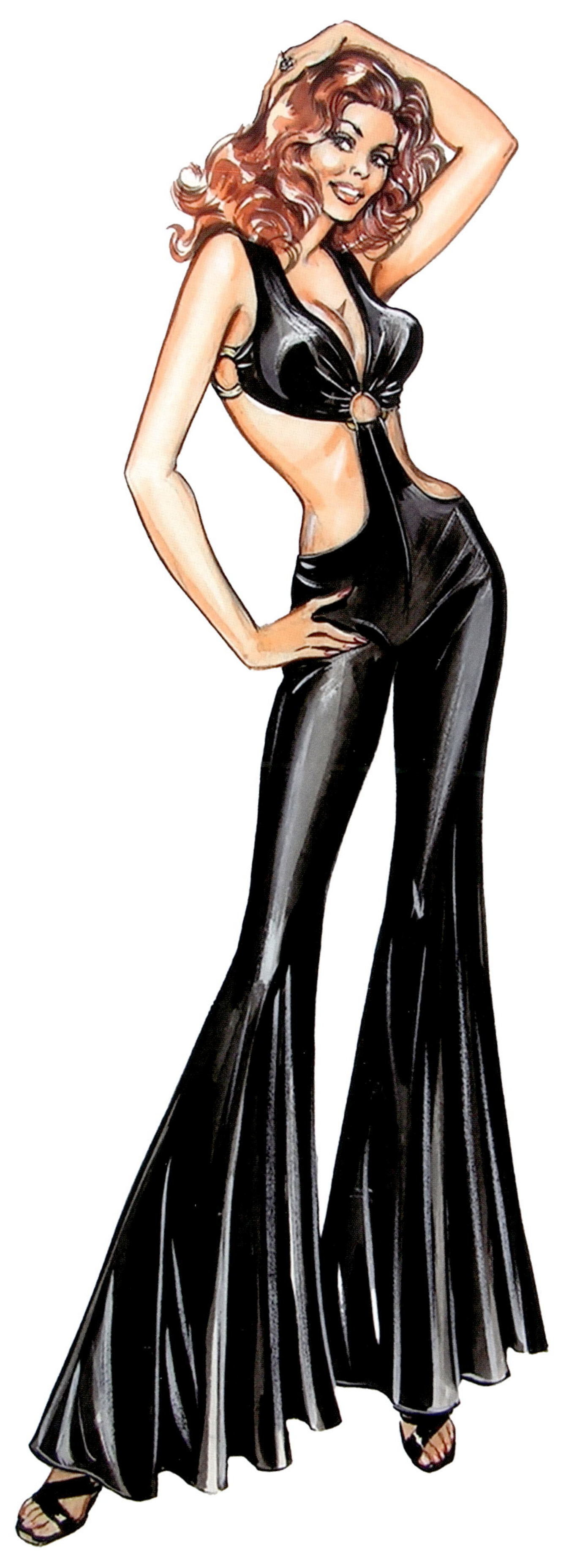

TAWNIE

Dazzling and dance floor ready, this model stuns in a two-piece ensemble. The spaghetti-strap top is a cascade of shimmering fringe, moving effortlessly with every step, while the form-fitting bell-bottom pants hug her curves before flaring out into fringe-accented drama. The silvery-white hue catches the light, making her the center of attention. With a look this electrifying, she's ready to steal the show and dance the night away!

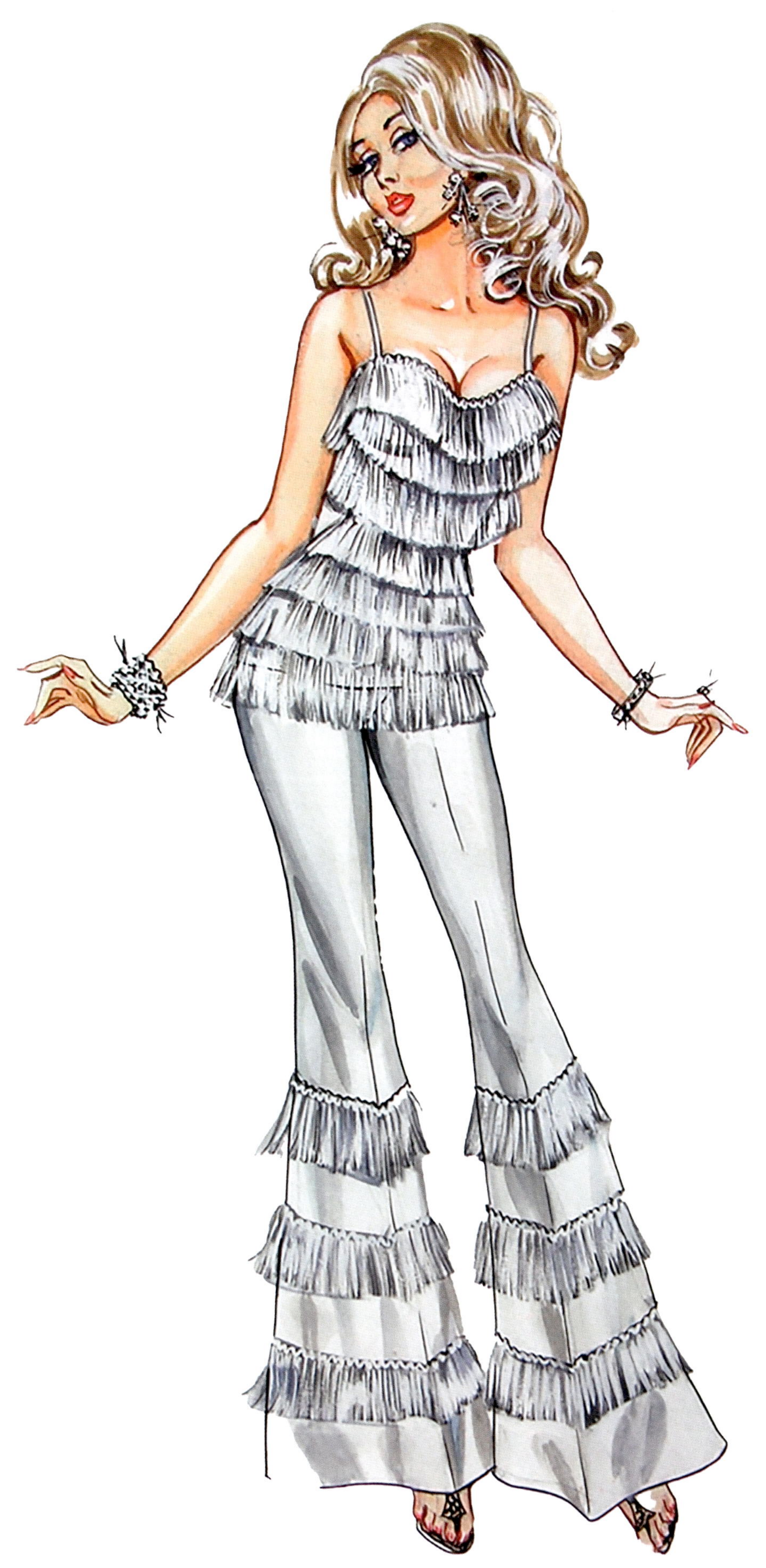

JANET

Bold and sultry, Janet turns heads in this daring two-piece black ensemble. Her plunge-neck crop top features dramatic flared sleeves and ladder-cut detailing along the arms, paired perfectly with high-waisted pants that sculpt her silhouette. Bold cutouts run the length of each leg before flowing into floor-skimming flares. It is truly a sexy, show-stopping suit designed to make an entrance and leave a lasting impression.

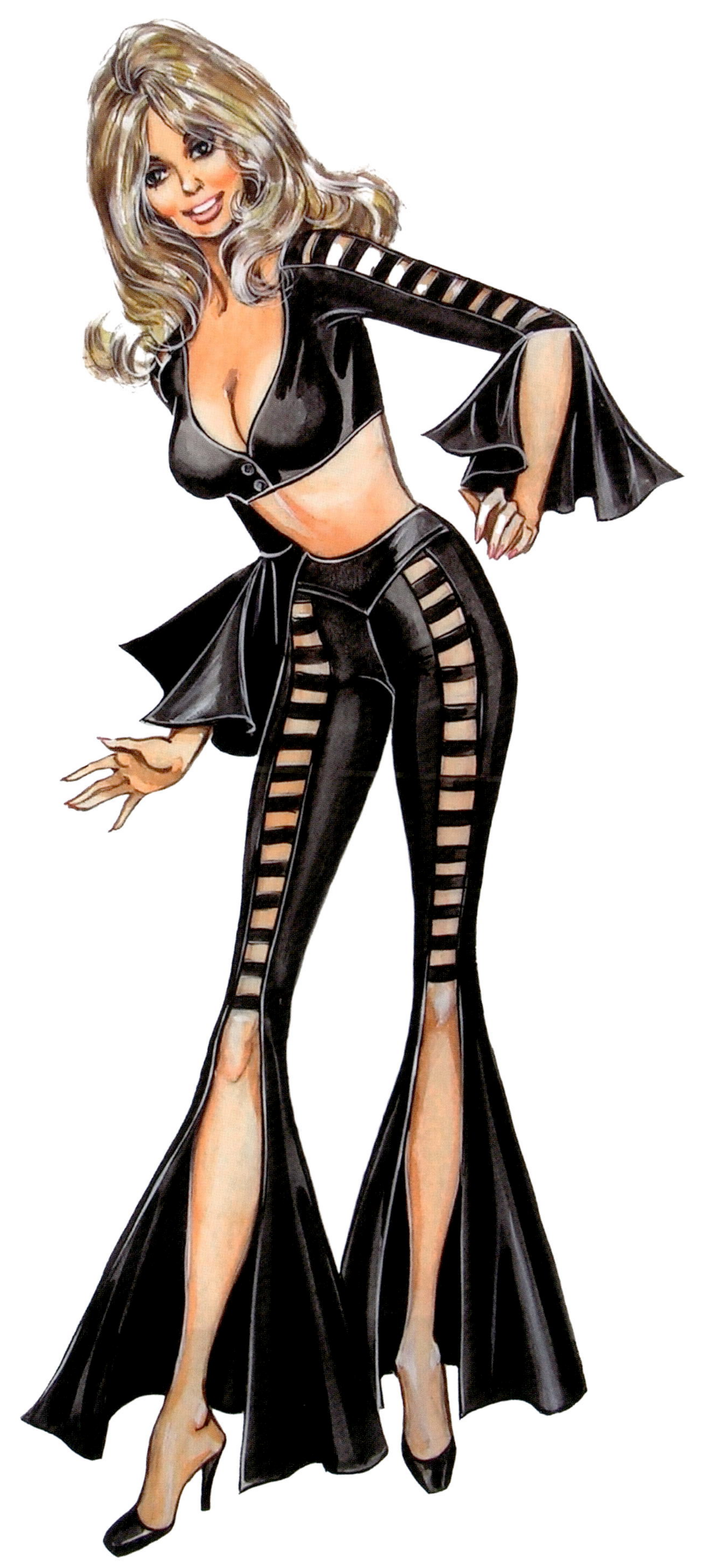

DIXIE

This fiery-red two-piece ensemble turns heads with its bold '70s country-disco flair. The plunging neckline and exposed midriff bring undeniable sex appeal, while layers of fringe cascade from the neckline down the open-front top and along the dramatic long sleeves. The high-rise, form-fitting bell-bottoms hug every curve before flaring out. Kneeling confidently on one knee, the model radiates sexy, showstopping confidence with undeniable stage presence.

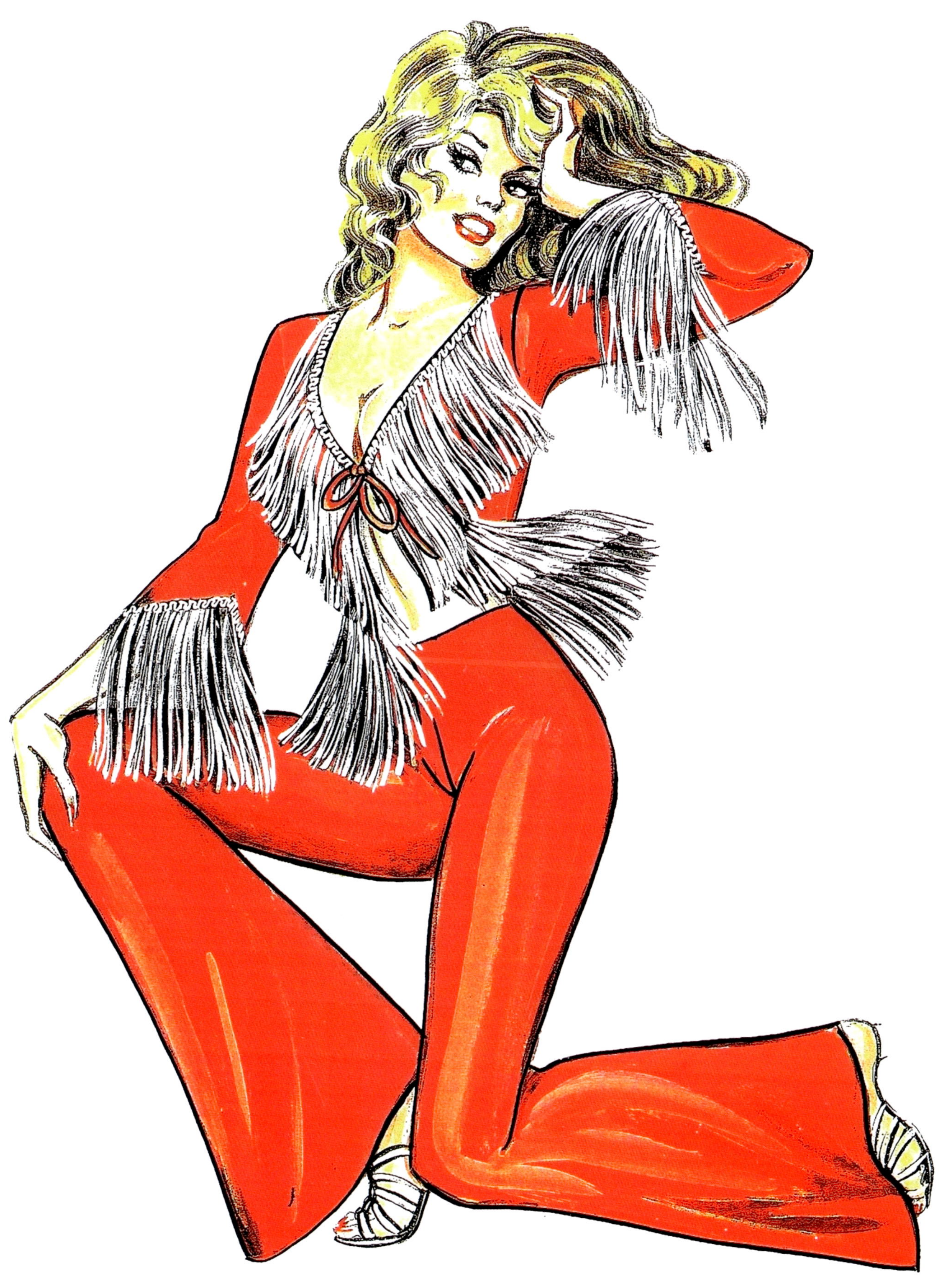

JASMINE

A daring deep-purple jumpsuit with a sleek, form-fitting silhouette. The plunging neckline ties at the bust, while the top fastens to the pants only at the sides, leaving the midriff fully bare for a striking, revealing look. The low-cut V of the bell-bottom pants dips below the belly button, adding extra edge. Long, fitted sleeves provide balance, while matching purple heels and a voluminous curly updo complete this unforgettable statement.

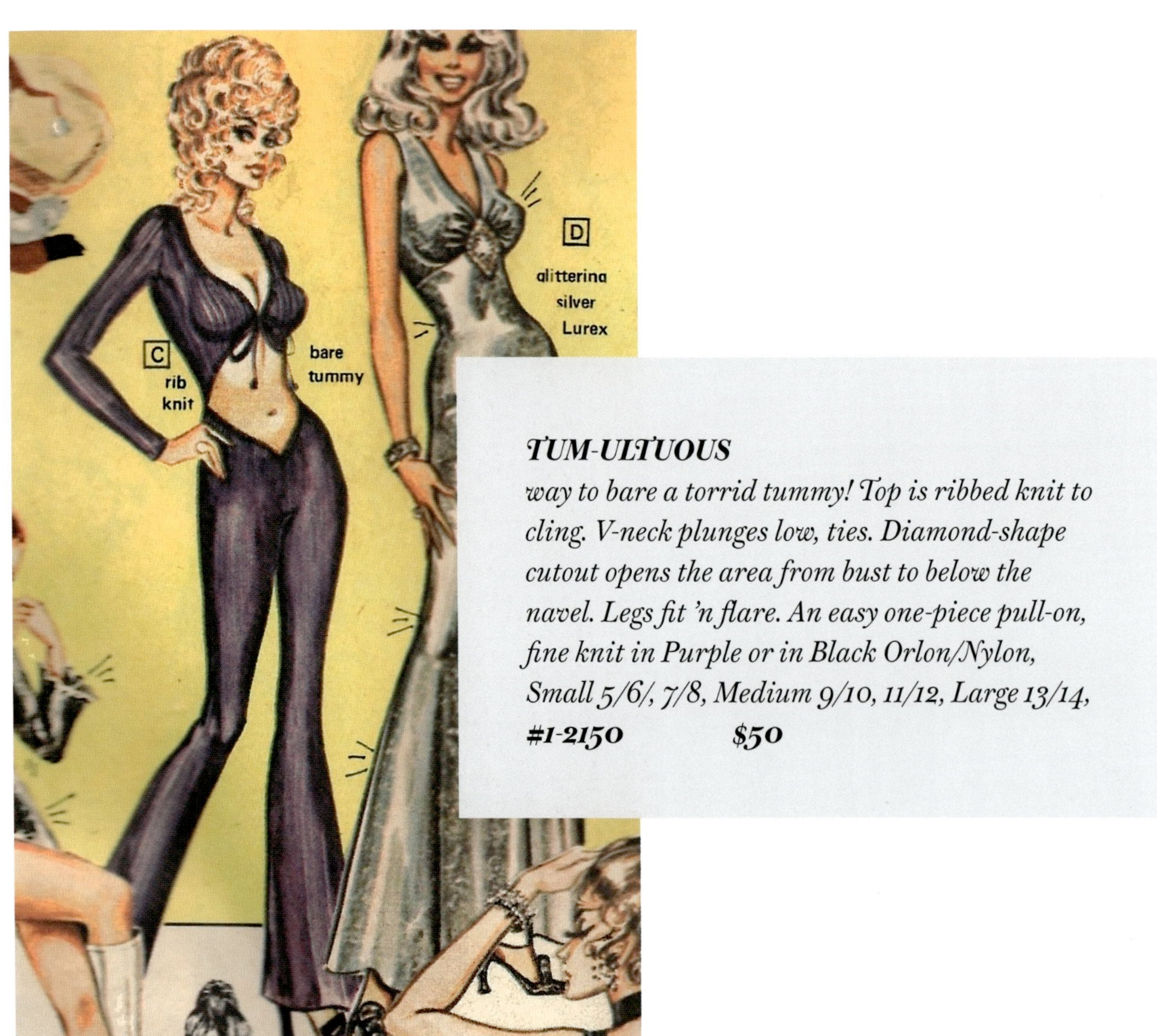

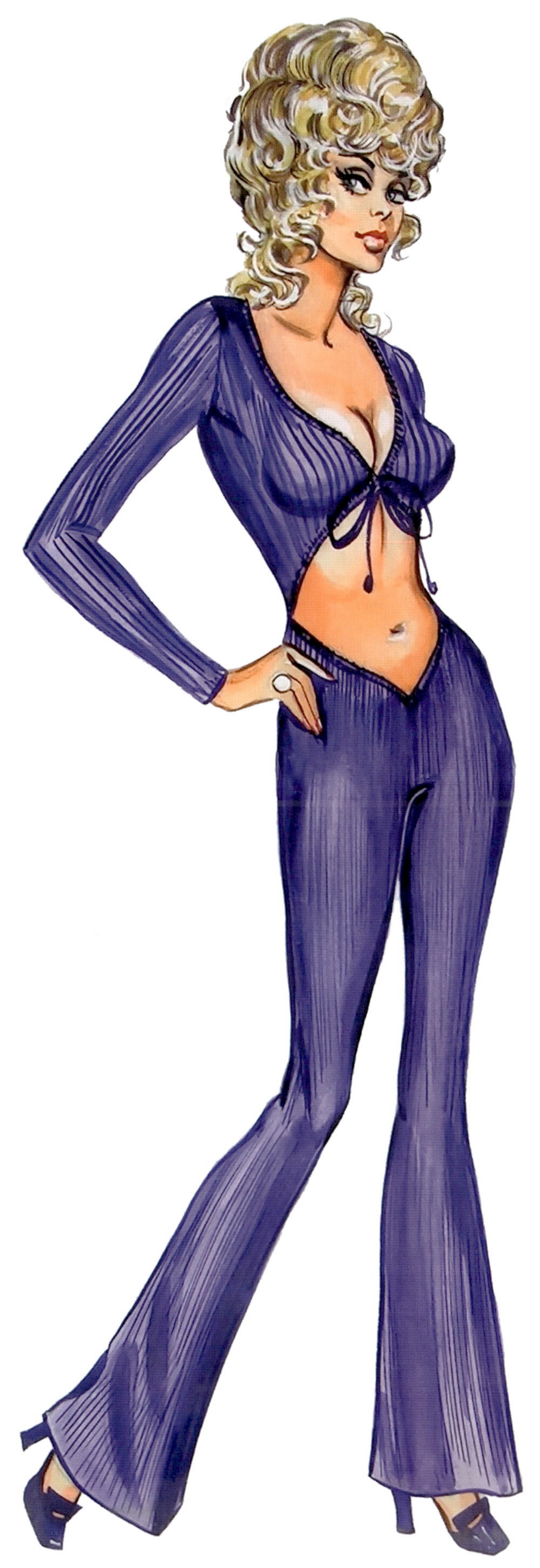

DESIREE

An ultra-sexy, striking-red jumpsuit, with sleek leatherlike sheen. The long-sleeved top features a deep V-neckline and bold button detailing beneath the bust, leading to a wide, structured waistband that cinches the figure. Below, matching buttons run down each leg to the knee—left unfastened from the upper thigh to reveal a sultry flash of leg. Knee-high slits add extra movement as the flared legs flow with each step. Strappy block heels complete the look with confident flair.

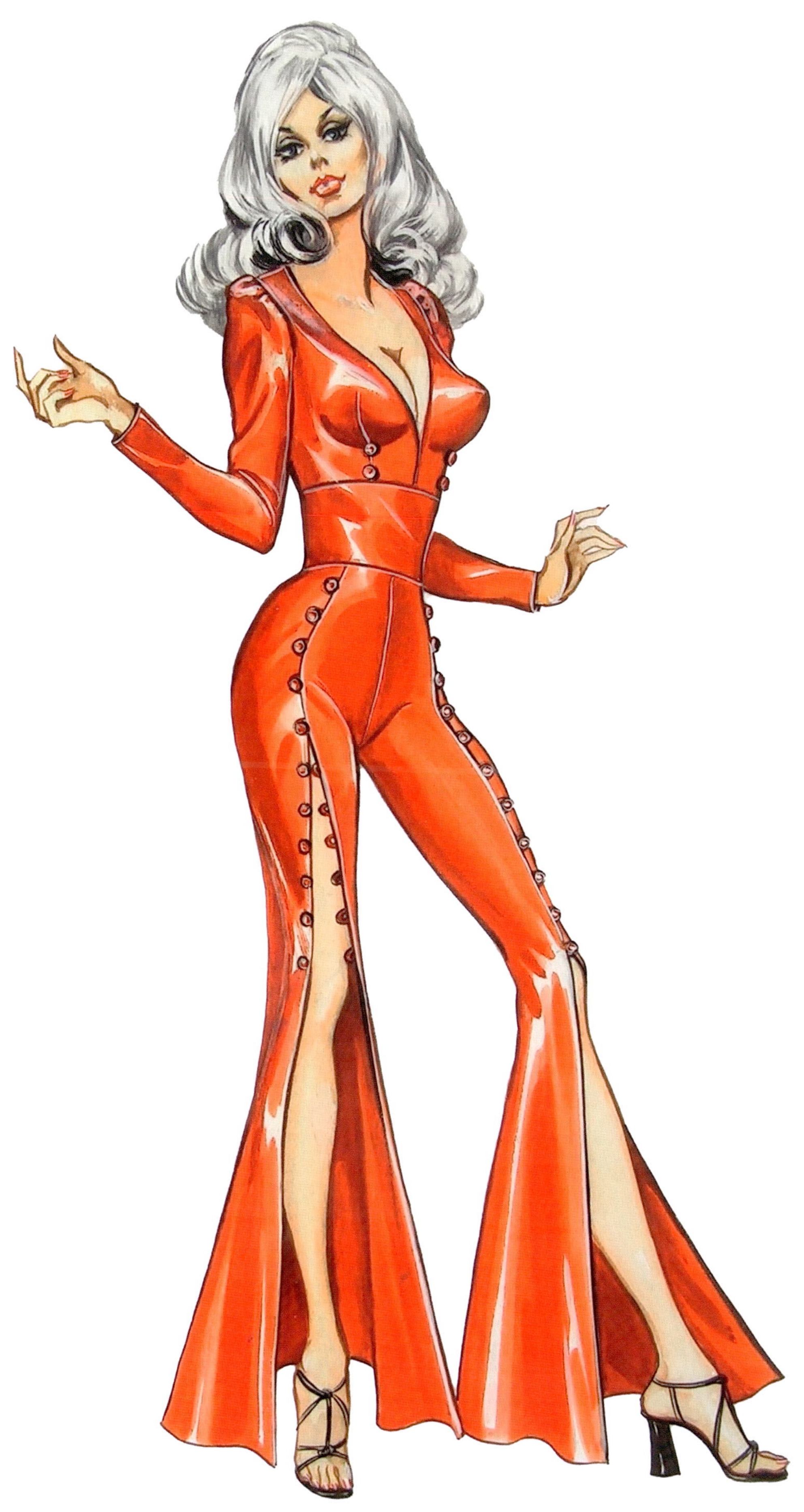

DEBORAH

This refined beauty channels old-Hollywood grace in a lustrous satin, knee-length dress that highlights her hourglass silhouette. A sheer, brocade-style cropped jacket fastened at the bust adds elegance, with sleeves ending just past the elbows to reveal her satin gloves. Simple black pumps and a single strand of pearls complete the timeless, sophisticated look.

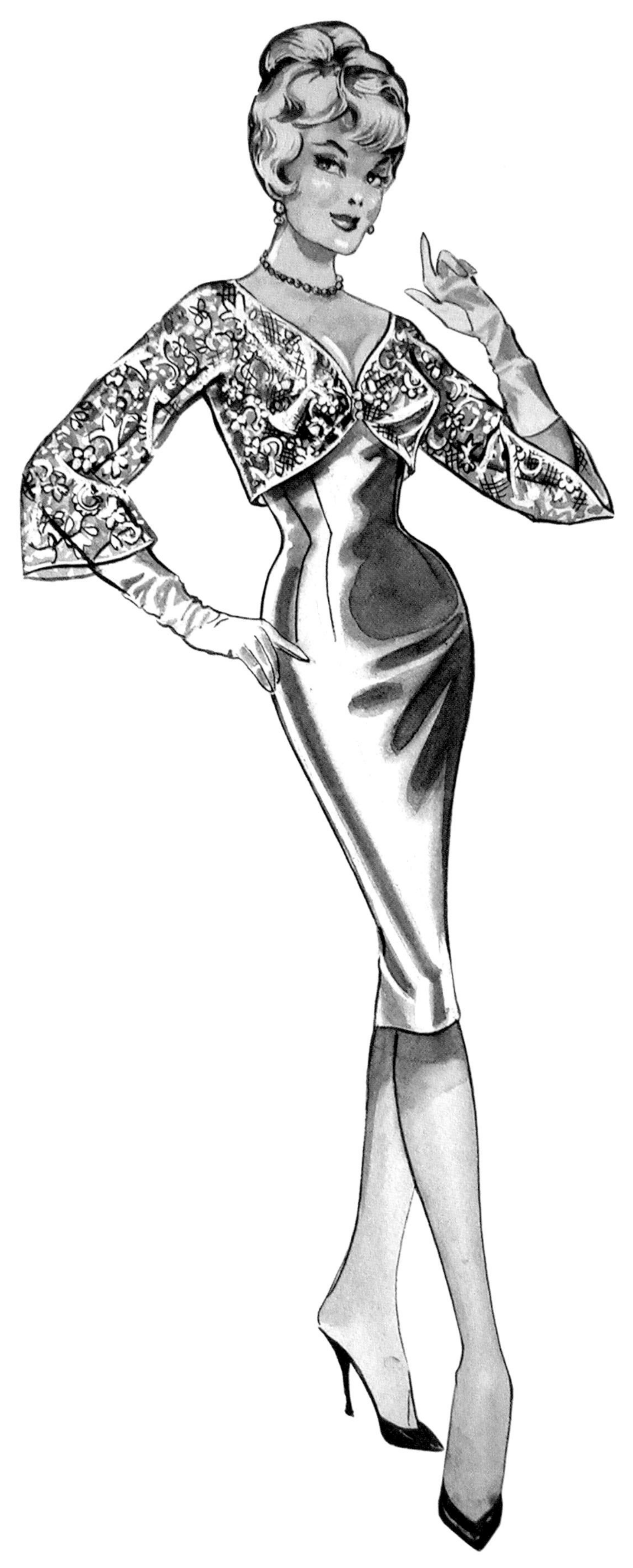

LINDA

A confident, alluring woman stands with poise, holding a cigarette in a long, stylish holder. Her figure is highlighted by a beautifully ruched, sleeveless knee-length dress, which perfectly complements her hourglass shape. The dress features a pointed bustline, a signature style of the 1960s. Satin gloves stretch gracefully past her elbows, while simple black heels and bold statement earrings add the finishing touches to her glamorous look.

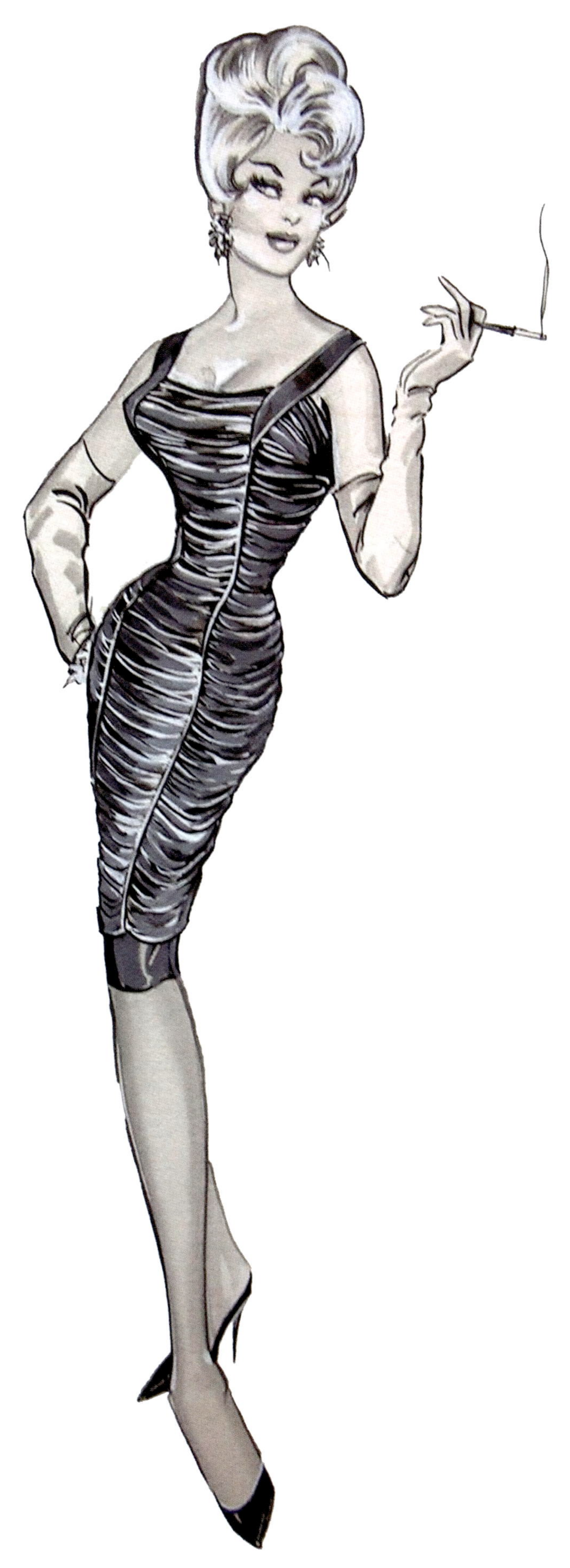

BARBARA

This beautiful, classy model looks effortlessly sophisticated in a knee-length satin dress with a soft, elegant sheen. The dress features bold ruffles at the high neckline and at the knee, making a statement against its otherwise simple design. A delicate spaghetti-style tie cinches at the waist, adding a refined touch. She wears a single large bangle bracelet and bold statement earrings, perfectly capturing the "less is more" philosophy for a striking look. Her short, refined pixie haircut completes the ensemble, channeling timeless 1960s-era elegance.

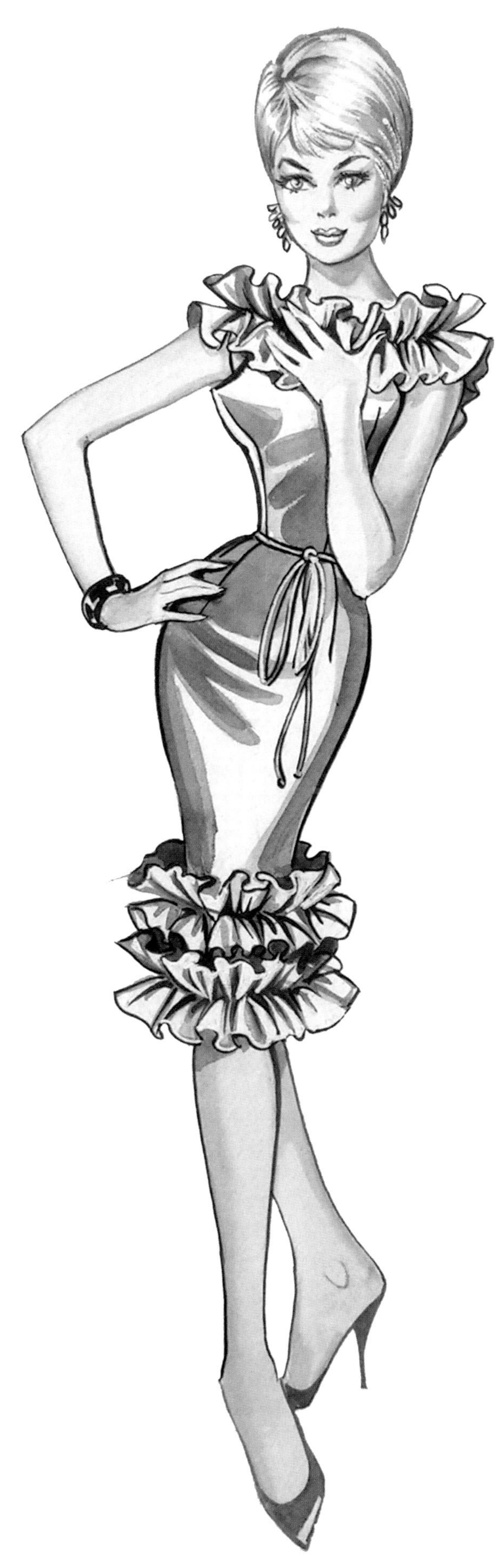

JULIE

This elegant dress channels the refined style of the 1950s with its full, flared skirt and structured bodice. The strapless design, paired with the delicate bow at the waist, reflects timeless charm that captures the essence of classic femininity. Her poised posture and glamorous accessories, including the satin gloves, further enhance the sophisticated vibe of the era, making her a picture of grace and style. A perfect representation of mid-century fashion, she embodies the poised and polished essence of '50s glamour.

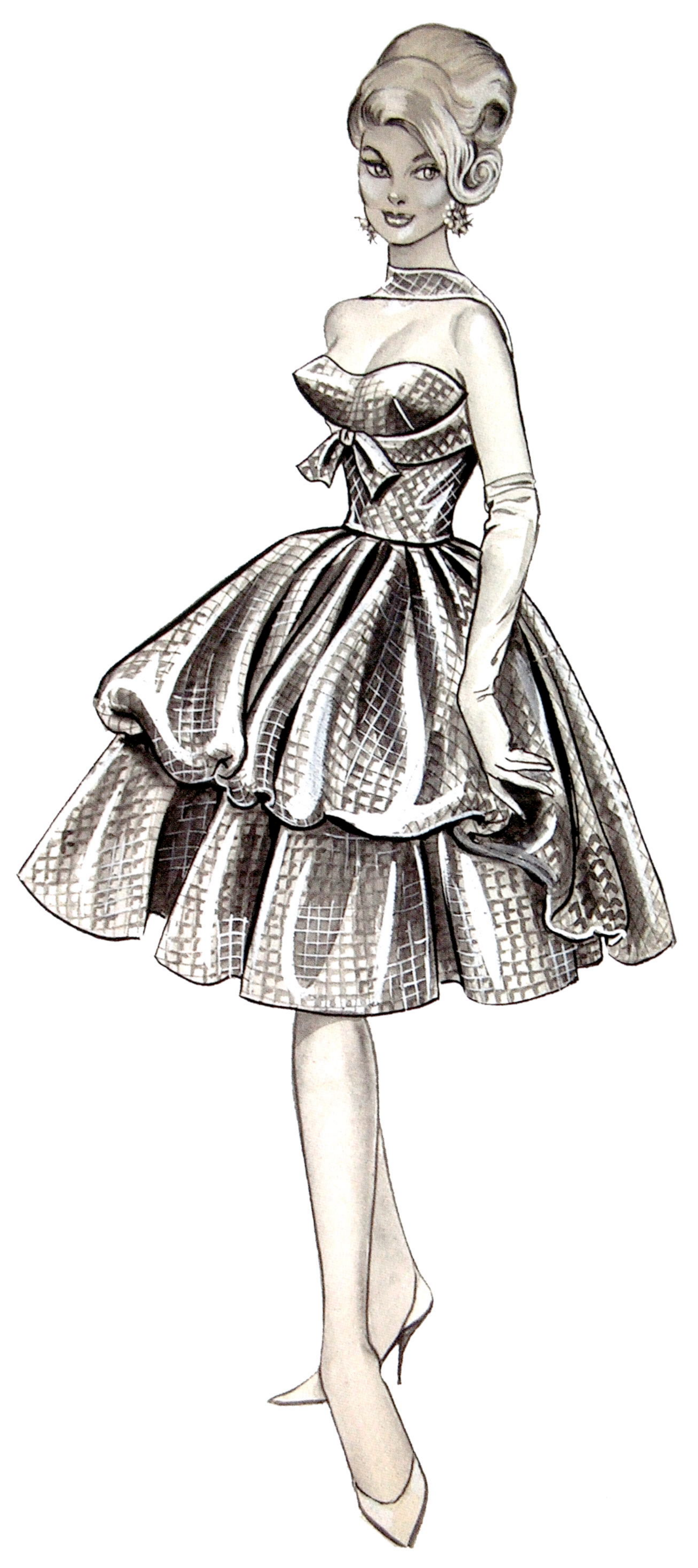

ROSE

This chic, shimmering silver dress embodies the elegance and glamour of the early 1960s. With its sleek, form-fitting silhouette and delicate ruffle detailing at the neckline, it perfectly captures the refined, polished style of the era. The waist is cinched with a jeweled belt, adding a touch of sophistication, while her playful, confident pose and stylish accessories complete the look, evoking the bold yet graceful spirit of '60s fashion.

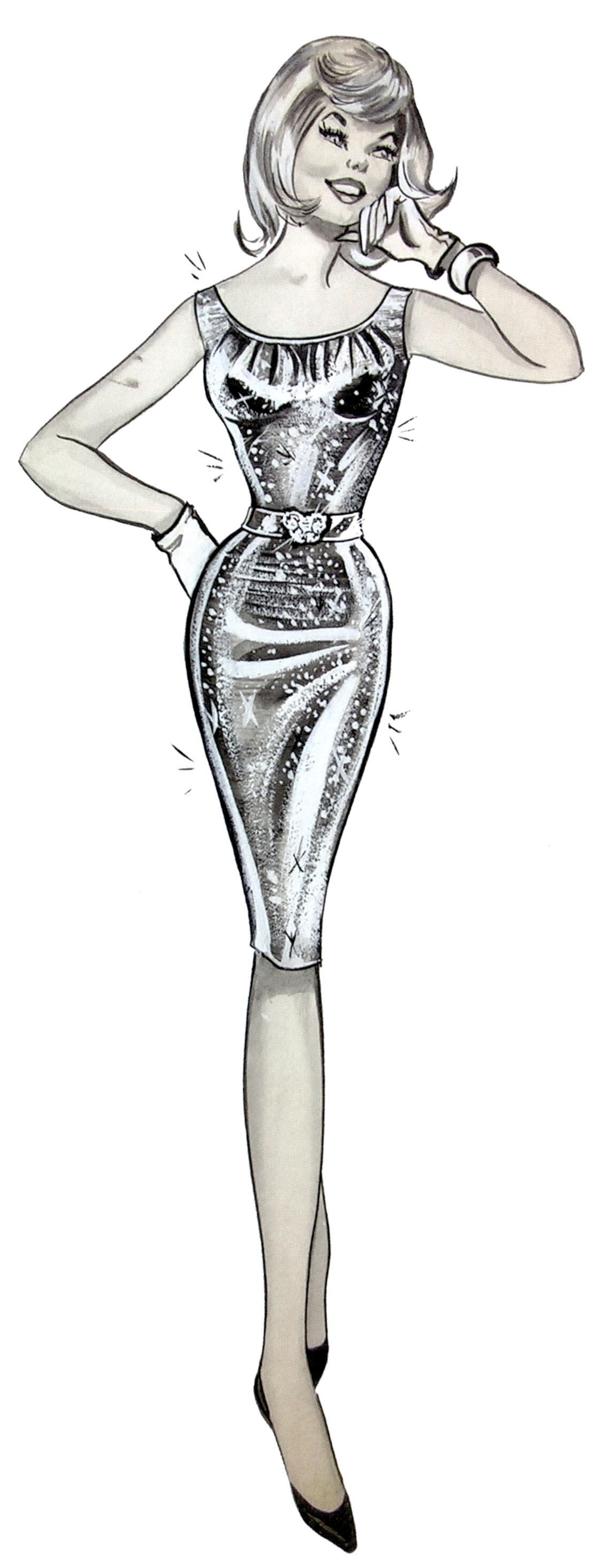

JACKIE

Playful, flirty, and effortlessly chic, this fringed dress is designed for movement and fun. Layers of delicate ruffles cascade softly, creating graceful motion with every step. The dress is paired perfectly with her voluminous curls and bold cat-eye makeup, as she radiates confidence and playful charm. This is a look made for catching the spotlight–bold, glamorous, and full of youthful energy.

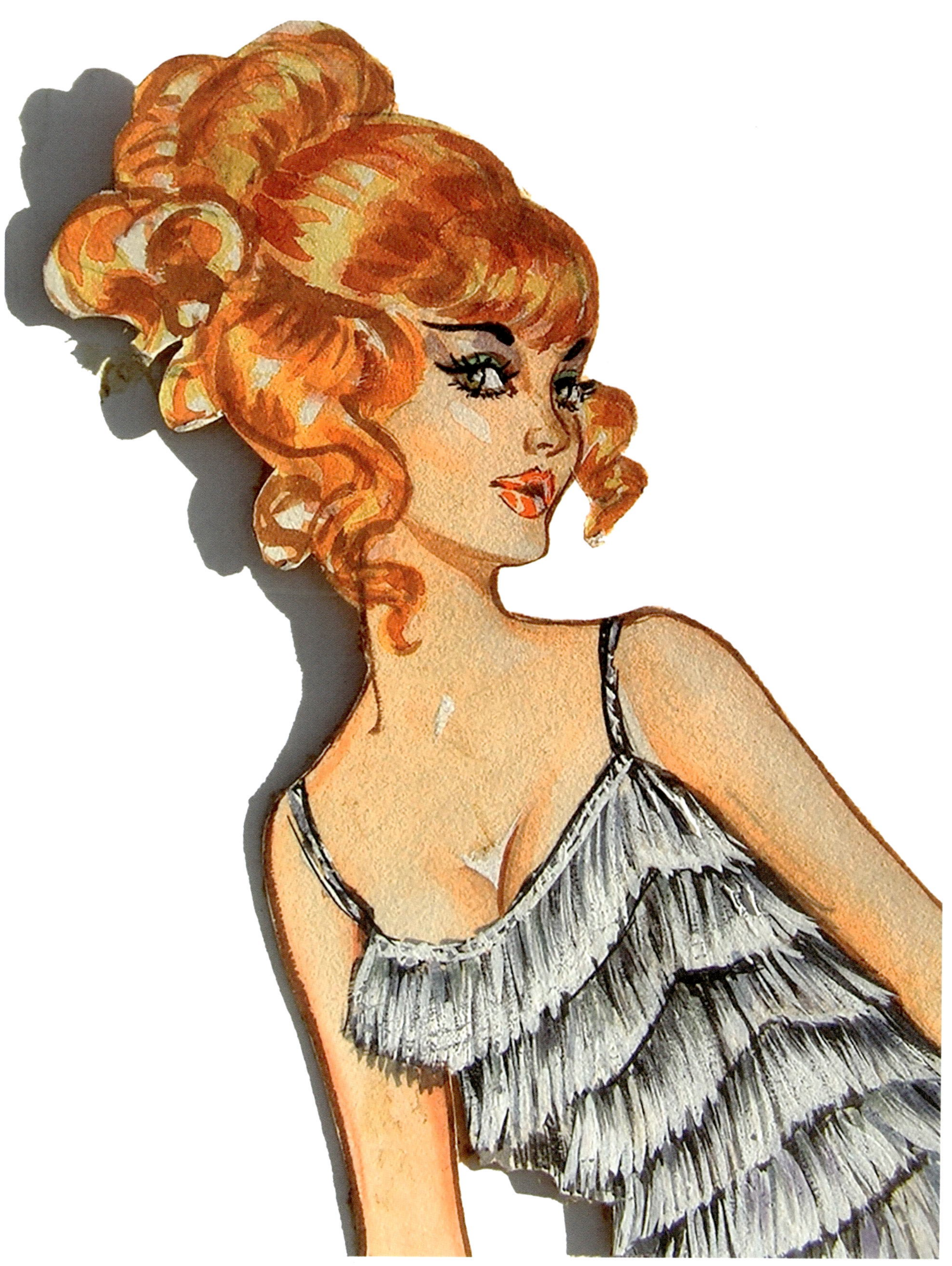

LOIS

Bold, vibrant, and effortlessly stylish, this bright-pink jumpsuit makes an undeniable fashion statement. With its fitted waist, dramatic wide-leg flares, and button-front detailing, this piece is as flattering as it is eye-catching. The sleek collar and matching belt add structure and sophistication, while the model's softly curled hair and confident pose amplify the glamorous, head-turning effect. This look is made for someone ready to command attention with grace and confidence.

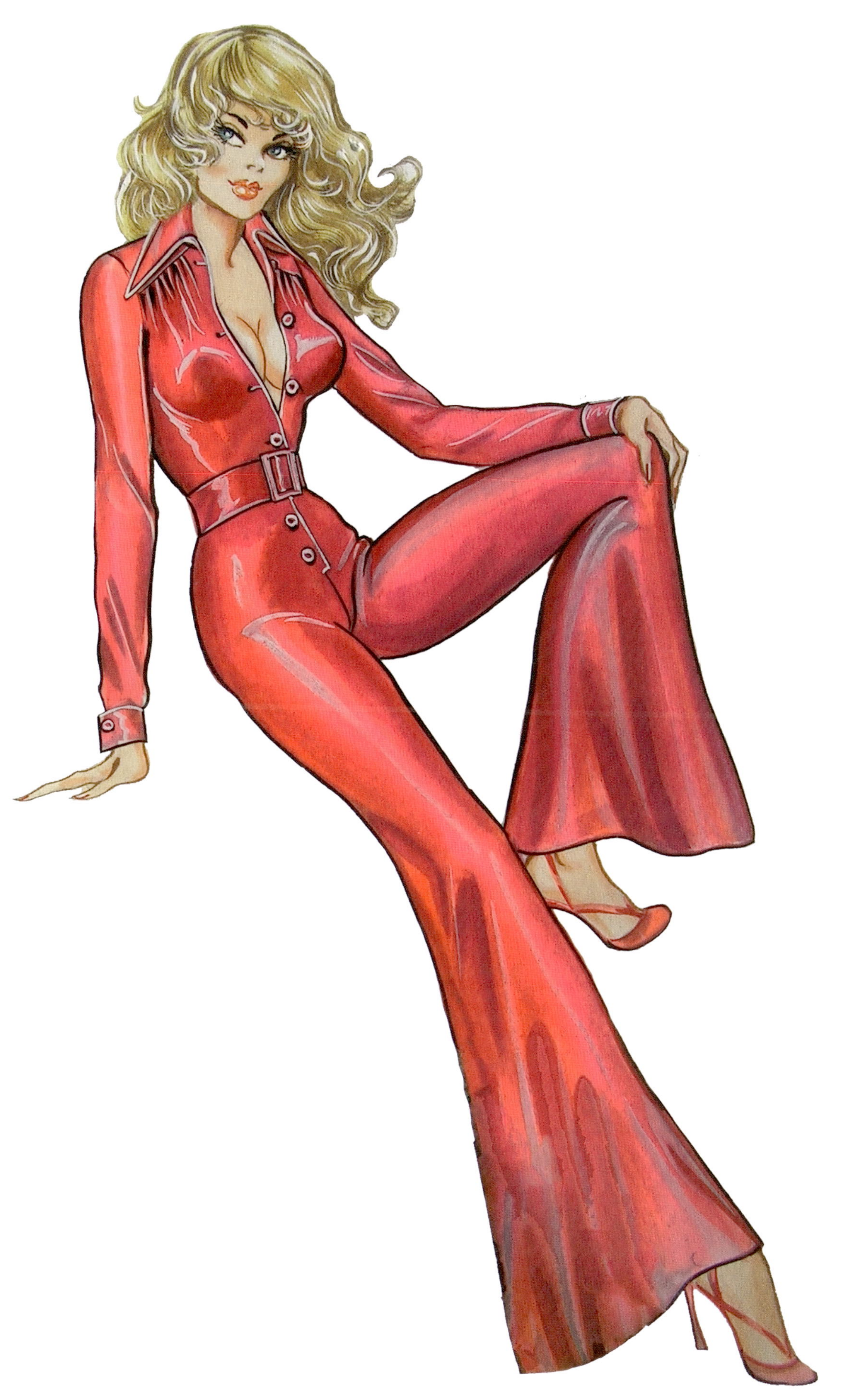

GEORGIA

This sleek jumpsuit features a structured bodice and dramatic bell-bottom flared pants. The figure-skimming silhouette is paired beautifully with an elegant fringed shawl, adding texture and graceful movement. A striking snake-inspired jewelry piece wraps around her upper arm, lending a daring and exotic touch.

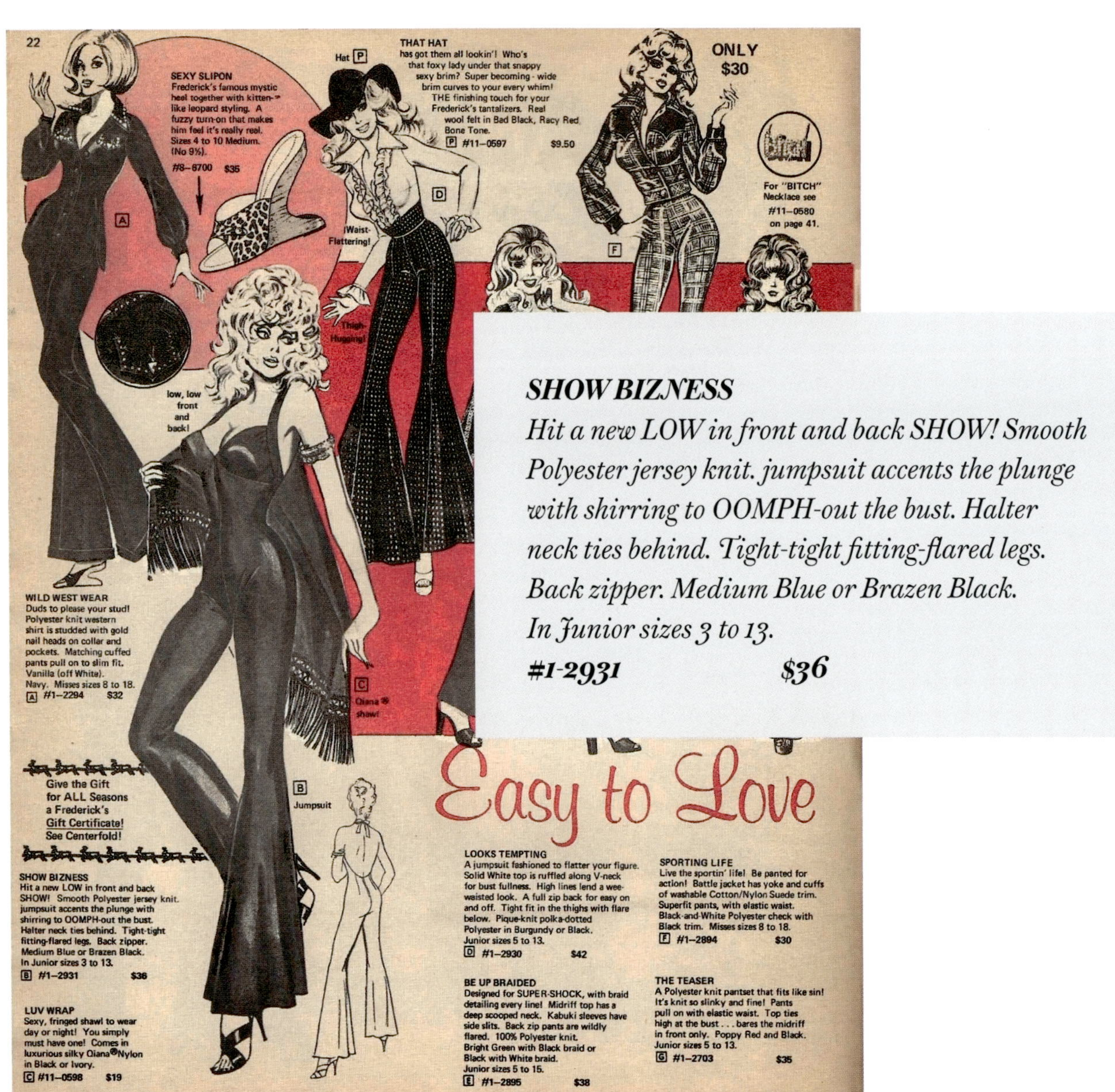

22

SEXY SLIPON
Frederick's famous mystic heel together with kitten-like leopard styling. A fuzzy turn-on that makes him feel it's really real. Sizes 4 to 10 Medium. (No 9½).
#8–6700 $35

Hat P

THAT HAT
has got them all lookin'! Who's that foxy lady under that snappy sexy brim? Super becoming - wide brim curves to your every whim! THE finishing touch for your Frederick's tantalizers. Real wool felt in Bad Black, Racy Red Bone Tone.
P #11–0597 $9.50

ONLY $30

For "BITCH" Necklace see #11–0580 on page 41.

Waist-Flattering!

Thigh-Hugging!

low, low front and back!

C Qiana shawl

B Jumpsuit

WILD WEST WEAR
Duds to please your stud! Polyester knit western shirt is studded with gold nail heads on collar and pockets. Matching cuffed pants pull on to slim fit. Vanilla (off White). Navy. Misses sizes 8 to 18.
A #1–2294 $32

Give the Gift for ALL Seasons a Frederick's Gift Certificate! See Centerfold!

SHOW BIZNESS
Hit a new LOW in front and back SHOW! Smooth Polyester jersey knit. jumpsuit accents the plunge with shirring to OOMPH-out the bust. Halter neck ties behind. Tight-tight fitting-flared legs. Back zipper. Medium Blue or Brazen Black. In Junior sizes 3 to 13.
B #1–2931 $36

LUV WRAP
Sexy, fringed shawl to wear day or night! You simply must have one! Comes in luxurious silky Qiana® Nylon in Black or Ivory.
C #11–0598 $19

Easy to Love

LOOKS TEMPTING
A jumpsuit fashioned to flatter your figure. Solid White top is ruffled along V-neck for bust fullness. High lines lend a wee-waisted look. A full zip back for easy on and off. Tight fit in the thighs with flare below. Pique-knit polka-dotted Polyester in Burgundy or Black. Junior sizes 5 to 13.
D #1–2930 $42

BE UP BRAIDED
Designed for SUPER-SHOCK, with braid detailing every line! Midriff top has a deep scooped neck. Kabuki sleeves have side slits. Back zip pants are wildly flared. 100% Polyester knit. Bright Green with Black braid or Black with White braid. Junior sizes 5 to 15.
E #1–2895 $38

SPORTING LIFE
Live the sportin' life! Be panted for action! Battle jacket has yoke and cuffs of washable Cotton/Nylon Suede trim. Superfit pants, with elastic waist. Black-and-White Polyester check with Black trim. Misses sizes 8 to 18.
F #1–2894 $30

THE TEASER
A Polyester knit pantset that fits like sin! It's knit so slinky and fine! Pants pull on with elastic waist. Top ties high at the bust . . . bares the midriff in front only. Poppy Red and Black. Junior sizes 5 to 13.
G #1–2703 $35

SHOW BIZNESS
Hit a new LOW in front and back SHOW! Smooth Polyester jersey knit. jumpsuit accents the plunge with shirring to OOMPH-out the bust. Halter neck ties behind. Tight-tight fitting-flared legs. Back zipper. Medium Blue or Brazen Black. In Junior sizes 3 to 13.
#1-2931 ***$36***

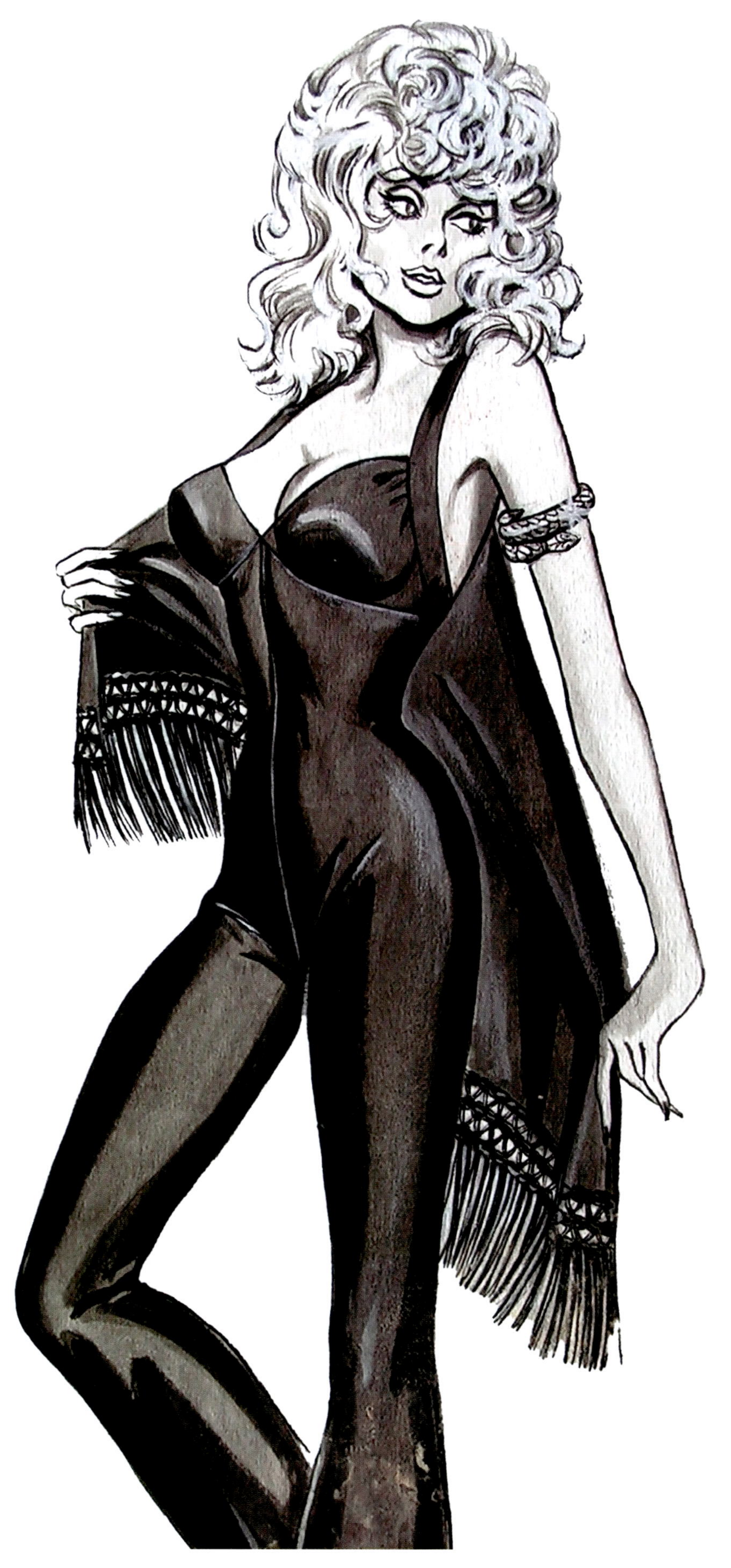

KIMBERLY

Sophisticated yet alluring, this sleek gown elegantly blurs the lines between luxurious evening wear and an enticing nightgown. Its silky, figure-skimming silhouette, accented by a delicate lace heart-shaped bodice, adds a romantic and sensual appeal with a high slit that gracefully reveals her legs.

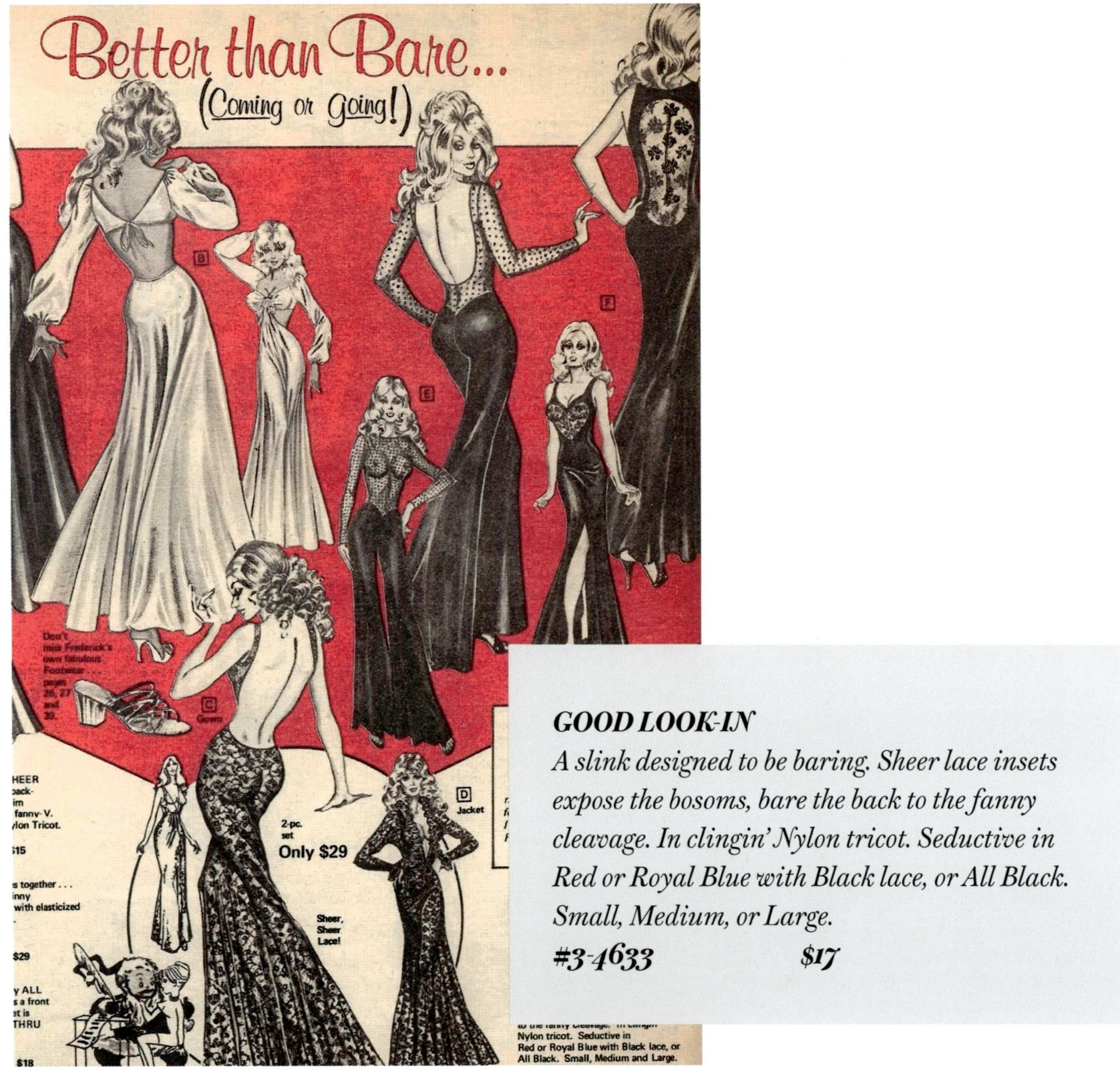

GOOD LOOK-IN

A slink designed to be baring. Sheer lace insets expose the bosoms, bare the back to the fanny cleavage. In clingin' Nylon tricot. Seductive in Red or Royal Blue with Black lace, or All Black. Small, Medium, or Large.

#3-4633 ***$17***

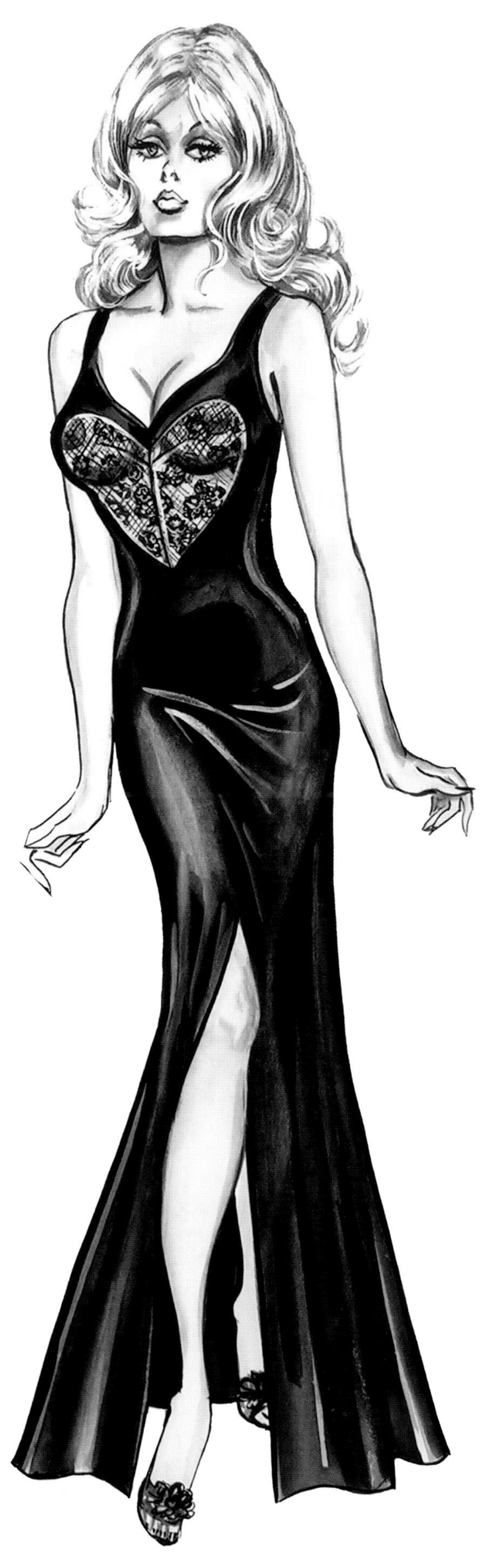

ANASTASIA

Another elegant, silky floor-length gown designed to turn heads. Its sophisticated silhouette is brought to life by a playful floral pattern, which adds a whimsical touch. The plunging neckline and daring thigh-high slit enhance the gown's allure, while the model's poised and captivating stance adds an extra layer of glamour, making this look undeniably chic and memorable.

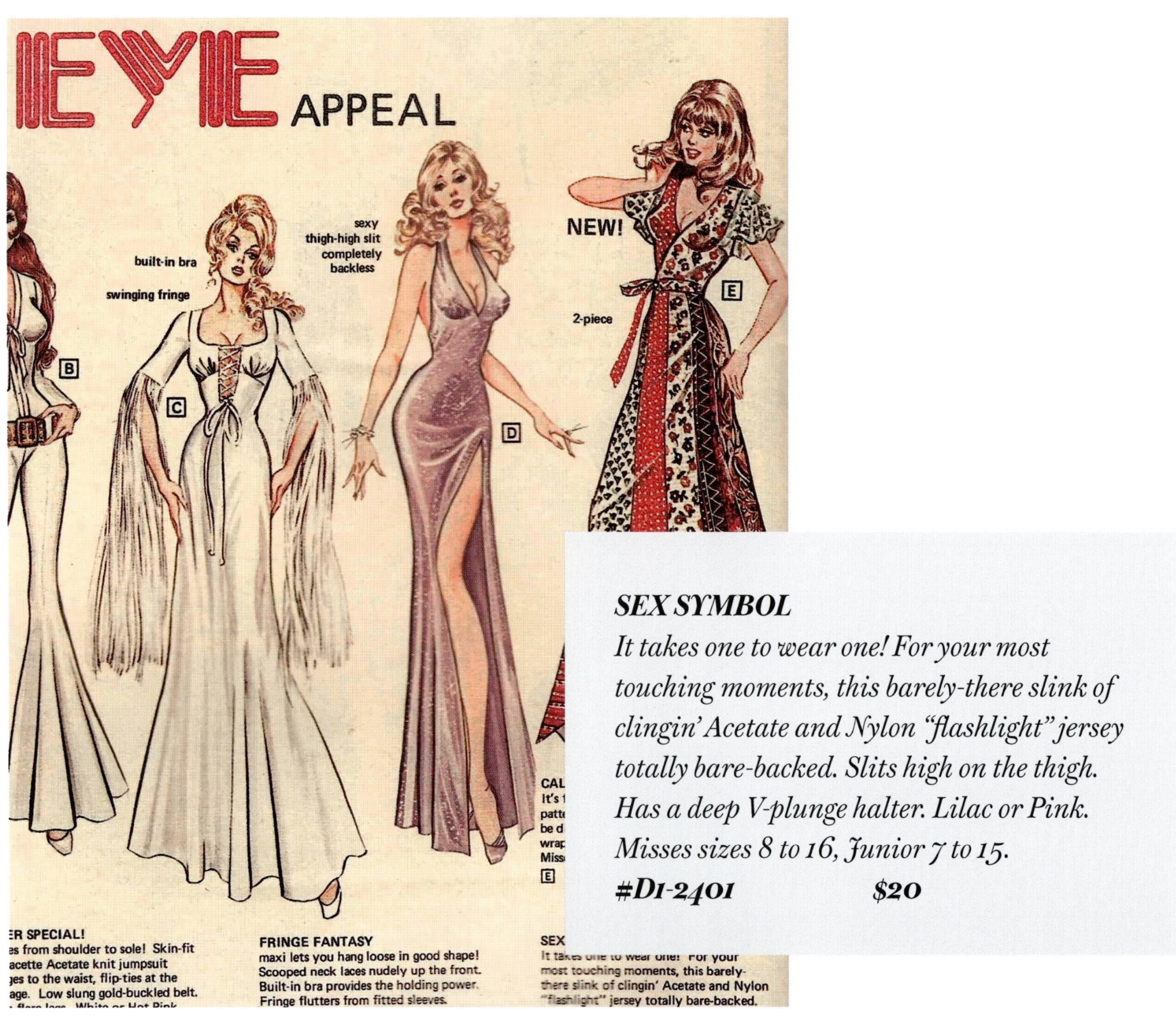

SEX SYMBOL

It takes one to wear one! For your most touching moments, this barely-there slink of clingin' Acetate and Nylon "flashlight" jersey totally bare-backed. Slits high on the thigh. Has a deep V-plunge halter. Lilac or Pink. Misses sizes 8 to 16, Junior 7 to 15.

#D1-2401 ***$20***

Like the paper dolls of the era, Frederick's of Hollywood often reused their favorite models and poses. Here, an almost identical illustration of "Anastasia" is subtly retouched and dressed in lavender for a new season.

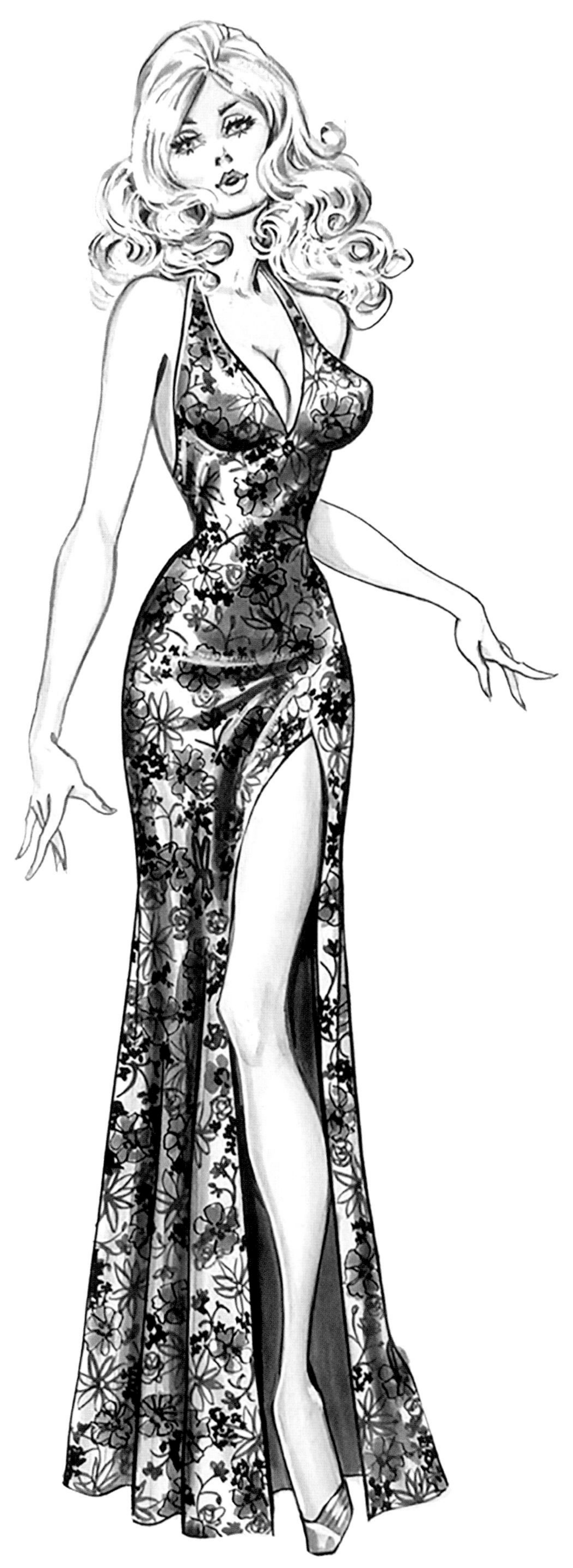

GAIL

A long-line button-up dress featuring a plunging neckline and a dramatic front slit created by buttons that reveal the model's long, alluring legs. The oversized collar is a classic '70s-inspired detail, bringing tailored elegance and retro charm. A delicate tie at the waist accentuates her figure, while the shimmering fabric adds glamour and sophistication.

Frederick's of Hollywood catalog description:

GLITTER ROBE
In a free-flowing caftan that glitters and glows as you go! Gold braid lifts the breasts, edges the neck, Elastic fit in the waist. Silvery White or Gold Rayon and Metallic. One size fits all.
#3-4178 ***$22***

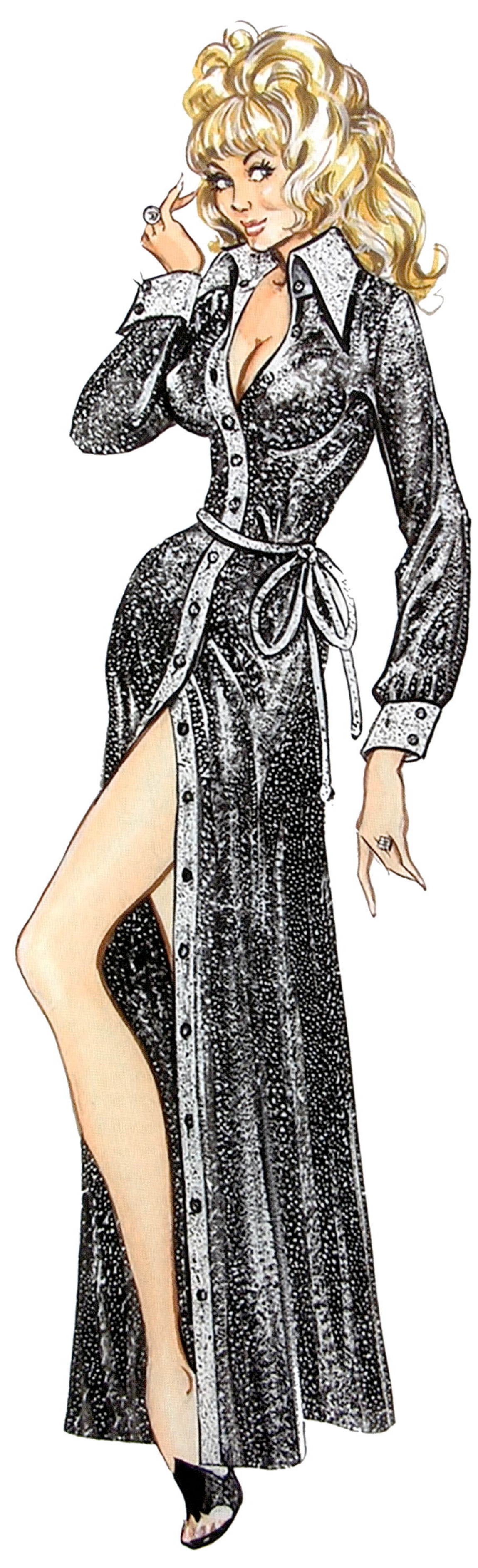

KAREN

This playful two-piece outfit is both youthful and flirty, featuring a charming polka-dot pattern that adds a fun, carefree vibe. The cropped top ties sweetly in front and is paired with a breezy miniskirt that shows the model's long, sexy legs, while strappy heels finish this fun look.

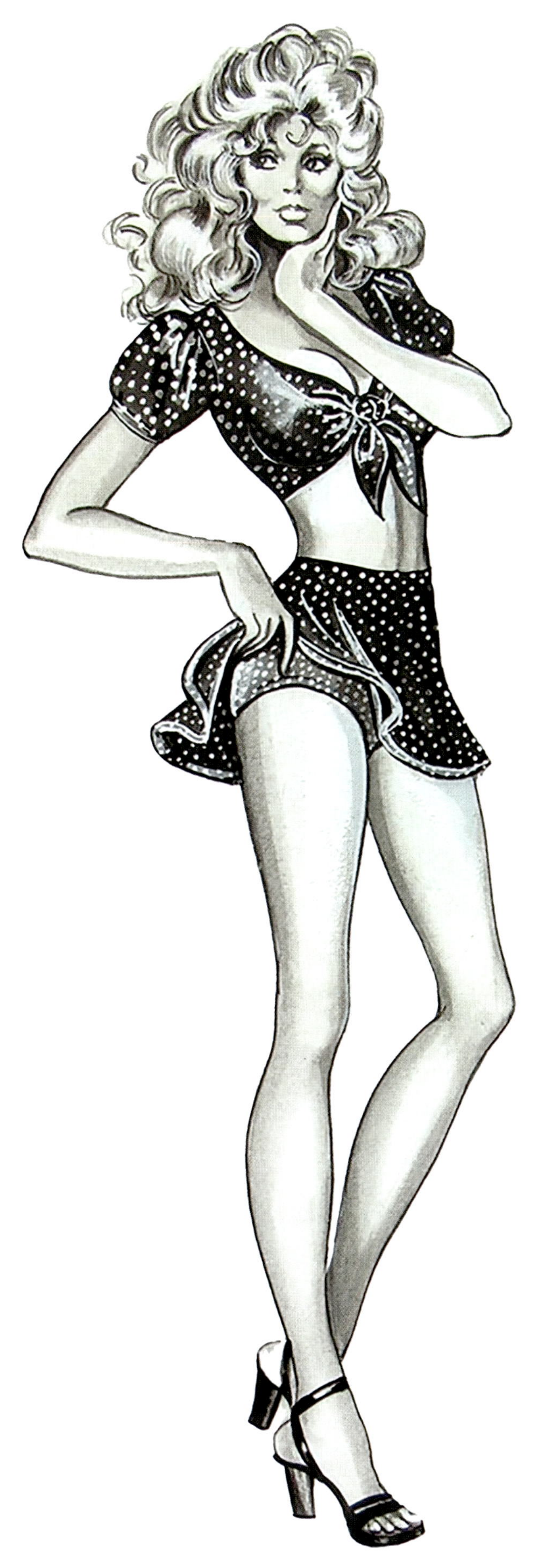

EVELYN

This sophisticated, floor-length gown is a stunning statement piece that commands attention from every angle. Intricate, sheer detailing and bold, artistic motifs accentuate the curves, while the daring open back adds an unexpected yet elegant flair. The high side slit subtly highlights her legs, complementing her graceful, confident pose.

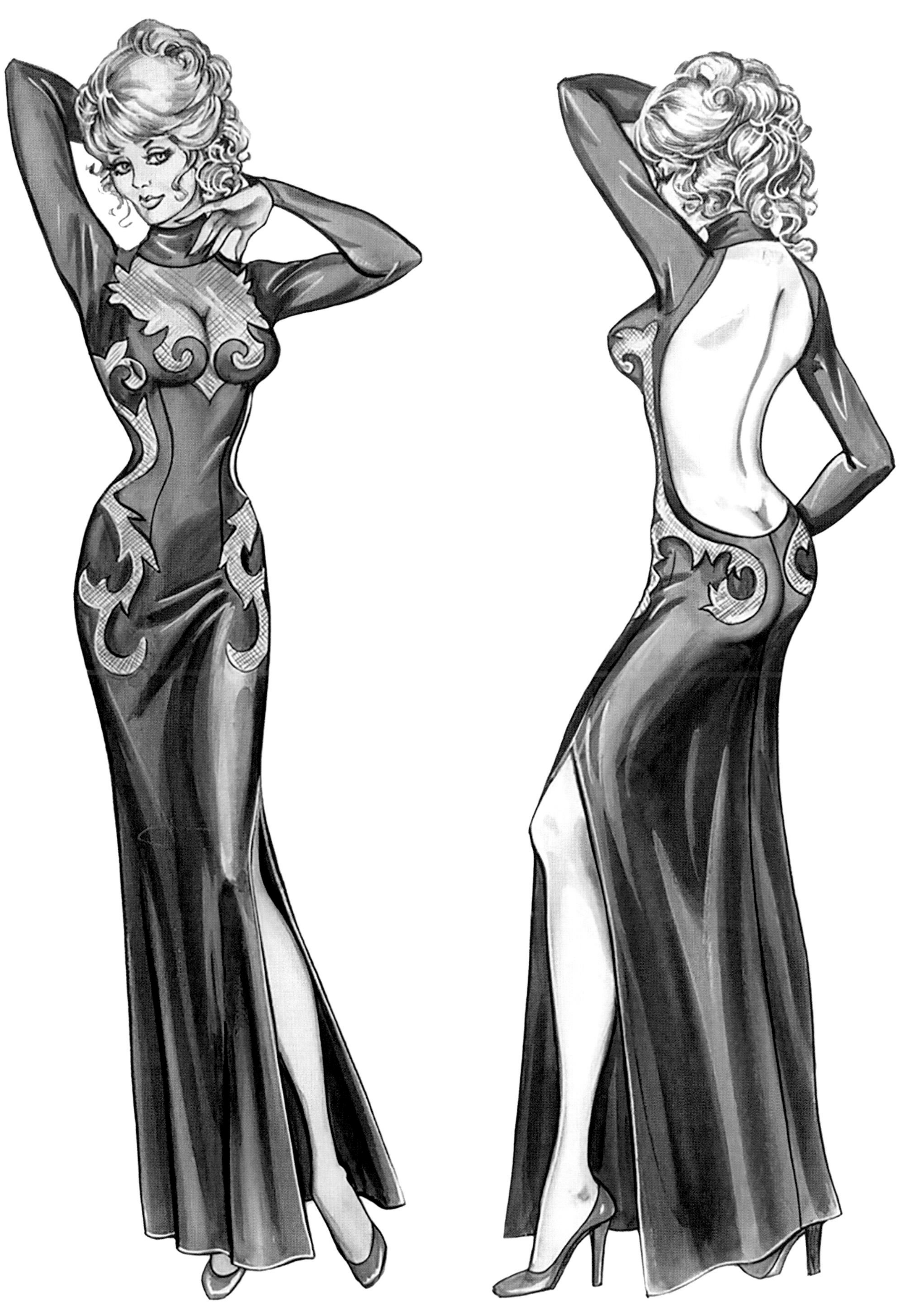

CYNTHIA

This dazzling ensemble is the epitome of 1970s glam. This model is dressed in a showstopping jumpsuit with a fitted bodice and dramatically flared pants. Sparkling embellishments decorate the wide lapels, belted waist, and panels running down the outer legs, adding a disco-era dazzle that practically radiates off the page. This piece captures both the flash and sophistication of the decade's fashion with flair.

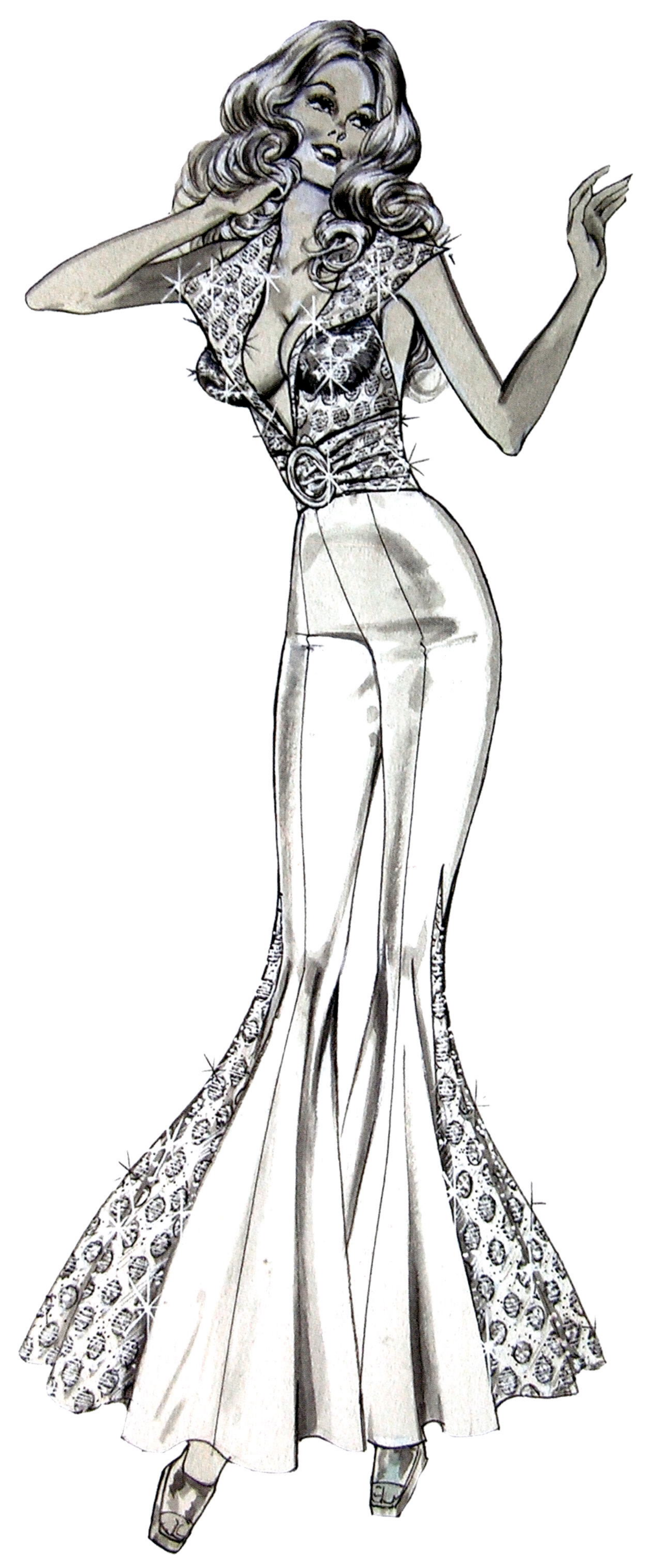

JUDITH

A curve-hugging, glossy black cocktail dress that exudes sophistication and allure. The off-the-shoulder neckline and three-quarter sleeves add a refined elegance, while the shiny, almost liquid-like texture of the fabric gives it a sleek, dramatic finish. Her voluminous beehive-style hair and bold starburst earrings are classic nods to early 1960s fashion, suggesting this design likely hails from that era. With her confident pose and hourglass silhouette, she perfectly embodies the glamorous, high-fashion look that defined the time.

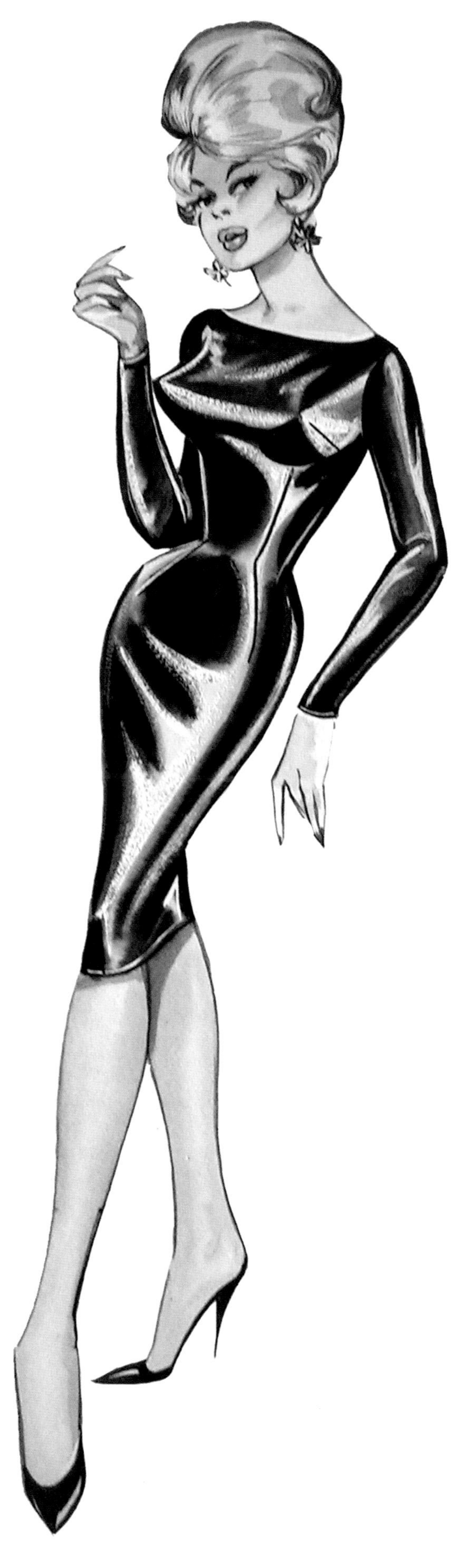

SANDRA

Bold, vibrant, and full of personality, this aqua jumpsuit is designed to make a statement. The form-fitting silhouette is enhanced by playful floral lace paneling, creating a striking visual effect from the neckline down to the dramatically flared bell-bottom legs. The halter neckline with delicate ties adds feminine charm, while her curly hairstyle and confident, stylish pose amplify the fun, youthful energy of this showstopping look.

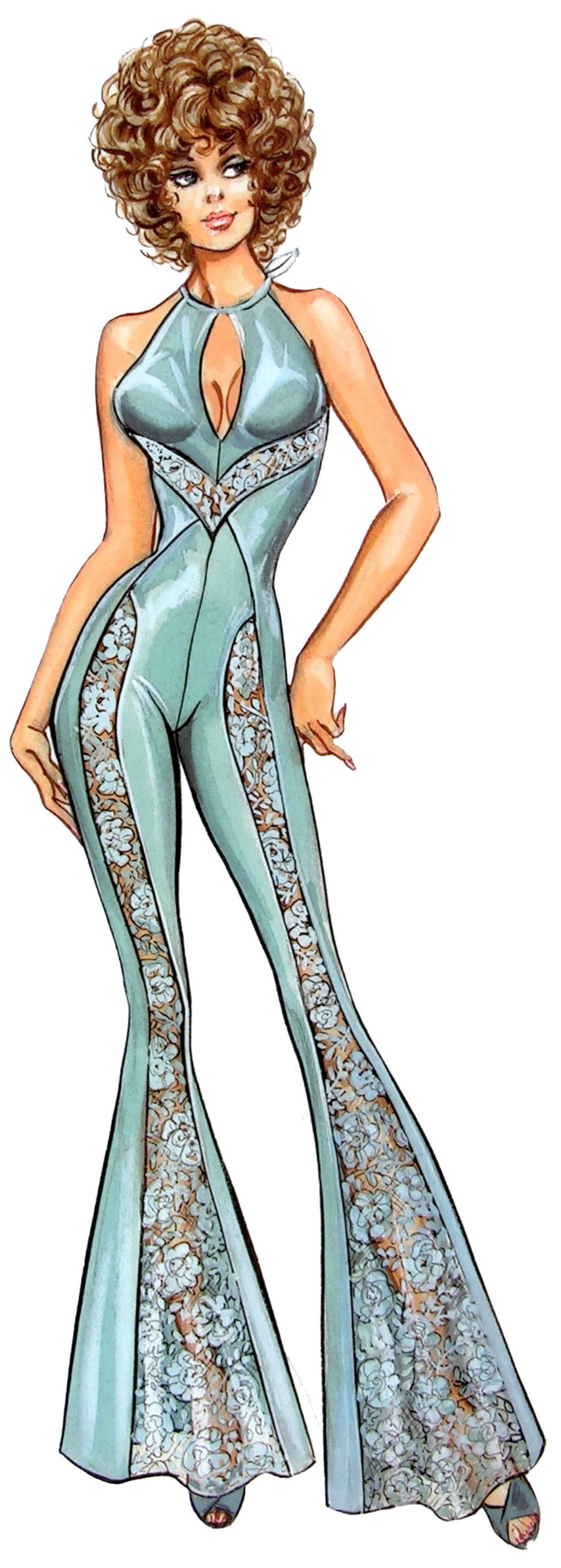

MAURINE

This vibrant floral jumpsuit is made for stealing the spotlight. Featuring a playful tie-front top, daring side cutouts, and dramatically flared legs, it's the perfect ensemble for dancing the night away. The model's carefree, striking pose suggests she's already the life of the party, captivating everyone around her with her confidence.

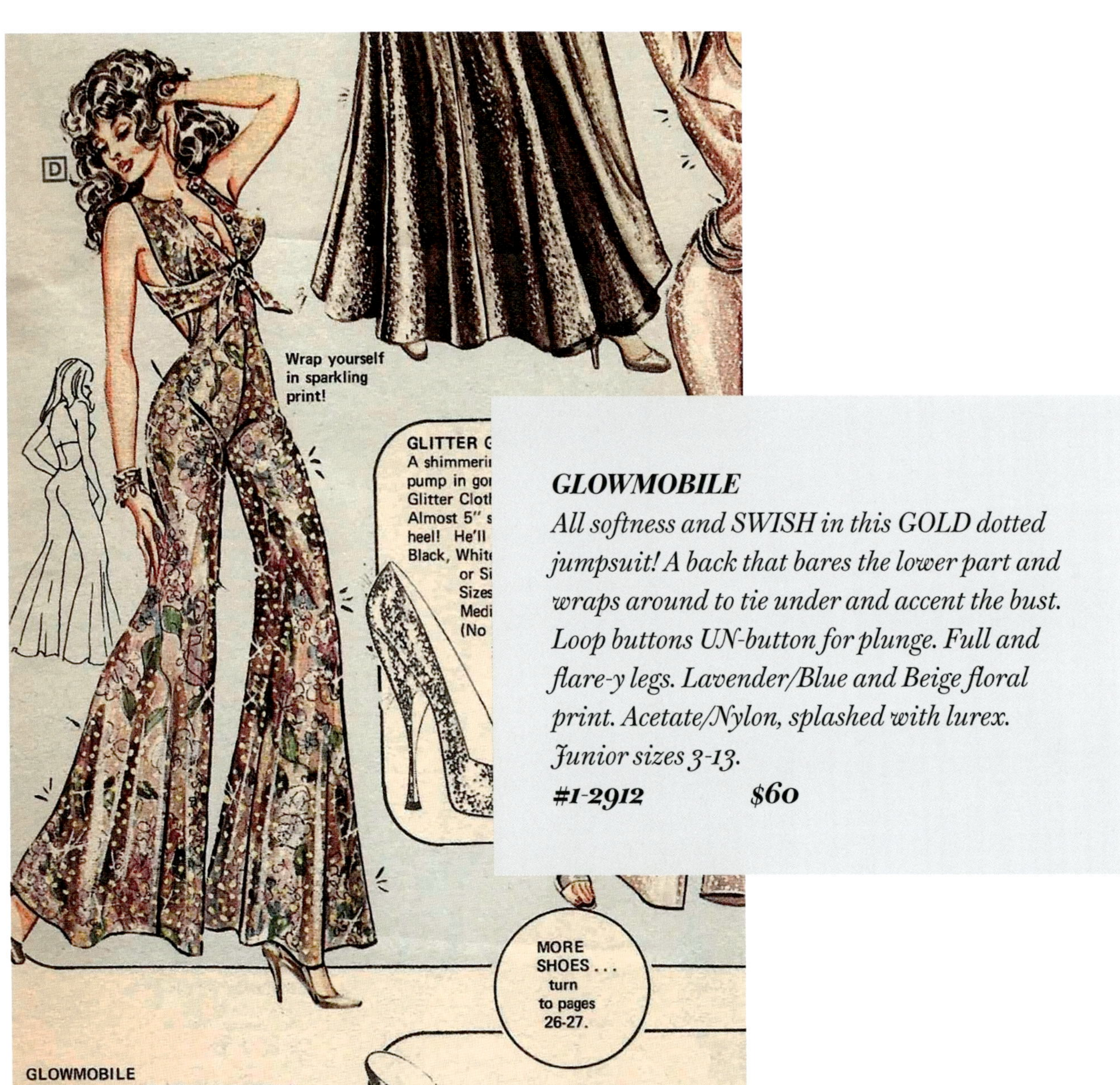

GLOWMOBILE
All softness and SWISH in this GOLD dotted jumpsuit! A back that bares the lower part and wraps around to tie under and accent the bust. Loop buttons UN-button for plunge. Full and flare-y legs. Lavender/Blue and Beige floral print. Acetate/Nylon, splashed with lurex. Junior sizes 3-13.
#1-2912 ***$60***

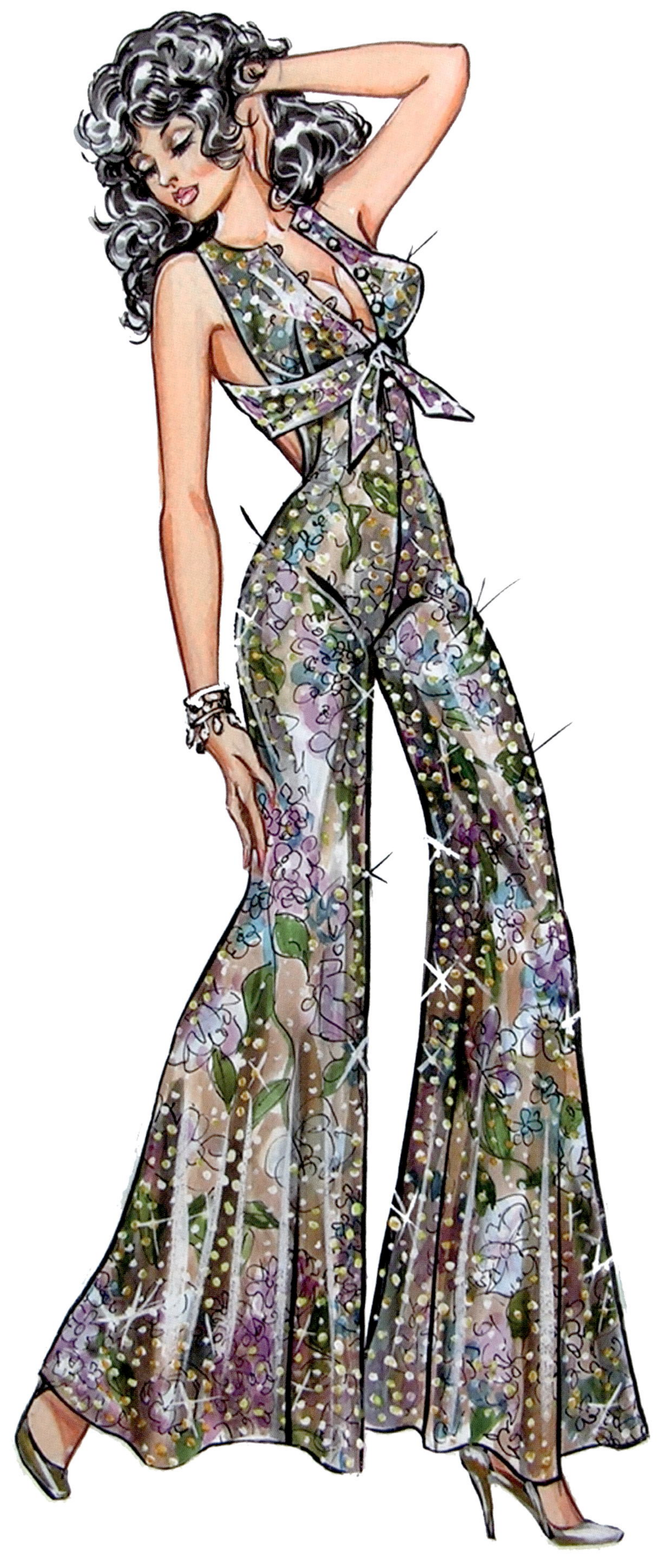

DANA

Radiant, bold, and full of charisma, this vibrant red jumpsuit makes an unforgettable impression. The wrap-style top, featuring a wide collar and sash tie, beautifully accentuates her figure, while the dramatically flared bell-bottom legs add movement and elegance.

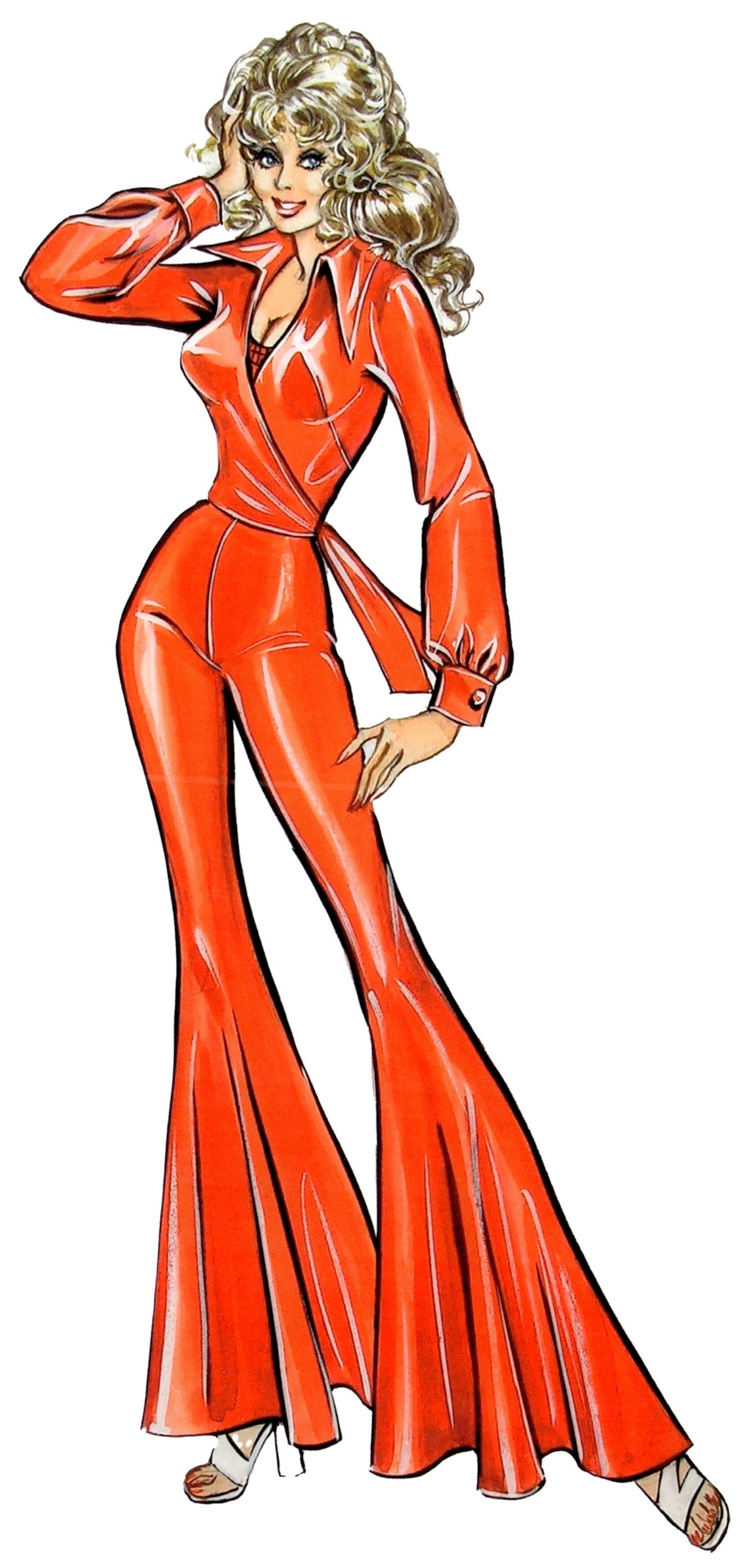

HOPE

Graceful, refined, and effortlessly elegant in a beautiful gown. The delicate fringe detail at the bodice adds movement and interest, perfectly complementing the simplicity of her flowing skirt. Her poised, proper stance enhances the overall sense of timeless beauty and understated glamour.

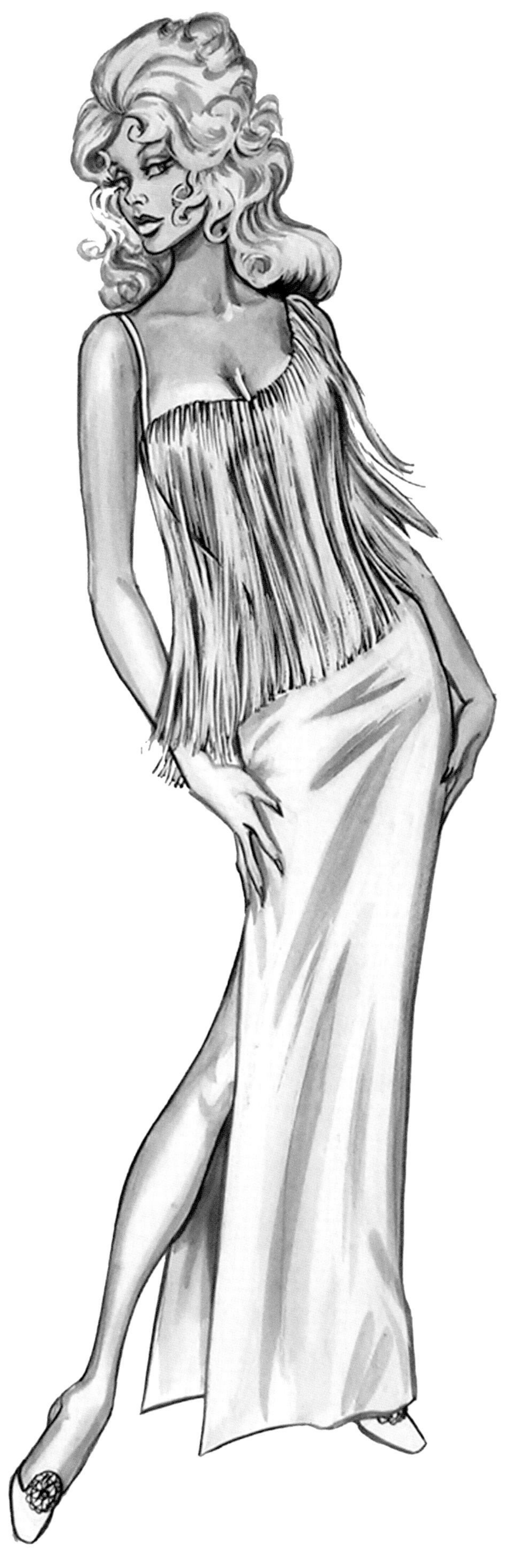

VALERIE

This playful, satiny lingerie piece blends flirty femininity with sophisticated charm. The delicate lace accents at the bust and hemline add a romantic touch, while the sleek, silky fabric hugs her figure beautifully.

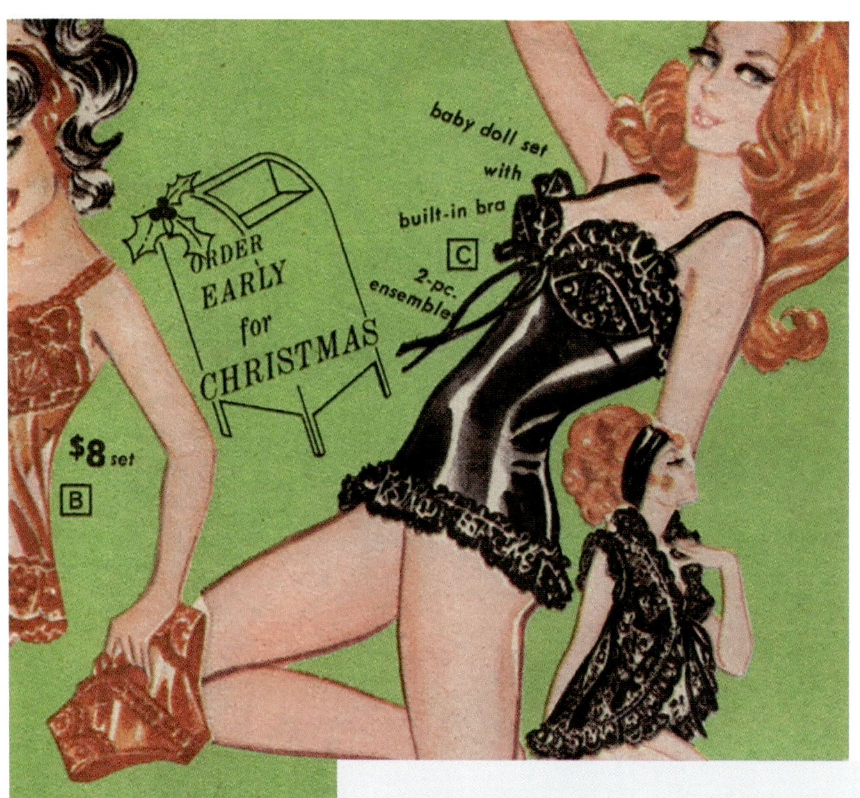

SLEEP SHAPER

Sleep in great shape in a baby doll with a built-in bra! Bust is contoured with 3-sectioned shell cups, shoulder straps adjust to fit. Lace-trimmed gown is 40 denier sheer nylon . . . all-lace topper ties at the cleavage. In Black or Red.

Sizes Small 32, Medium 34, and Large 36.

#3-4120 ***$17 THE SET***

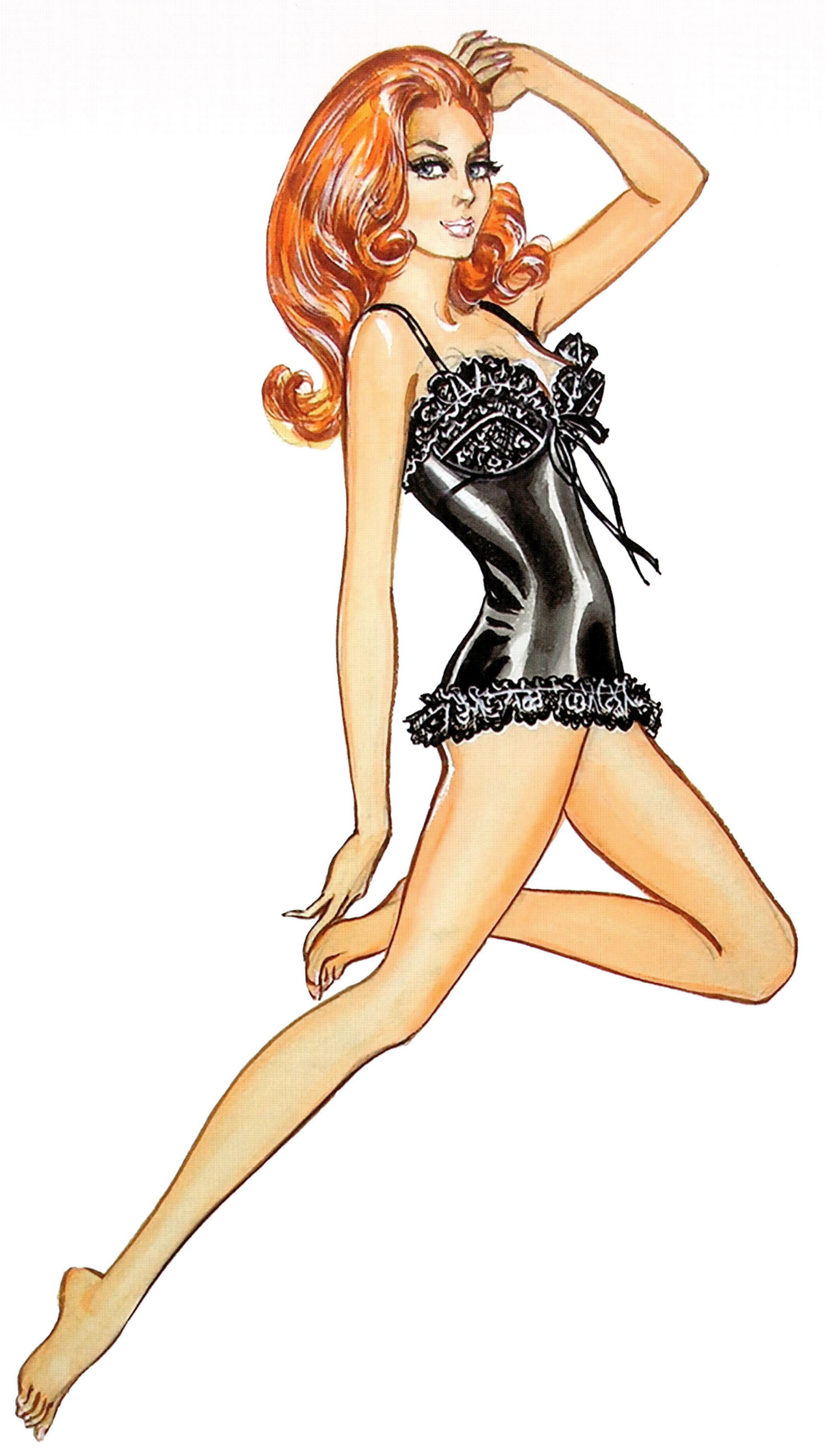

LUCINDA

An elegant yet playful lace sleep romper. The soft floral lace pattern and flattering tie waist create a relaxed, comfortable fit perfect for lounging. The deep neckline and playful hemline add a touch of flirtatiousness, while the overall silhouette keeps it effortlessly chic.

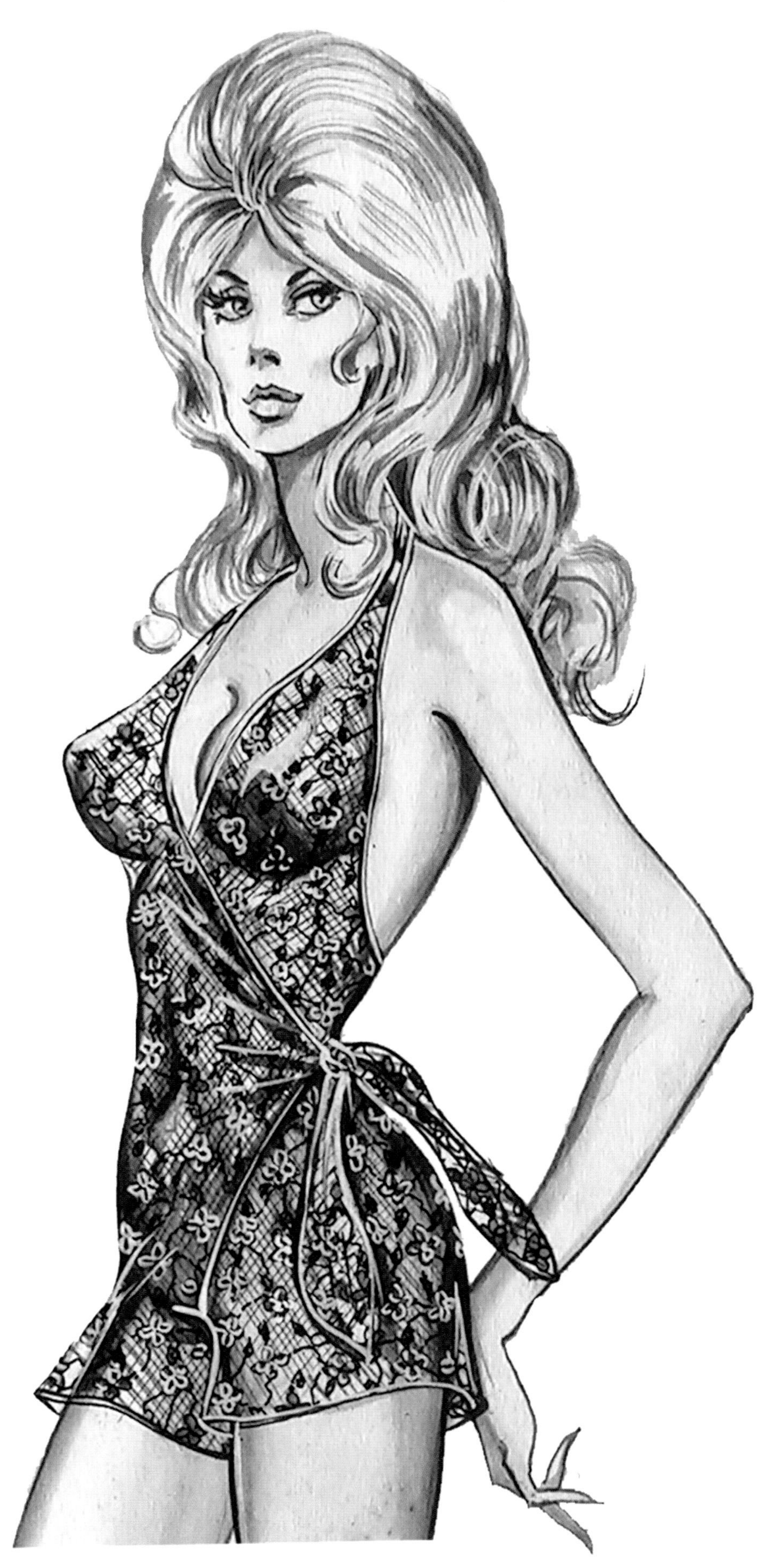

LORRAINE

An alluring leopard-print negligee with sheer detailing along the neckline and flirtatious side-tie accents, effortlessly blending elegance with a daring edge. Its sleek, figure-flattering shape makes it a captivating choice for an unforgettable evening—perfect for anyone looking to embrace glamour and femininity after dark.

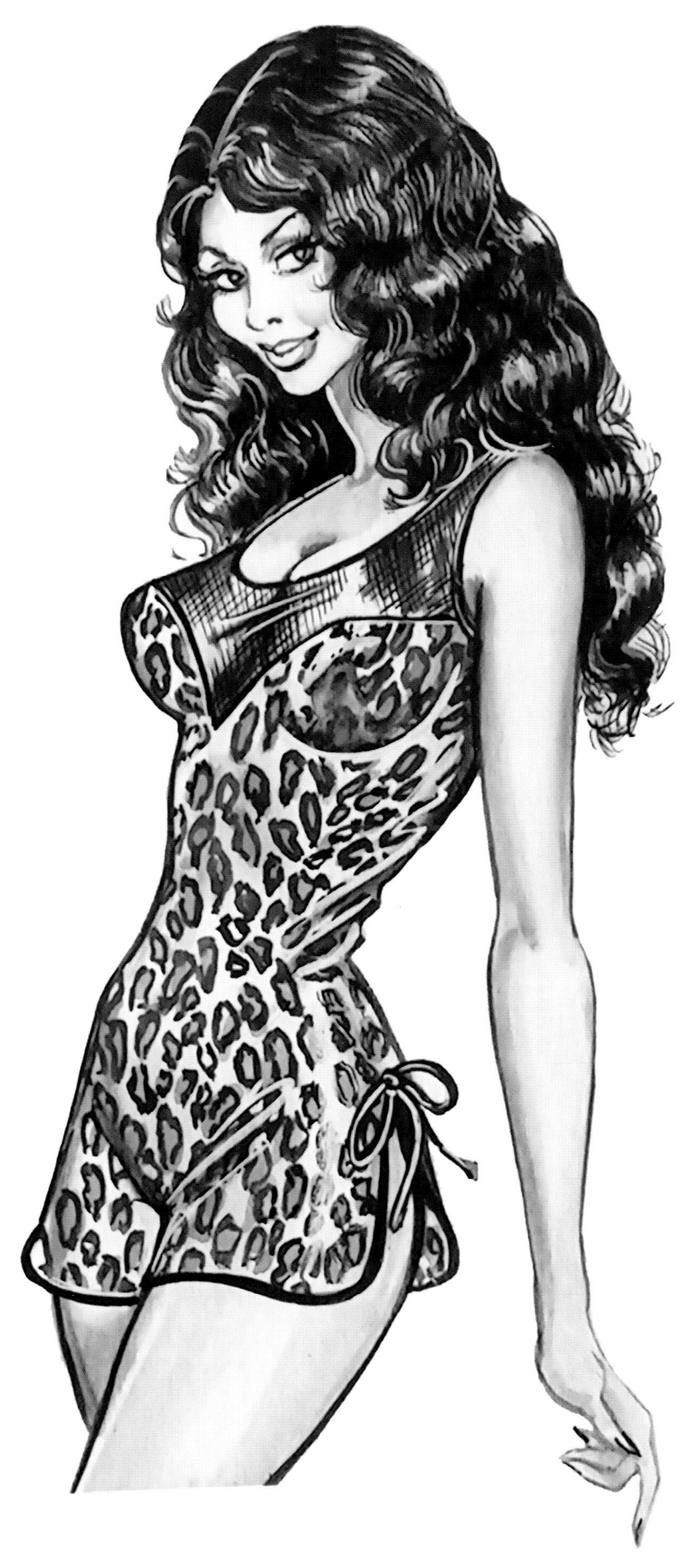

ELAINE

This dramatic lace gown features a plunging neckline framed with delicate ruffled edges. The sheer floral lace cascades elegantly to the floor, emphasizing a silhouette that's both romantic and enticing.

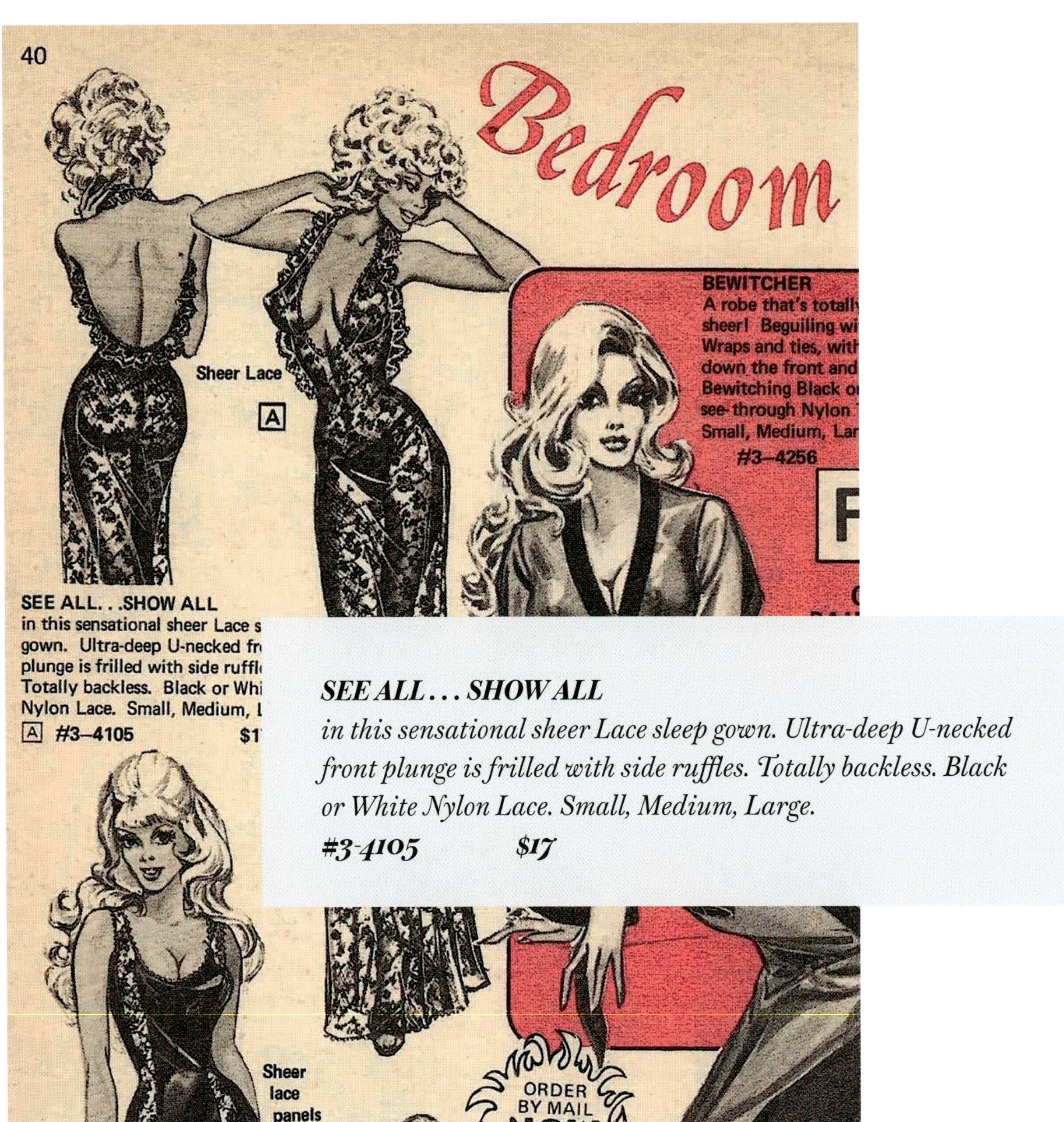

SEE ALL . . . SHOW ALL

in this sensational sheer Lace sleep gown. Ultra-deep U-necked front plunge is frilled with side ruffles. Totally backless. Black or White Nylon Lace. Small, Medium, Large.

#3-4105 ***$17***

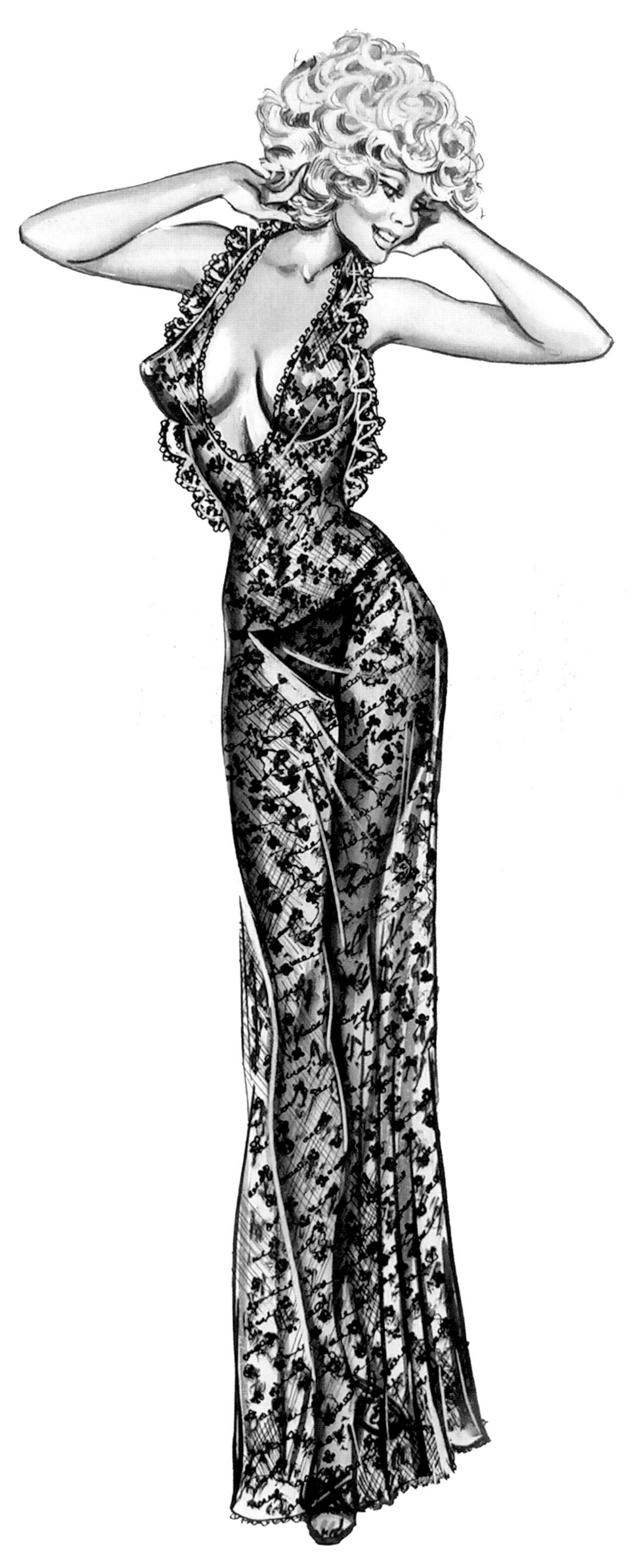

JOANNA

This revealing silky sheer floor-length gown with its high neckline and daring front cutout, tied with a delicate bow, plays with contrast in all the right ways.

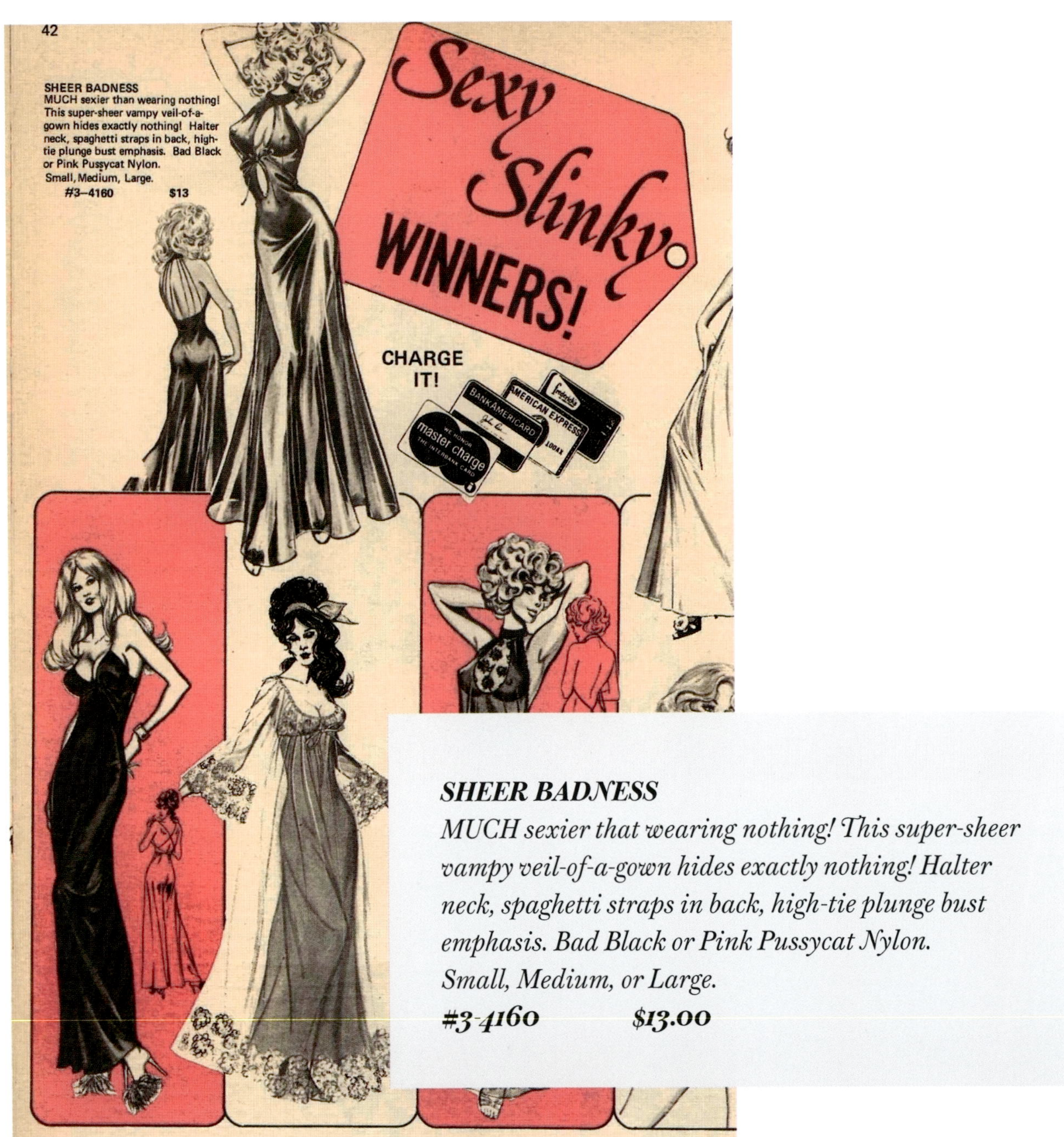

SHEER BADNESS
MUCH sexier that wearing nothing! This super-sheer vampy veil-of-a-gown hides exactly nothing! Halter neck, spaghetti straps in back, high-tie plunge bust emphasis. Bad Black or Pink Pussycat Nylon. Small, Medium, or Large.
#3-4160 $13.00

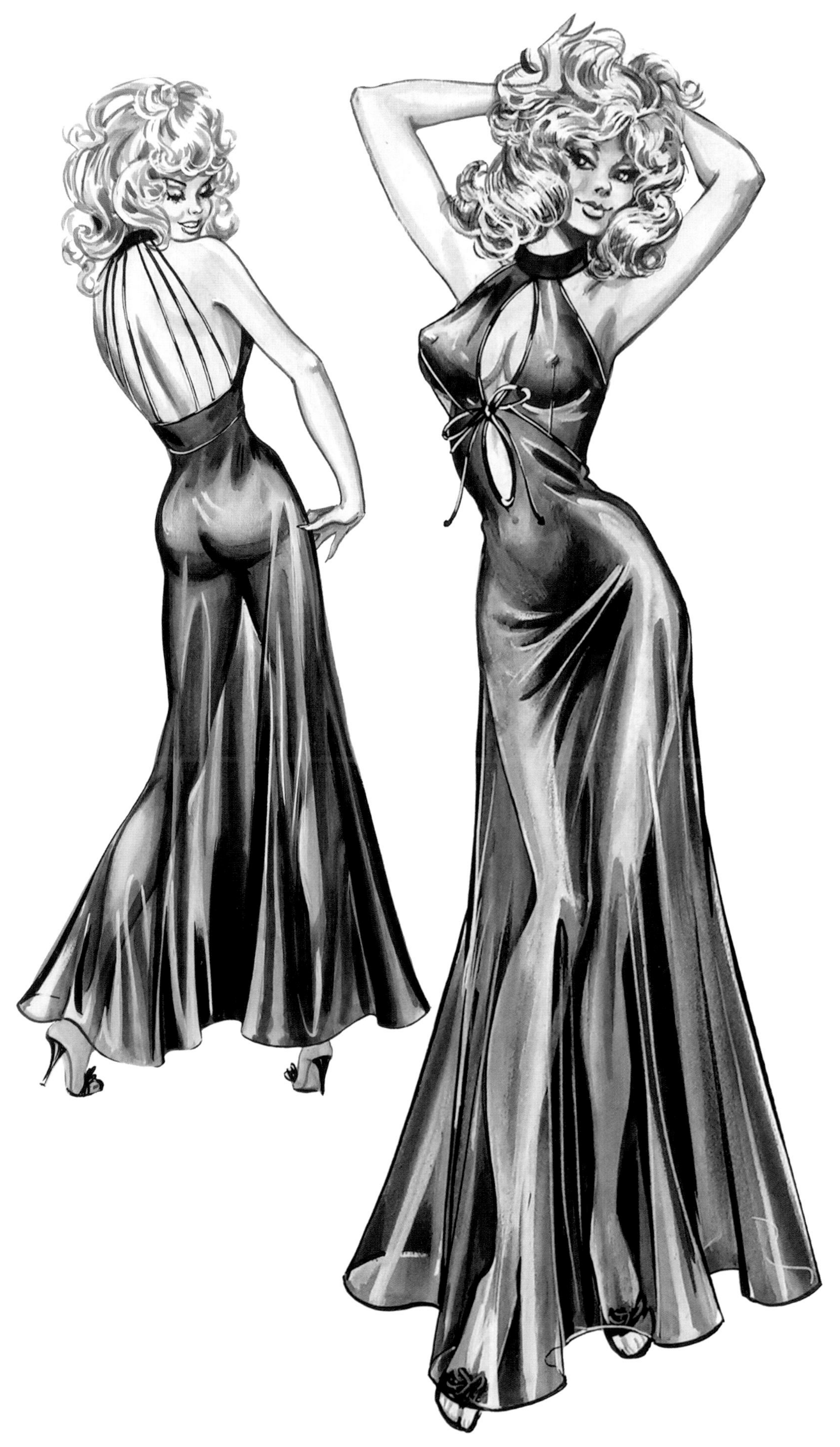

HEIDI

Sweet meets seductive in this flirty baby-blue negligee, trimmed in layers of playful ruffles that frame every curve. The sheer bodice, delicate bow, and matching marabou heels make the look feel like a vintage boudoir fantasy.

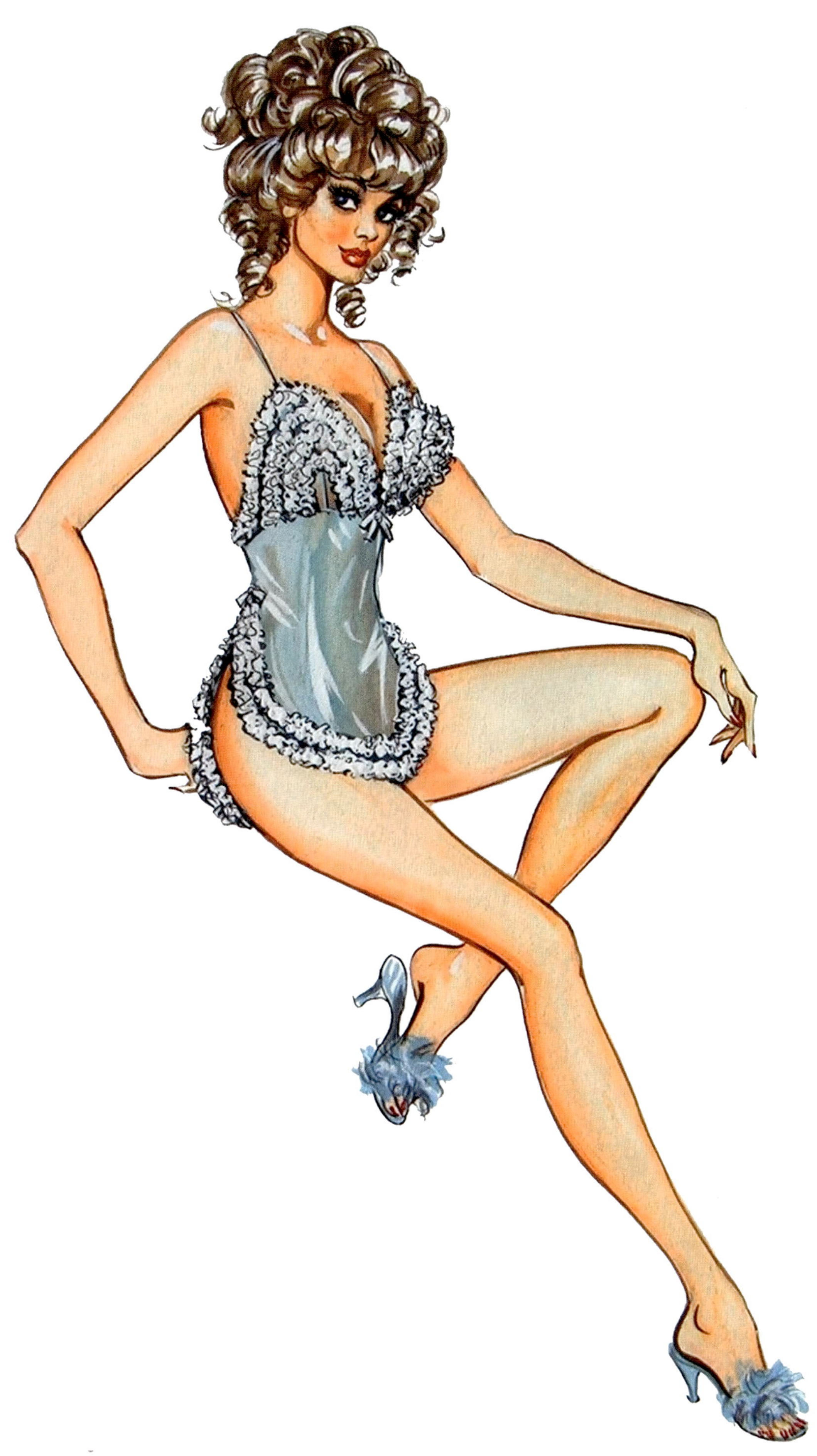

MONICA

The sleek satin finish and minimal design of this bodysuit make it perfect for layering under a fitted dress or styling solo for a confident statement. Delicate lace trim softens the look with a feminine edge, adding just the right amount of allure to this classic silhouette.

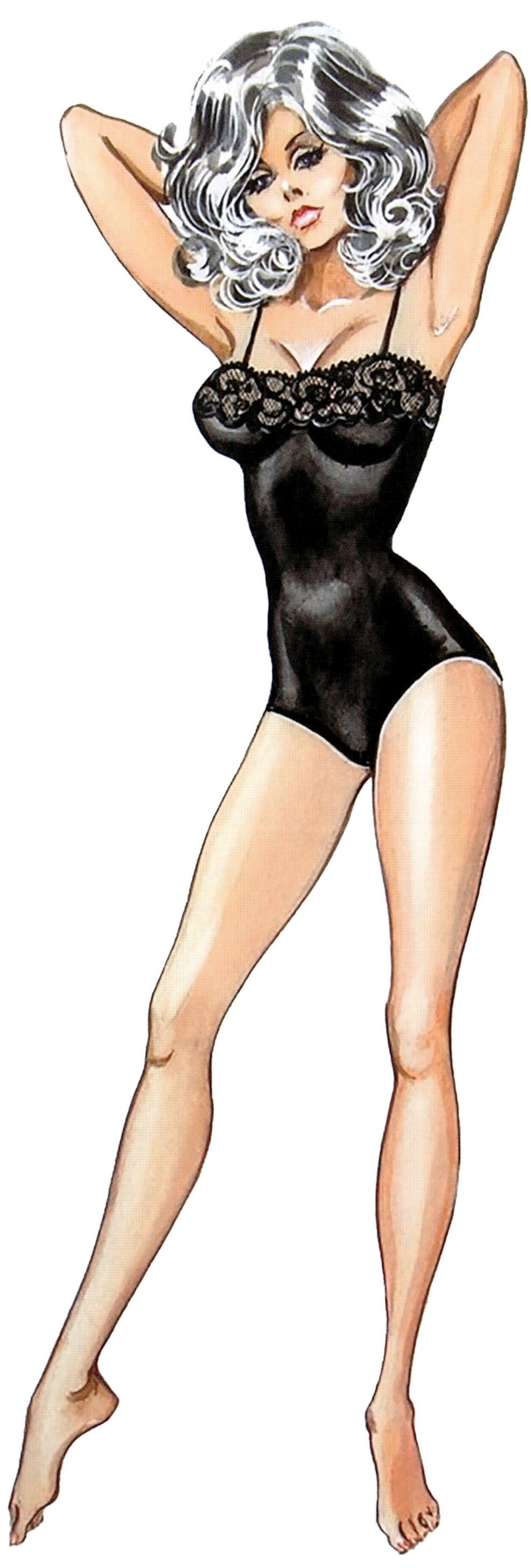

NANCY

This glossy black bodysuit is designed with shape wear in mind, offering firm support that lifts the breasts and hugs every curve. The structured seams and button-front detail add a bold, slightly edgy touch, while the high-cut leg creates a lengthening effect. Both functional and flattering, it sculpts the body beautifully.

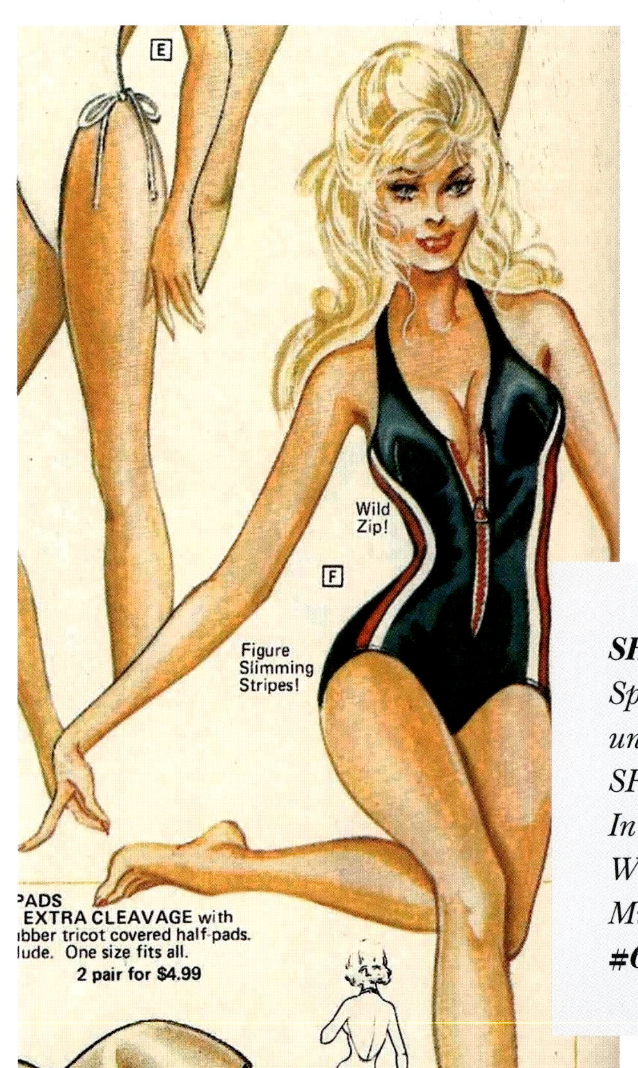

SHAPE SUIT

Spandex fits TIGHT to hold you right! Front unzips as low as you dare to go. Molded cups give SPECTACULAR shaping. BRAZENLY backless. In Navy with sensuously slimming Red and White stripes. Nylon and Lycra ® and Spandex. Misses sizes 8 to 16.

#6-1748 ***$27***

Shown here is "Nancy" adorned in a slight variation of this slimming bodysuit.

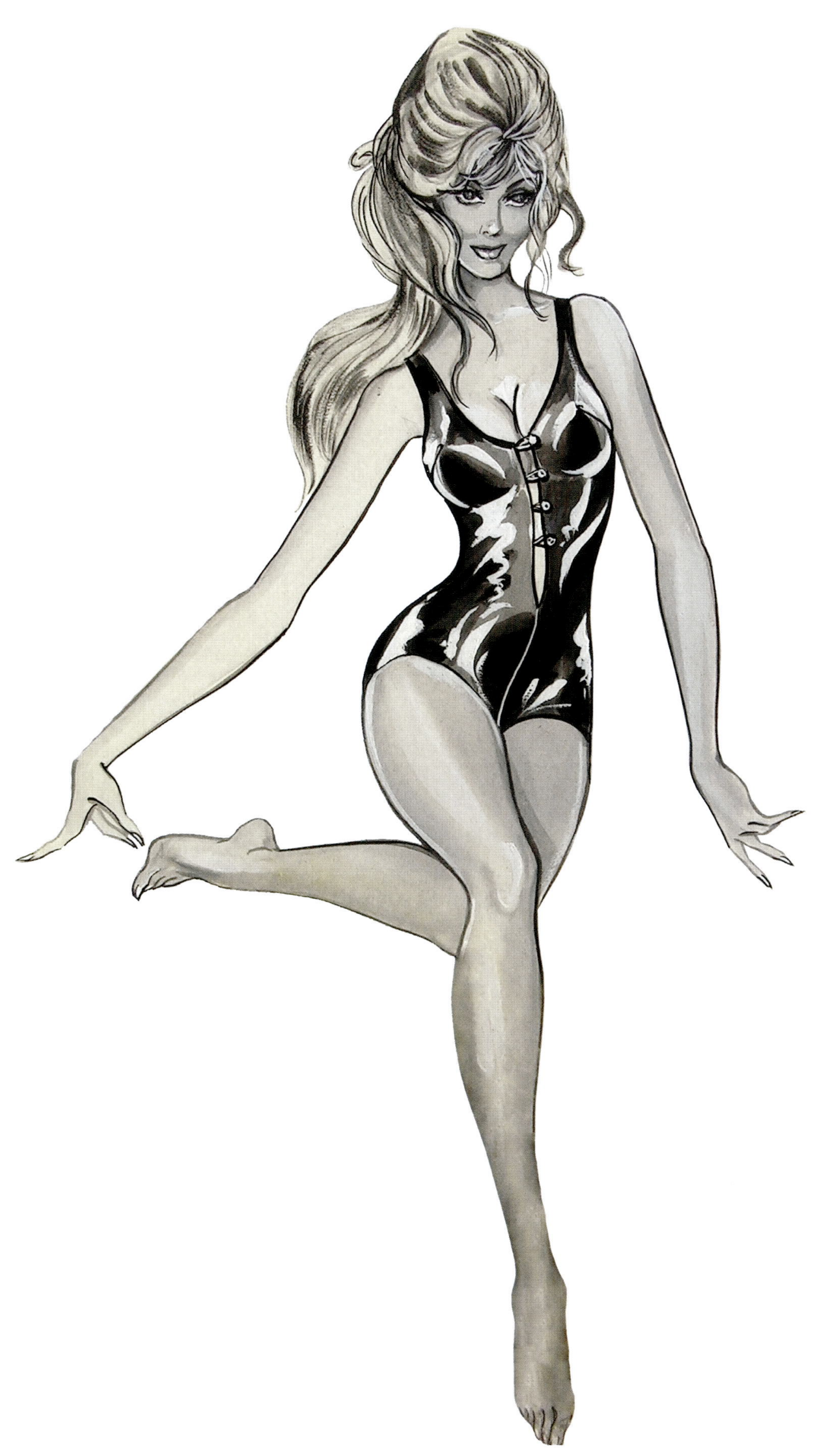

KATHLEEN

This elegant nightgown is both romantic and refined, in a soft satin with just the right amount of structure to accentuate the figure. The contrast floral embroidery on the bust adds a luxurious, vintage detail, while delicate ruffles trim the neckline and hem. A piece designed for lounging in glamour or slipping into something dreamy.

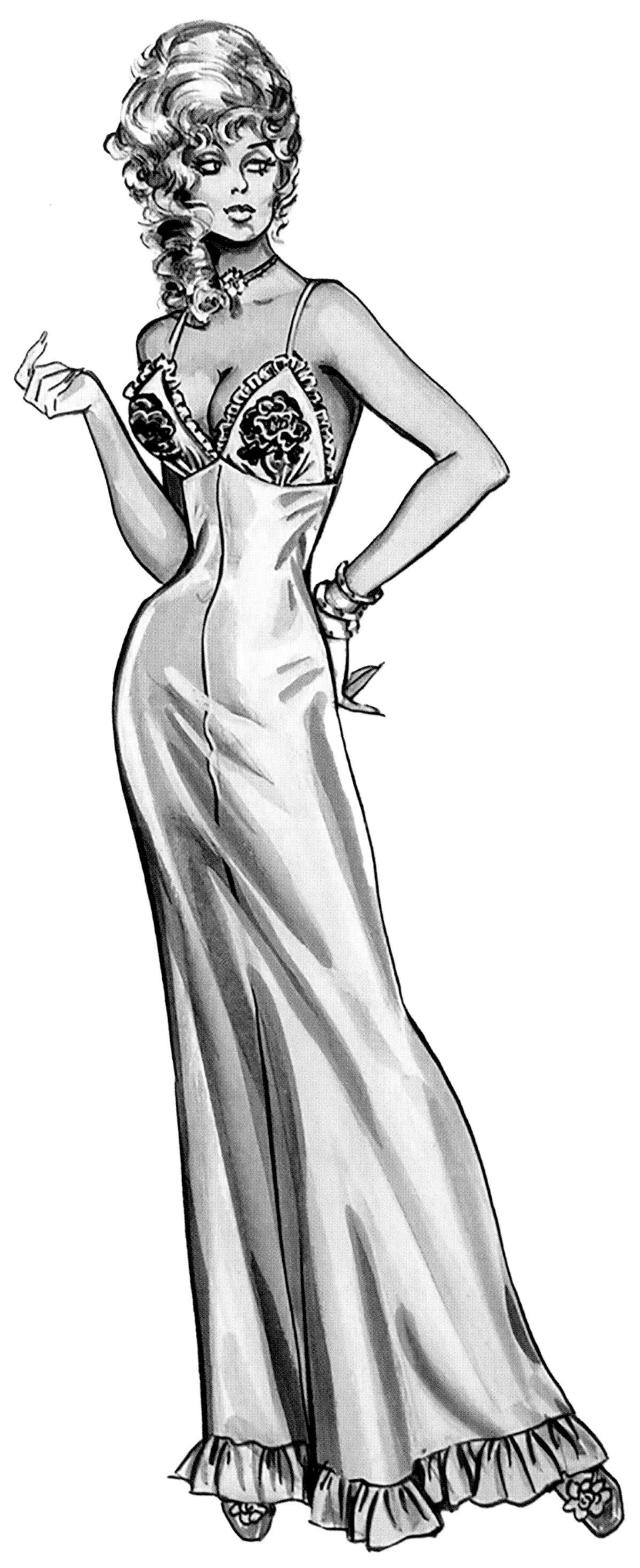

CANDACE

This playful baby-doll set is a sweet and flirty take on classic sleepwear. Sheer, airy fabric flows outward from the bodice, trimmed in ruffled lace that highlights the plunging neckline and hem. Finished with a satin bow at the center and matching panties underneath, it's the perfect piece for a fun bedtime look.

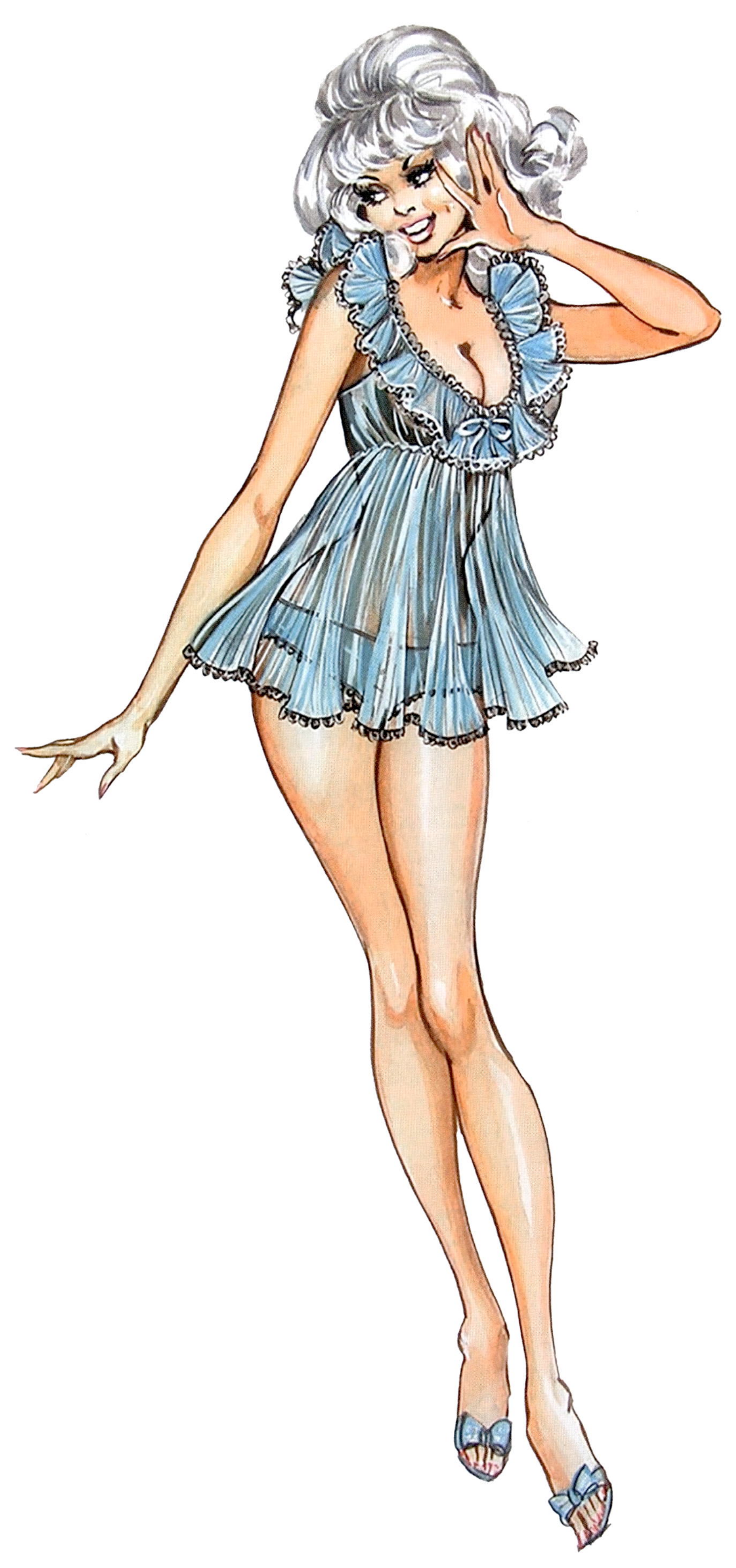

MARGARET

A glamorous satin nightgown that feels just as luxurious as it looks. The deep neckline is framed by bold ruffled trim edged in delicate lace, adding a dramatic flair to the otherwise smooth and flowing silhouette. Perfect for winding down in style or simply stealing the spotlight at home.

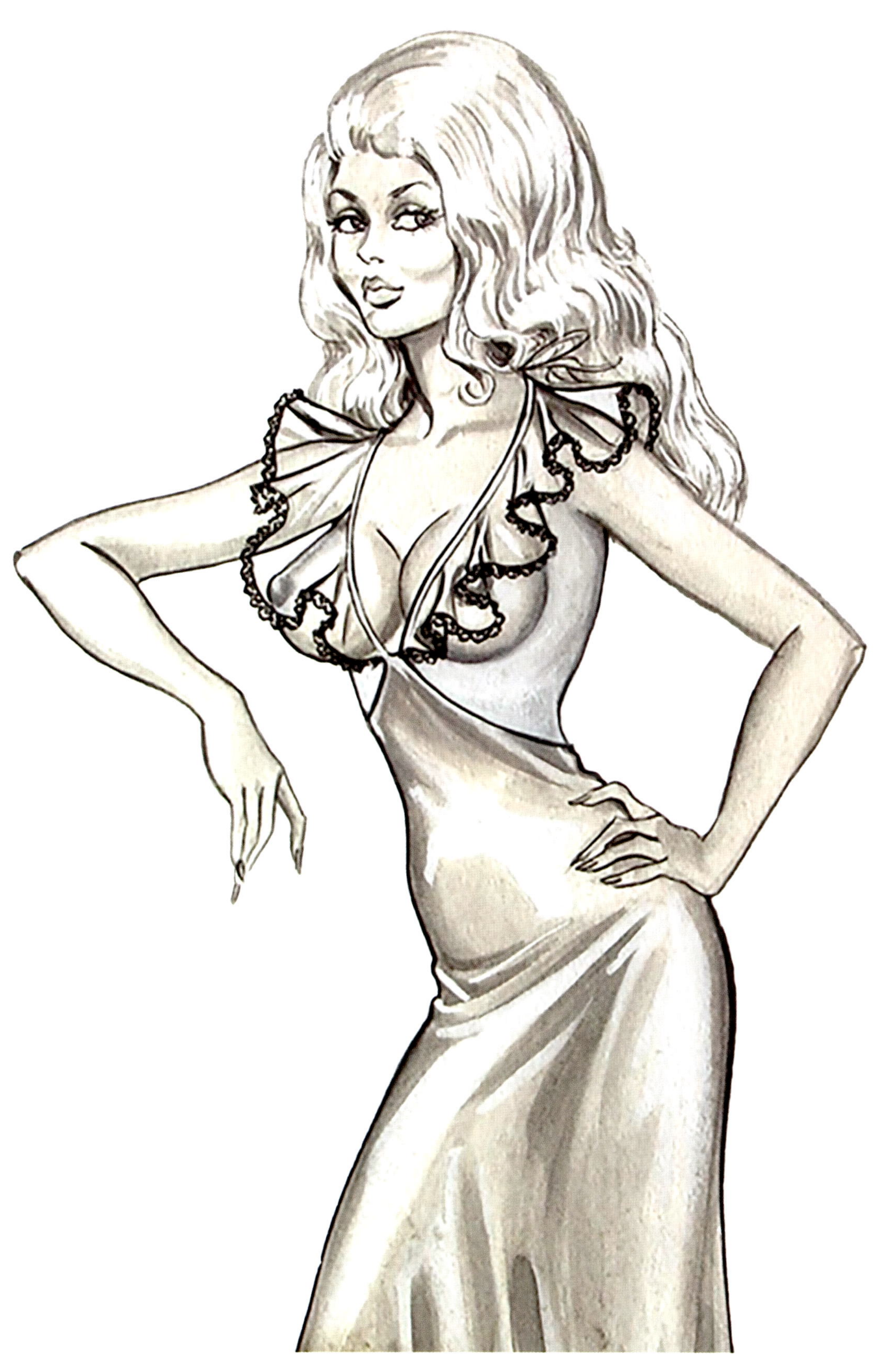

GAYLE

This sheer baby-doll set is flirty and fun with its airy, flowy shape and playful peekaboo sides. The pretty pink color is sweet but undeniably sultry, while the side ties add a touch of charm—and a hint of drama. A perfect blend of innocent and irresistible.

Frederick's of Hollywood catalog description:

SLEEP APRON
for bedtime home work! Sheer Nylon baby doll is striped with satin ribbons . . . held together by a tie on either side. Matching opaque bikinis. Purple or Shocking Pink.
Small, Medium, or Large.
#3-4194 ***$16***

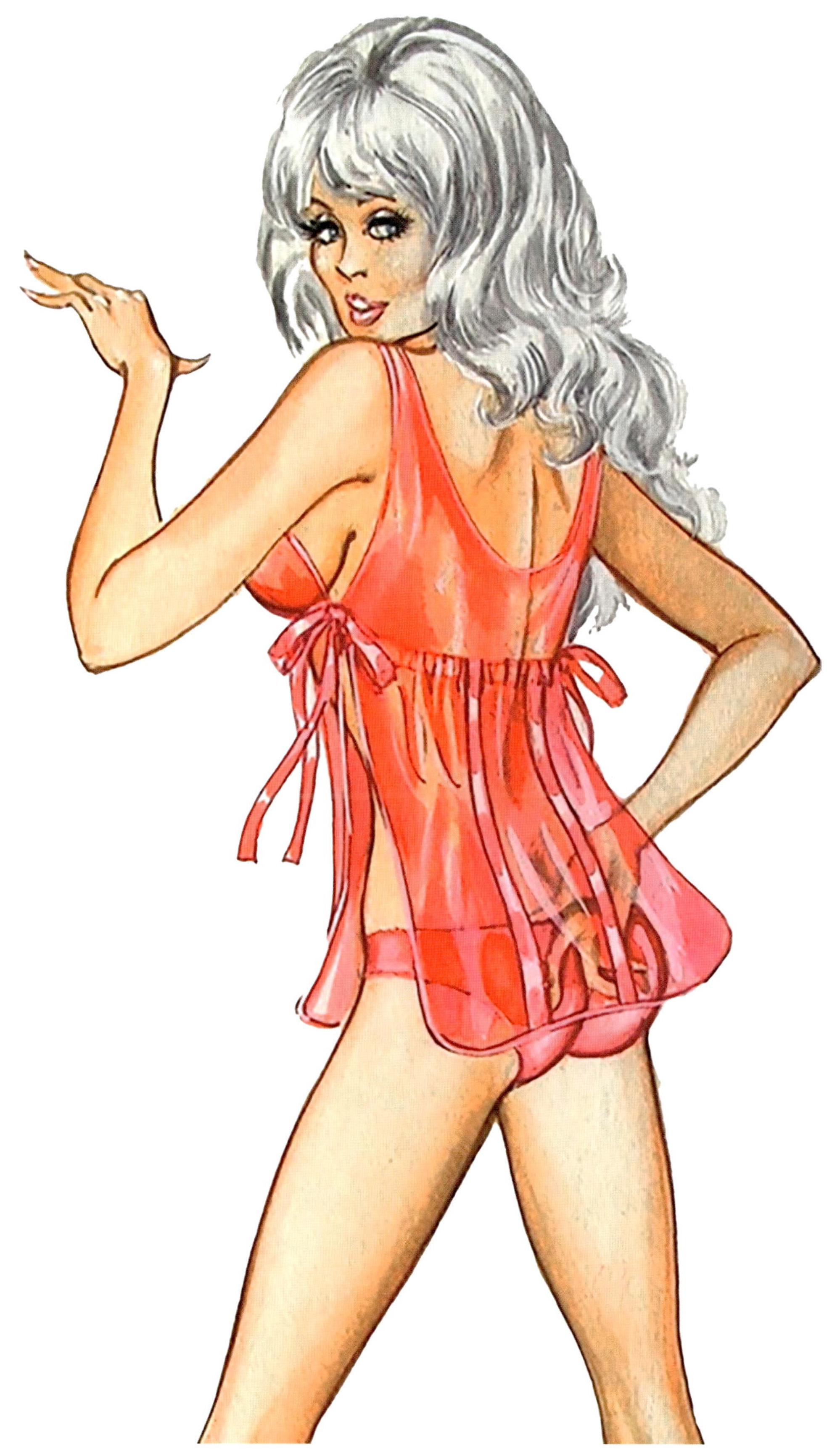

BRENDA

This front-hook bra is a classic example of 1960s lingerie design, sculpting the bust into the signature pointed silhouette of the era. With structured cups and strategic seaming, it shapes and lifts for that unforgettable vintage effect.

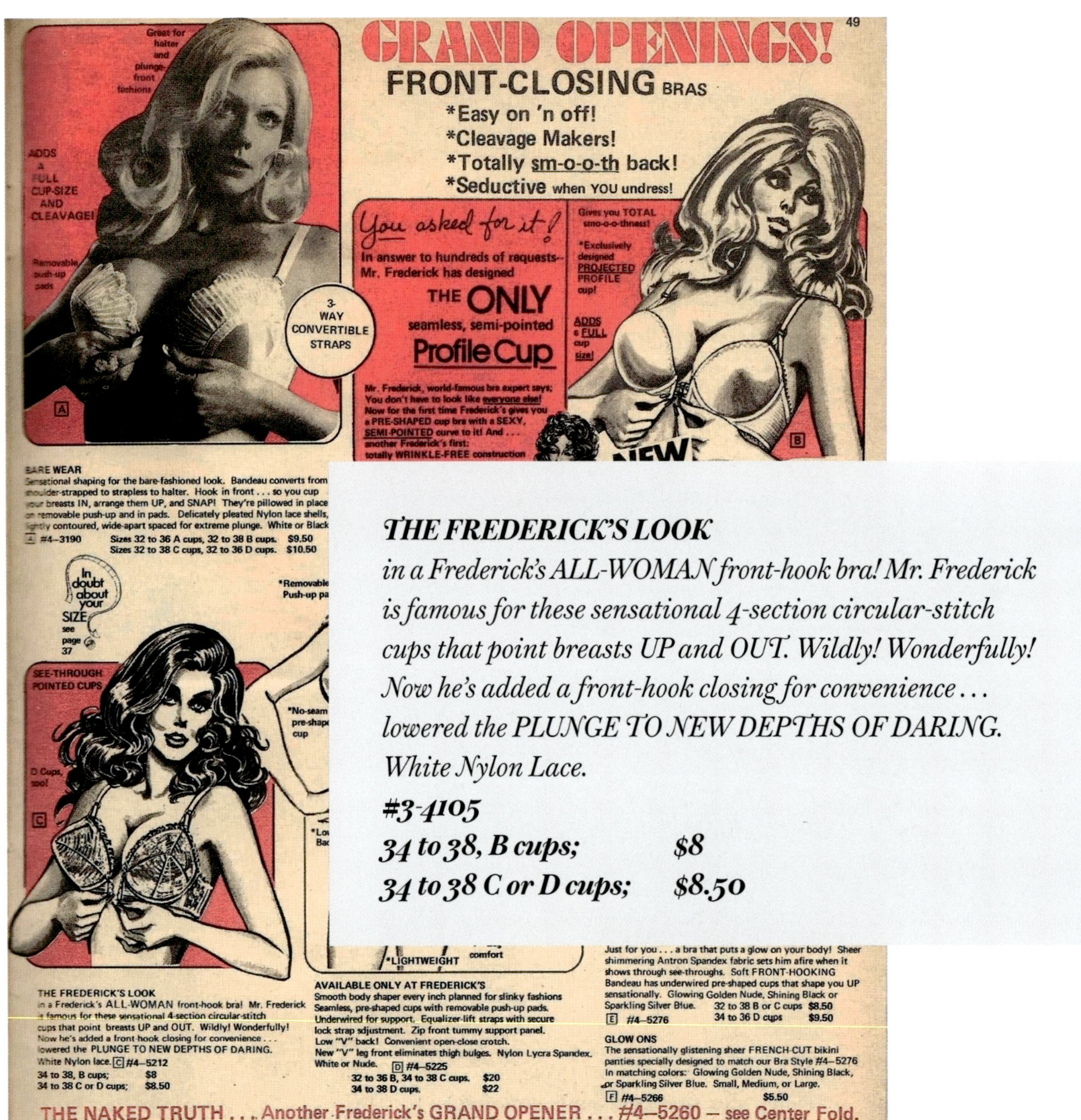

THE FREDERICK'S LOOK

in a Frederick's ALL-WOMAN front-hook bra! Mr. Frederick is famous for these sensational 4-section circular-stitch cups that point breasts UP and OUT. Wildly! Wonderfully! Now he's added a front-hook closing for convenience . . . lowered the PLUNGE TO NEW DEPTHS OF DARING. White Nylon Lace.

#3-4105

34 to 38, B cups;	***$8***
34 to 38 C or D cups;	***$8.50***

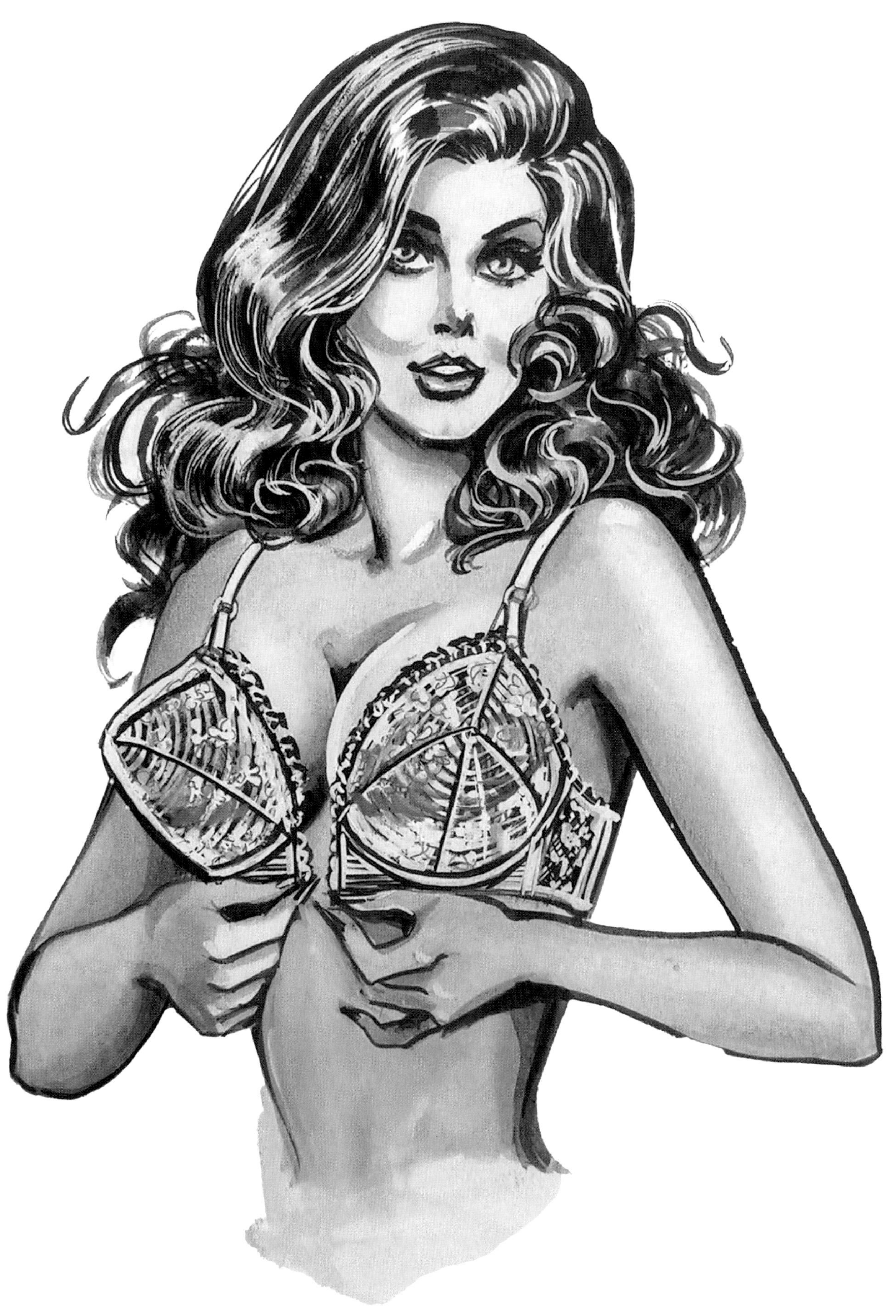

ANGELA

A simple yet timeless matching bra-and-panty set. The soft sheen of the fabric adds a touch of elegance, while the delicate bow detail brings just the right amount of charm. According to the Frederick's of Hollywood catalog, the panties have an exclusive "fanny former elastic seam," adding an unexpected touch. Perfect for everyday wear or as a foundational piece under something fabulous.

Frederick's of Hollywood catalog description:

Underwired push in . . . push-up BRA lifts and shows! Removable pads.
Bra sizes. 32 34 36 B or 32 34 36 C cups.
#6-1814 $16

End up with enticing rear cleavage! PANTY has exclusive Fanny Former elastic seam. Panty Hip Sizes:
Sm. (34 to 35 1/2). Med. (36 to 36 1/2) or Large (39 to 42).
#6-1815 $10

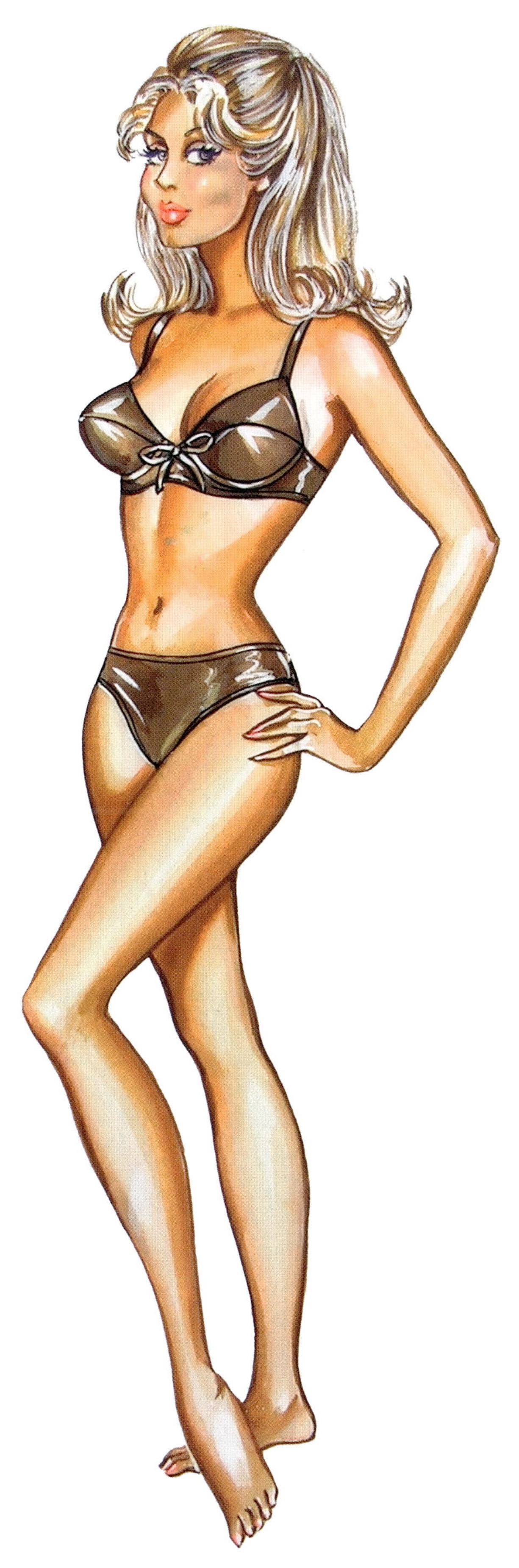

ANITA

Flirtatious and fun pajama set with a fitted tee and matching shorts, both adorned with bold "LOVE" patches for a groovy pop-art twist. It's soft, comfy, and made for lounging in style.

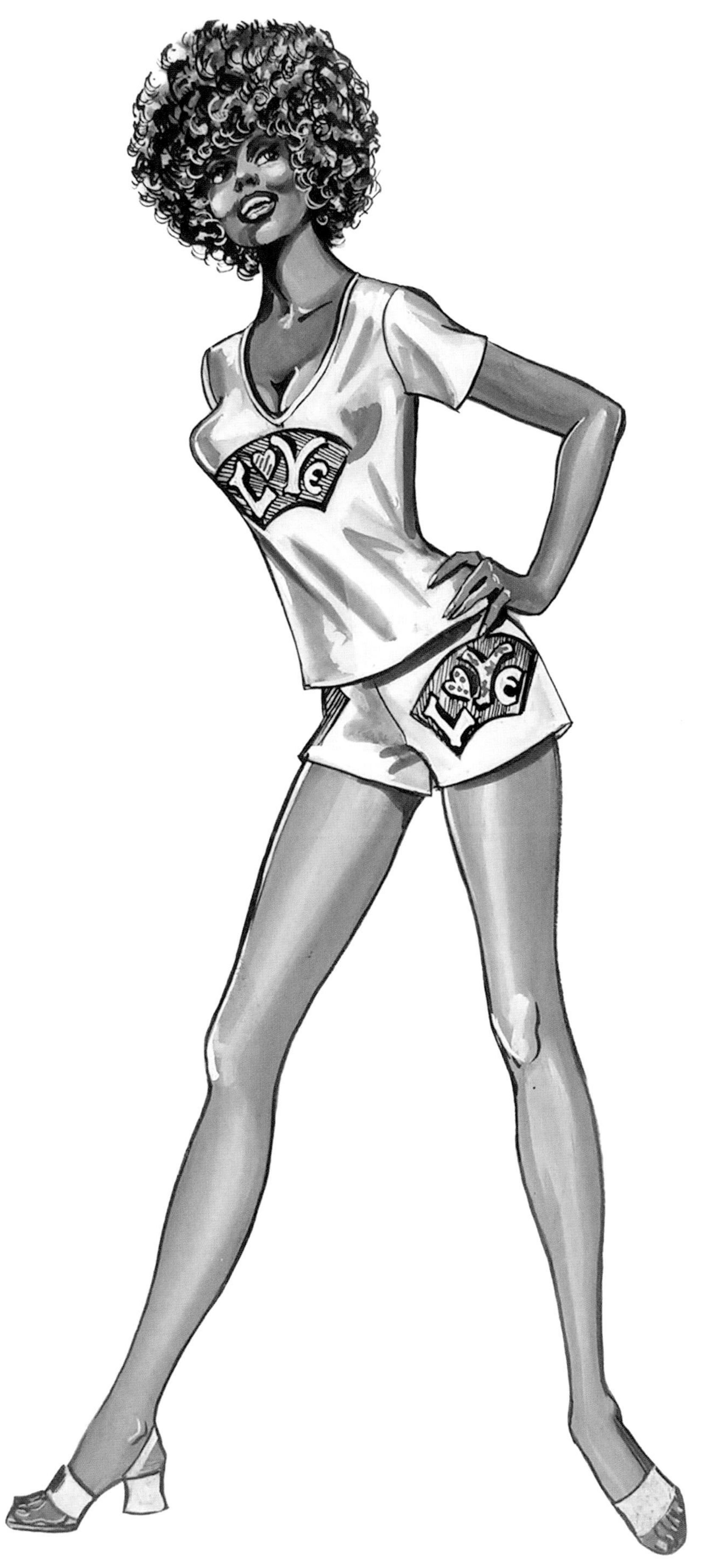
LOVE
LOVE

JANE

She's barely dressed but fully fabulous. Wearing nothing but sparkling pasties and the tiniest of panties, this model dons a look that is proof that daring fashion didn't start at Burning Man—Frederick's was already there decades ahead, turning up the heat and the glamour.

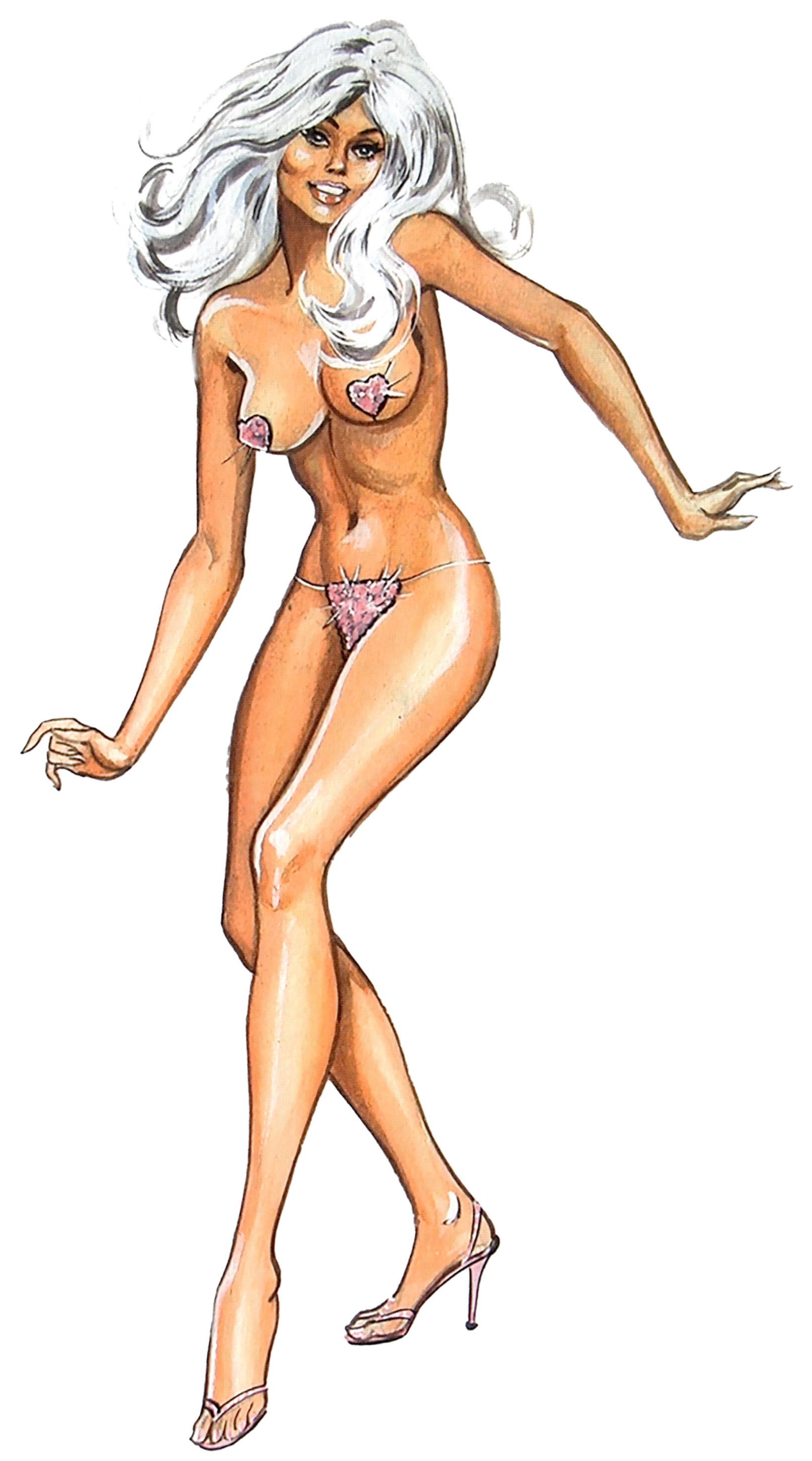

PATRICIA

This daring daisy set takes "flower power" to a whole new level. Barely there and boldly cheeky, it's a playful nod to the free-spirited flair of the era.

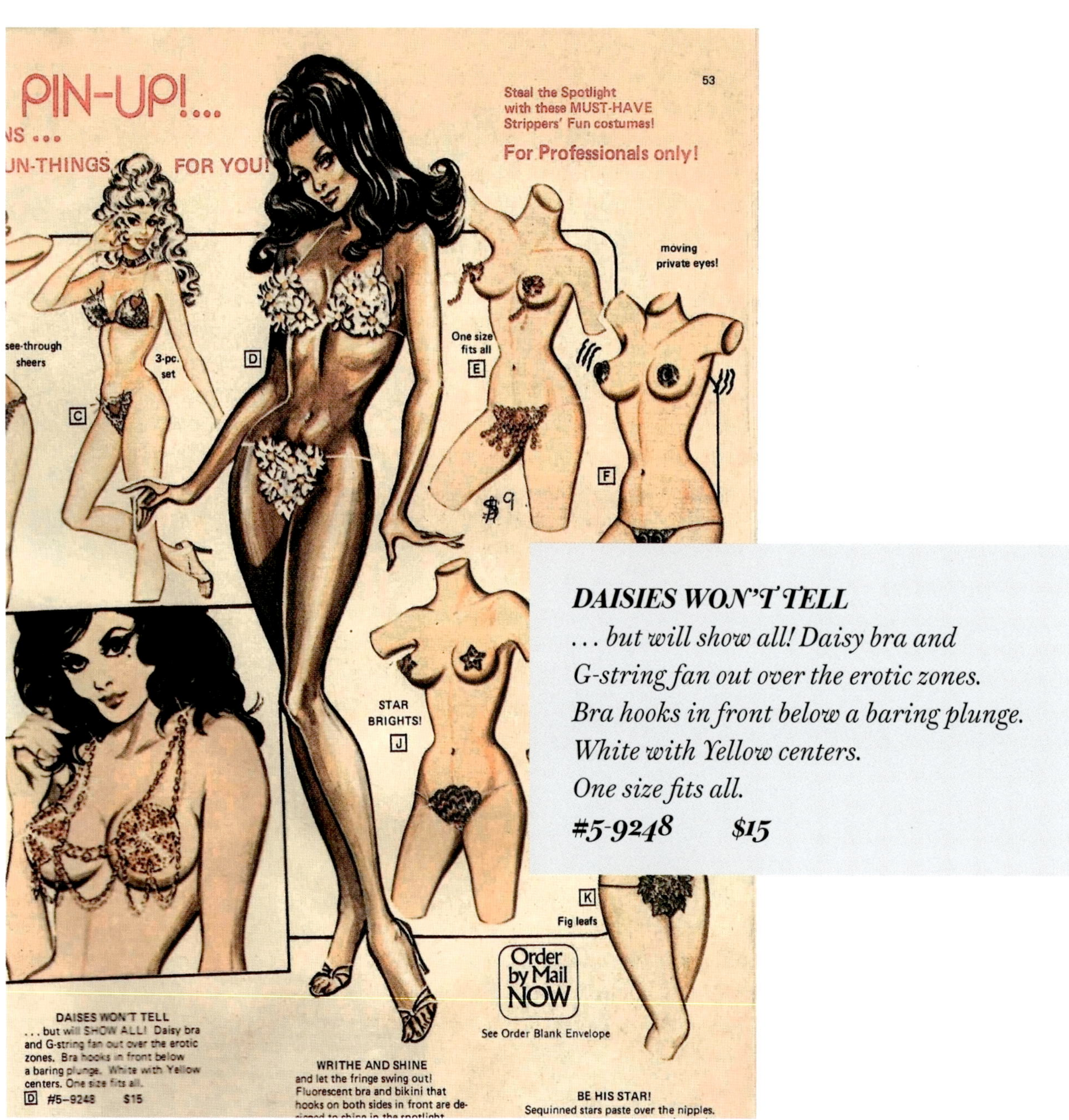

DAISIES WON'T TELL
. . . but will show all! Daisy bra and
G-string fan out over the erotic zones.
Bra hooks in front below a baring plunge.
White with Yellow centers.
One size fits all.
#5-9248 $15

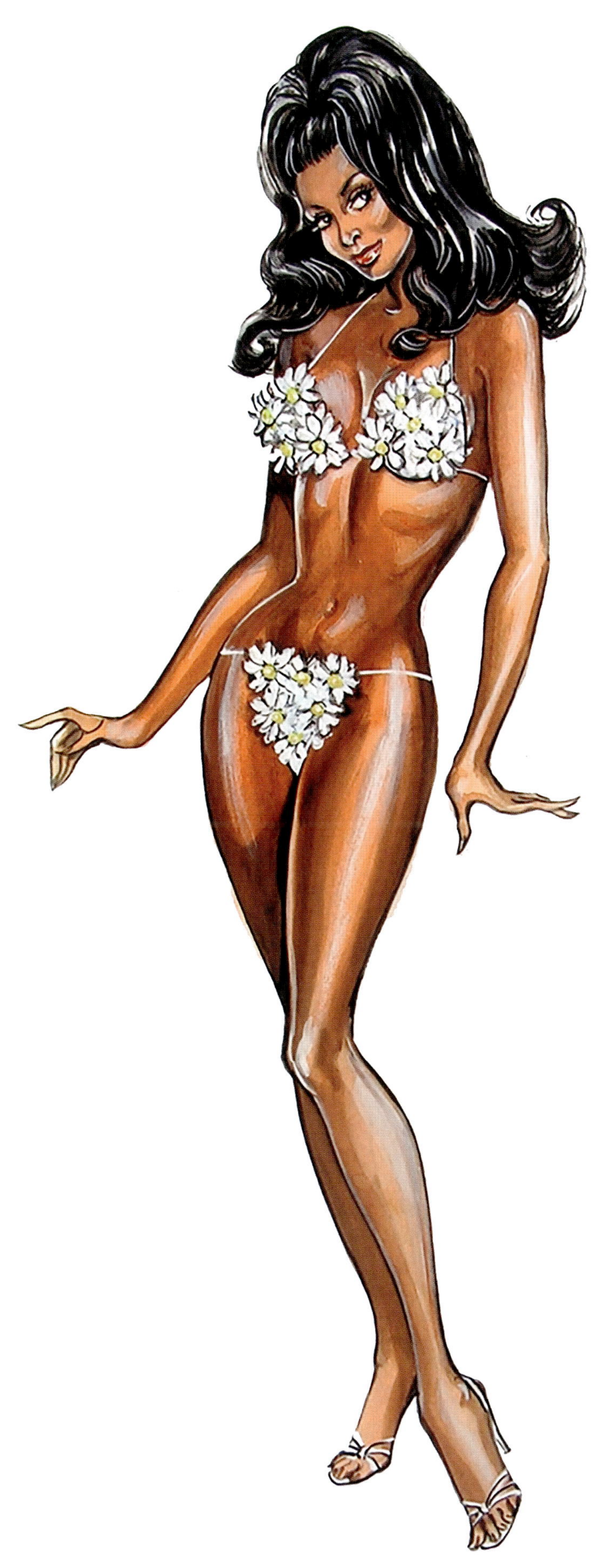

VERONICA

Business in the front, bombshell in the back. This barely there red thong and crisscross tie top is a flirty take on minimal coverage with maximum impact. A true showstopper that leaves little to the imagination.

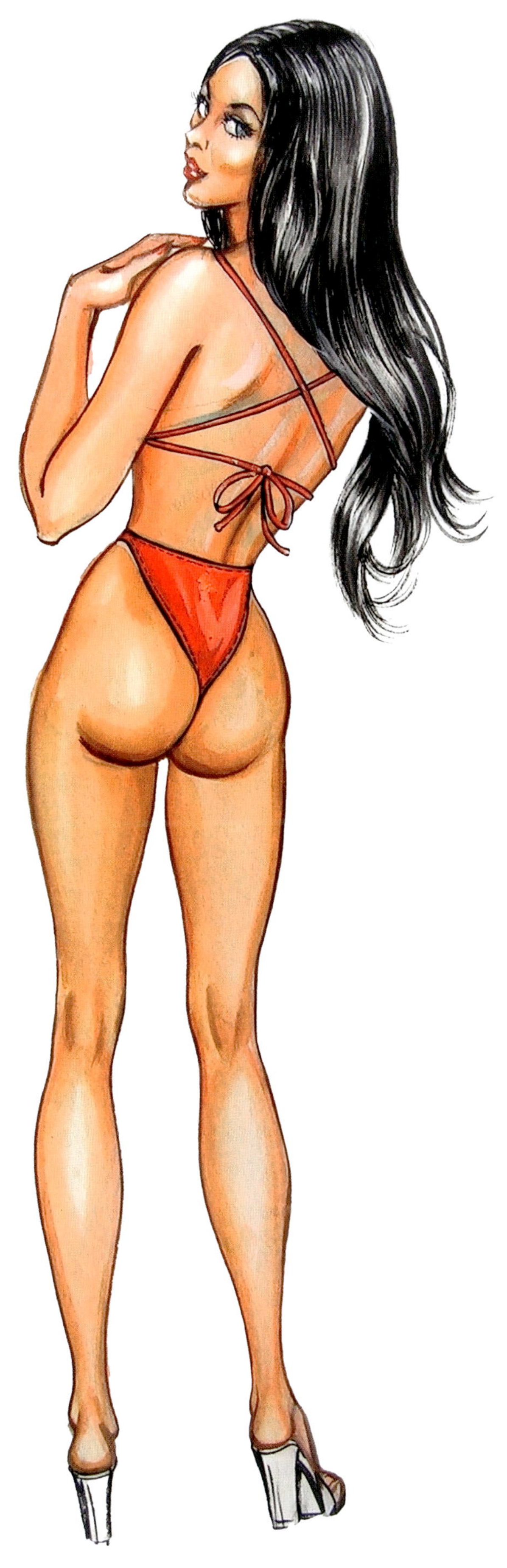

DENISE

This dramatic pink peignoir, complete with ruffled trim and billowy sleeves, is made for lounging in luxury—preferably with a cocktail in hand.

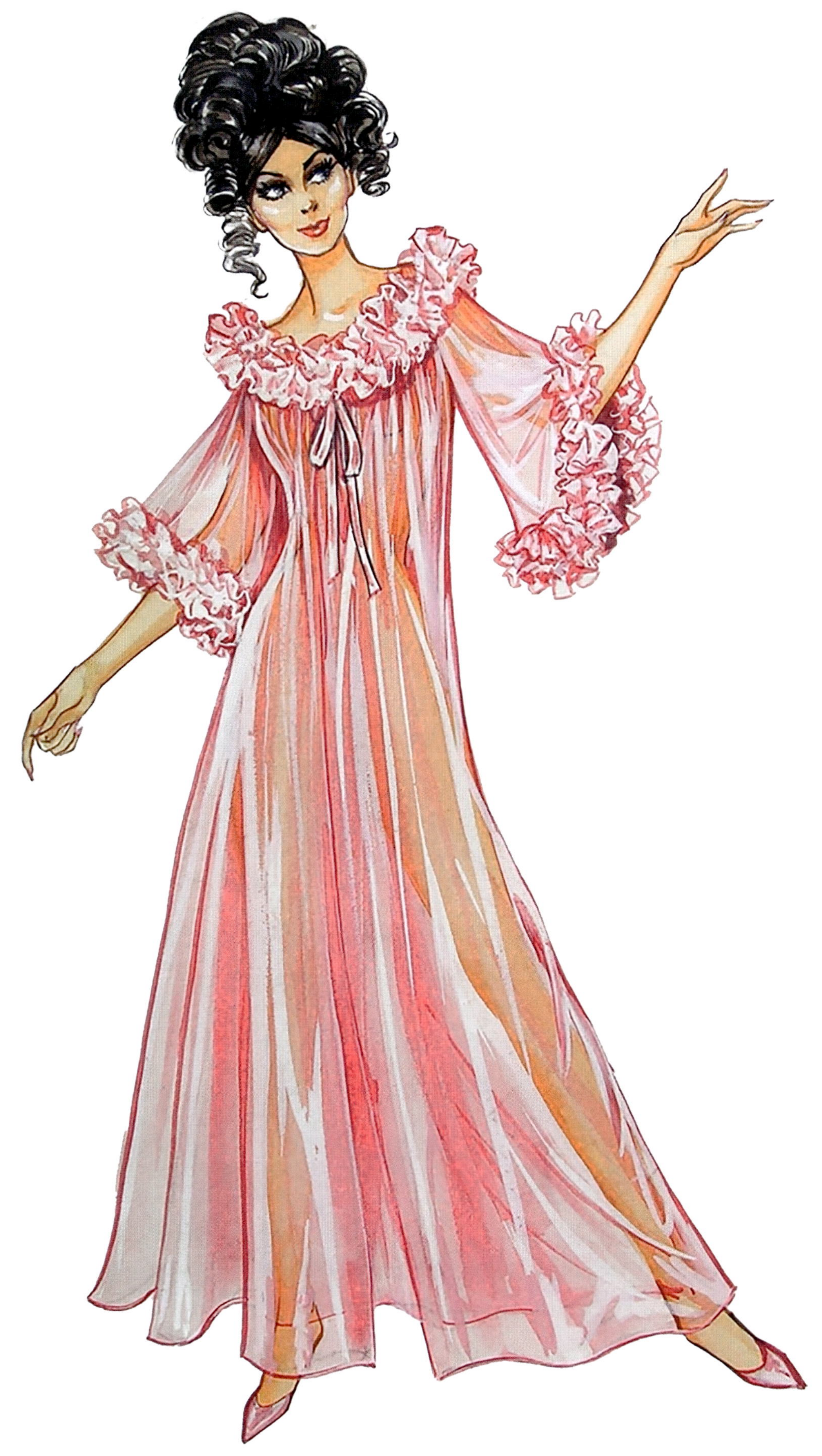

CAMILLE

This lace-up teddy has curve-hugging satin, flirty frills, and just the right amount of peekaboo detail, giving it a vintage bombshell feel. The kind of piece you slip into when you want to feel fabulous.

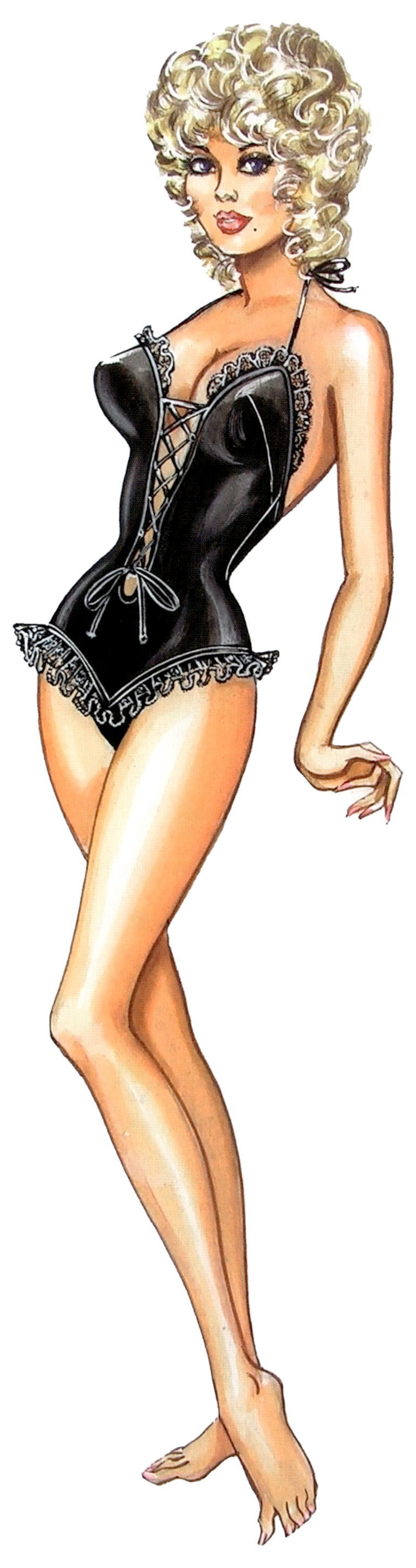

VANESS

Elegant and seductive, this black floor-length gown stuns in silky fabric that glides over her curves. The bust is delicately gathered with a tie, accented by a soft pink rose for a touch of romantic charm. Feminine ruffles trace the neckline, while sheer black balloon sleeves cinch at the wrist with flirty ruffled cuffs. Her curly ponytail and shy, downward gaze add a graceful softness to this sultry, sophisticated look.

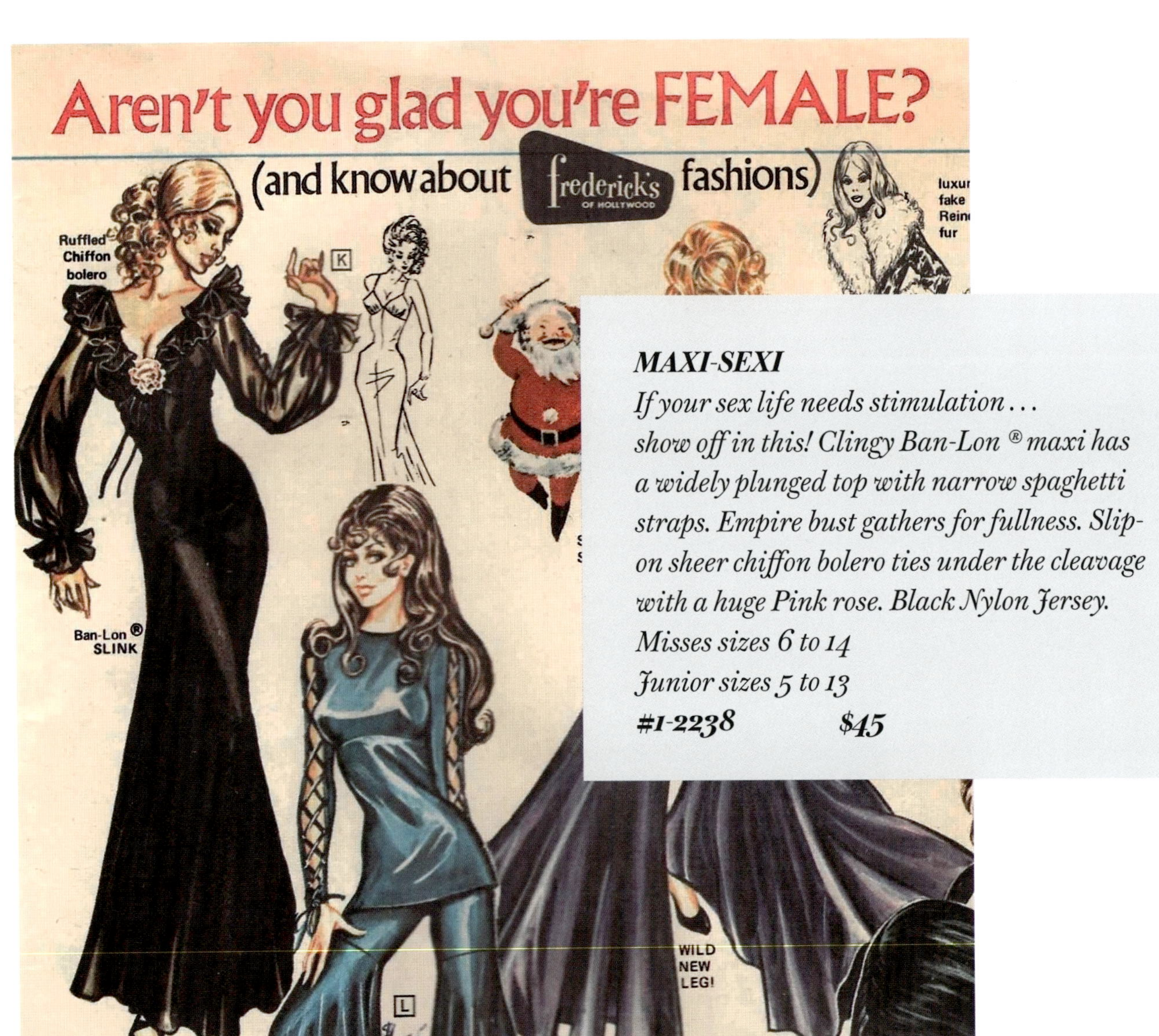

MAXI-SEXI

If your sex life needs stimulation . . . show off in this! Clingy Ban-Lon ® maxi has a widely plunged top with narrow spaghetti straps. Empire bust gathers for fullness. Slip-on sheer chiffon bolero ties under the cleavage with a huge Pink rose. Black Nylon Jersey.
Misses sizes 6 to 14
Junior sizes 5 to 13
#1-2238 $45

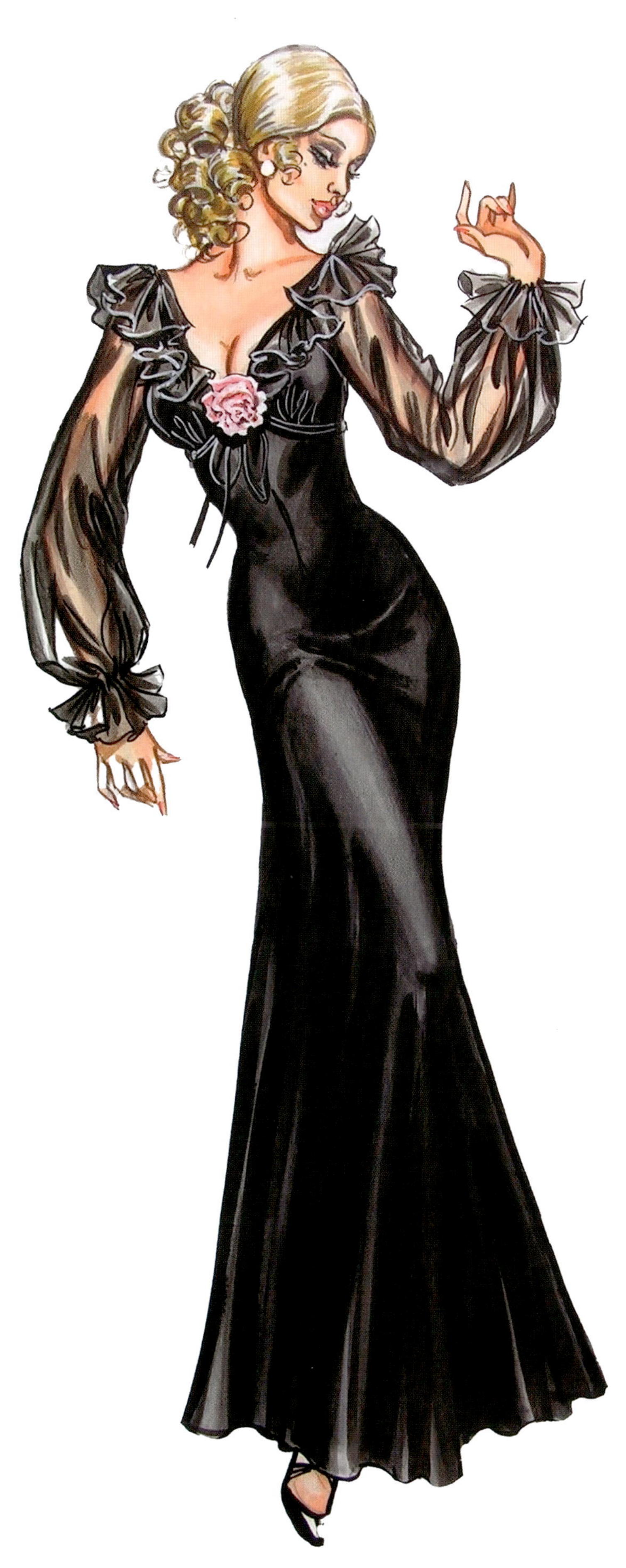

JENNIFER

Definitely one of the more daring and unique pieces, this sheer, full-body fishnet catsuit is equal parts sexy and bold. The fitted silhouette hugs every curve while the crisscross pattern adds texture and intrigue. Something you'd expect from a vintage vixen who isn't afraid to push the envelope.

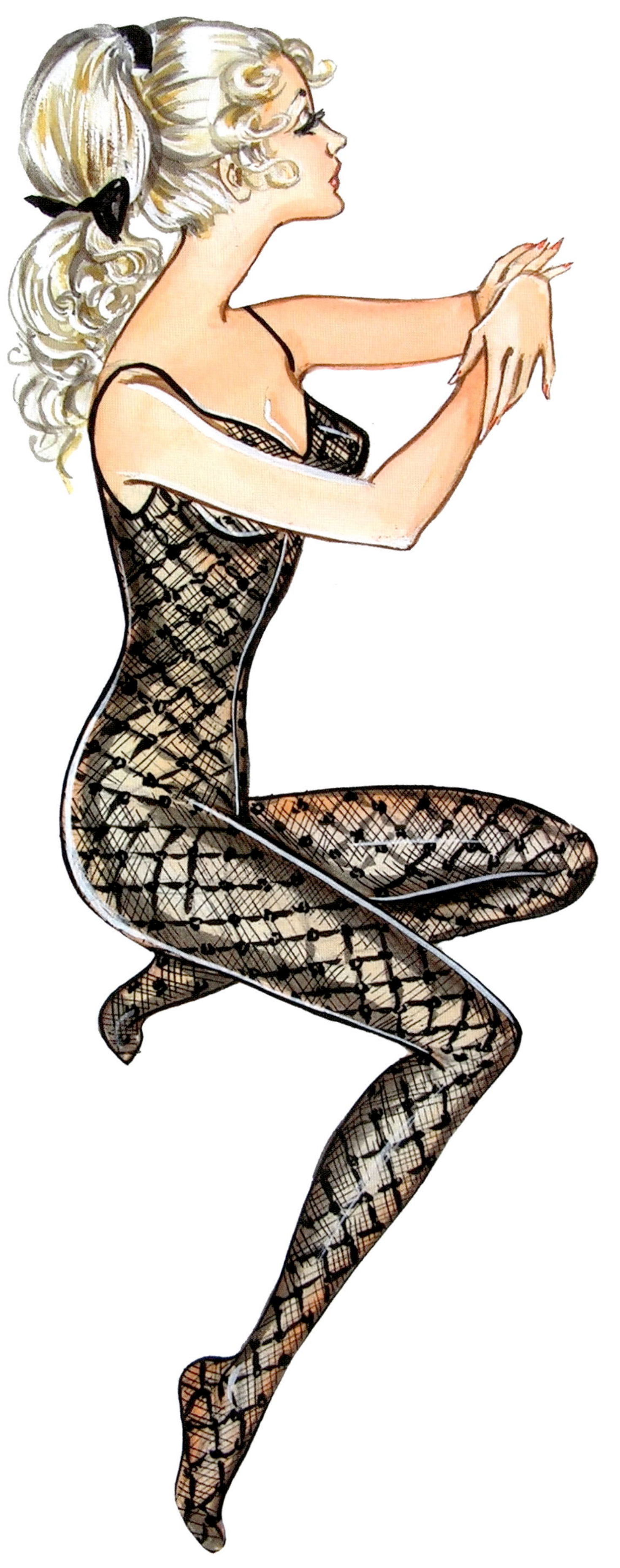

SHANNON

This corset is all about cinched elegance and vintage glamour. With its intricate lace detailing and structured boning, it shapes the waist and lifts the bust, creating that signature hourglass silhouette. The ribbon tie adds just the right touch of romance—perfect for pairing with a long skirt or wearing all on its own for a sultry boudoir look.

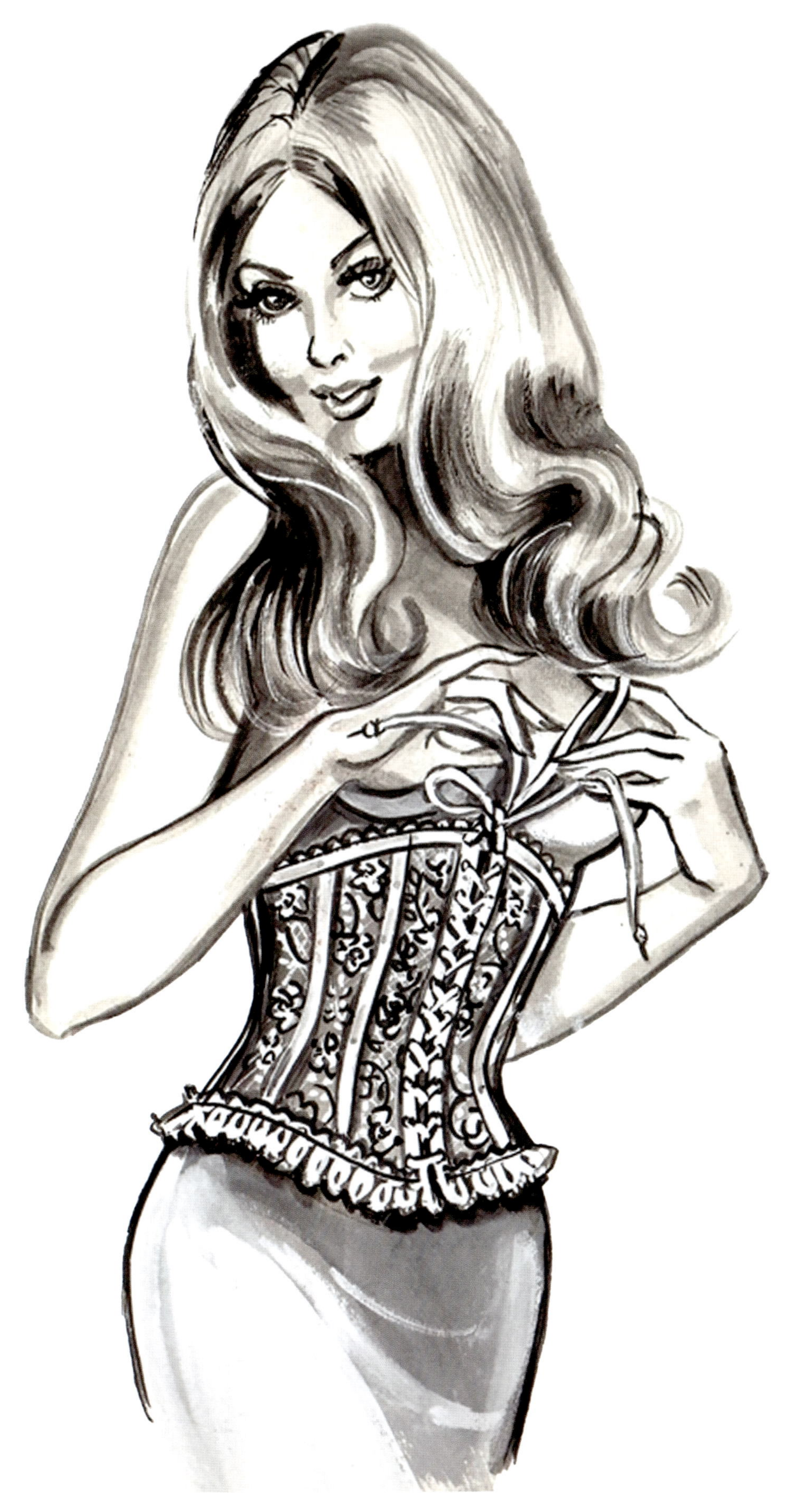

ELIZABETH

A glamorous vintage set featuring a structured bra with pointed cups and a high-waisted garter belt. Satin paneling and crisscross details add extra drama, while delicate ruffles bring a playful touch.

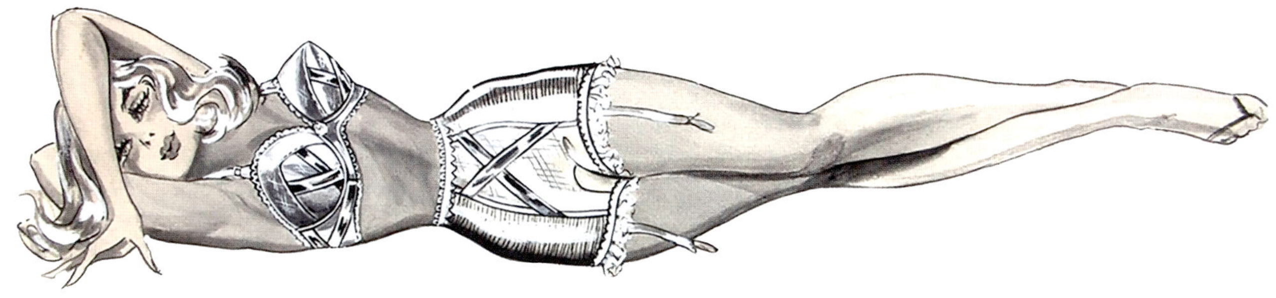

DAWN

This cheeky little number looks like the lovechild of a vintage playsuit and classic sleepwear. With bold striped trim and a buttoned bodice, it's part pajama, part pin-up, and 100 percent fabulous. Perfect for when you're feeling playful but still want to keep it comfy.

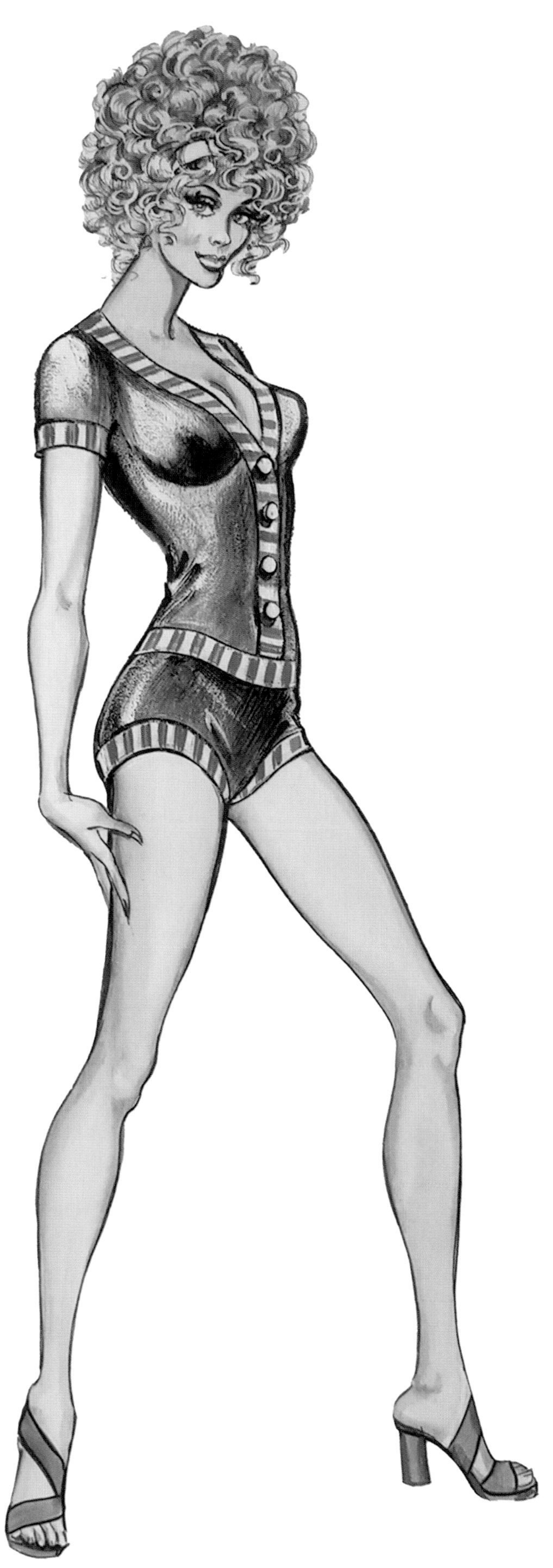

KATHY

A bold animal-print top paired with glossy high-cut bottoms that make a striking impression. The button-down neckline adds a touch of flirtation, while the overall ensemble feels equal parts fierce and fashionable.

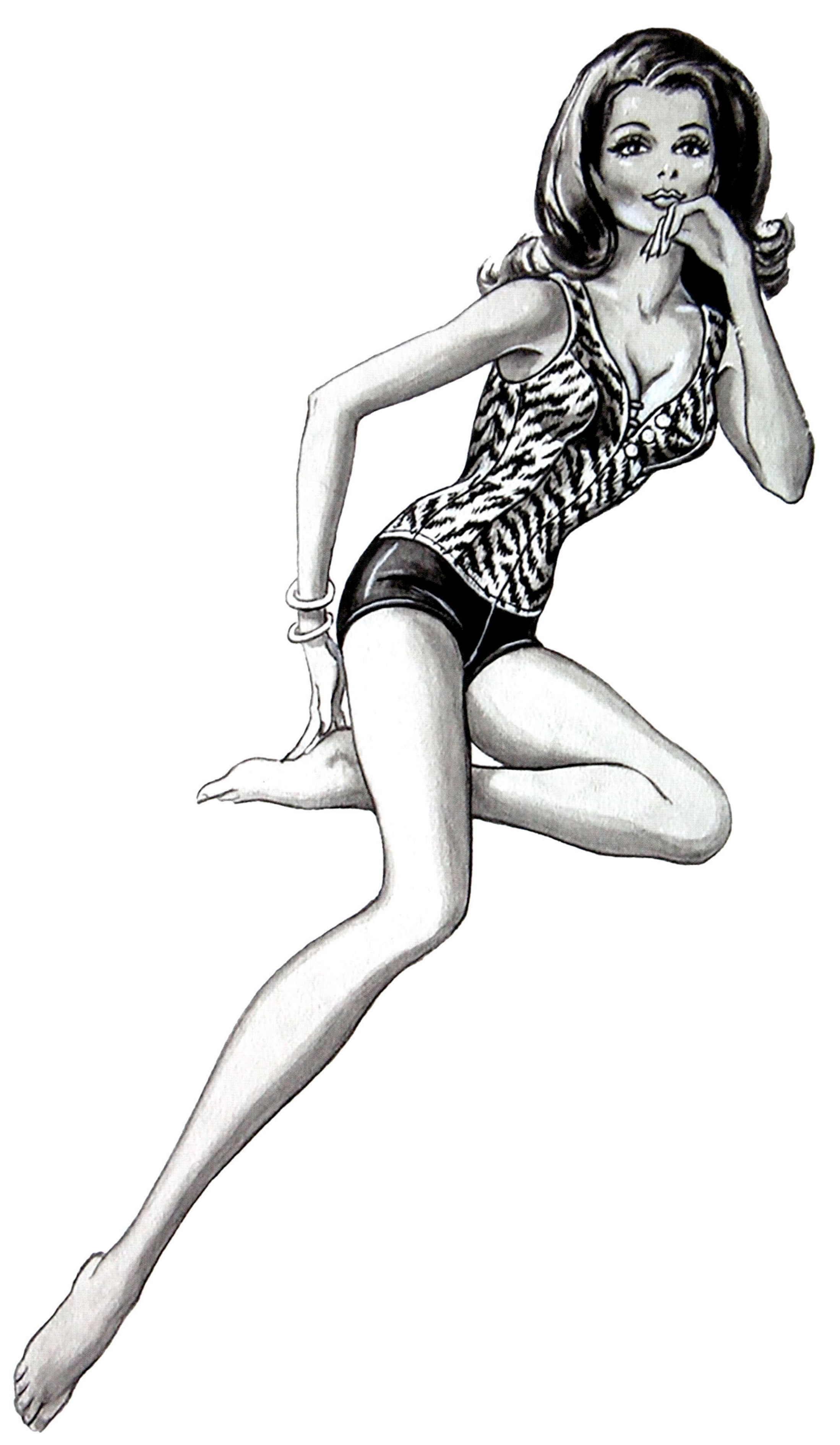

MONIQUE

This sweet and sexy baby-doll set is the perfect blend of playful and provocative. With embroidered triangle cups, a flouncy hem, and matching panties peeking through, it's giving classic pin-up energy with plenty of boudoir glam.

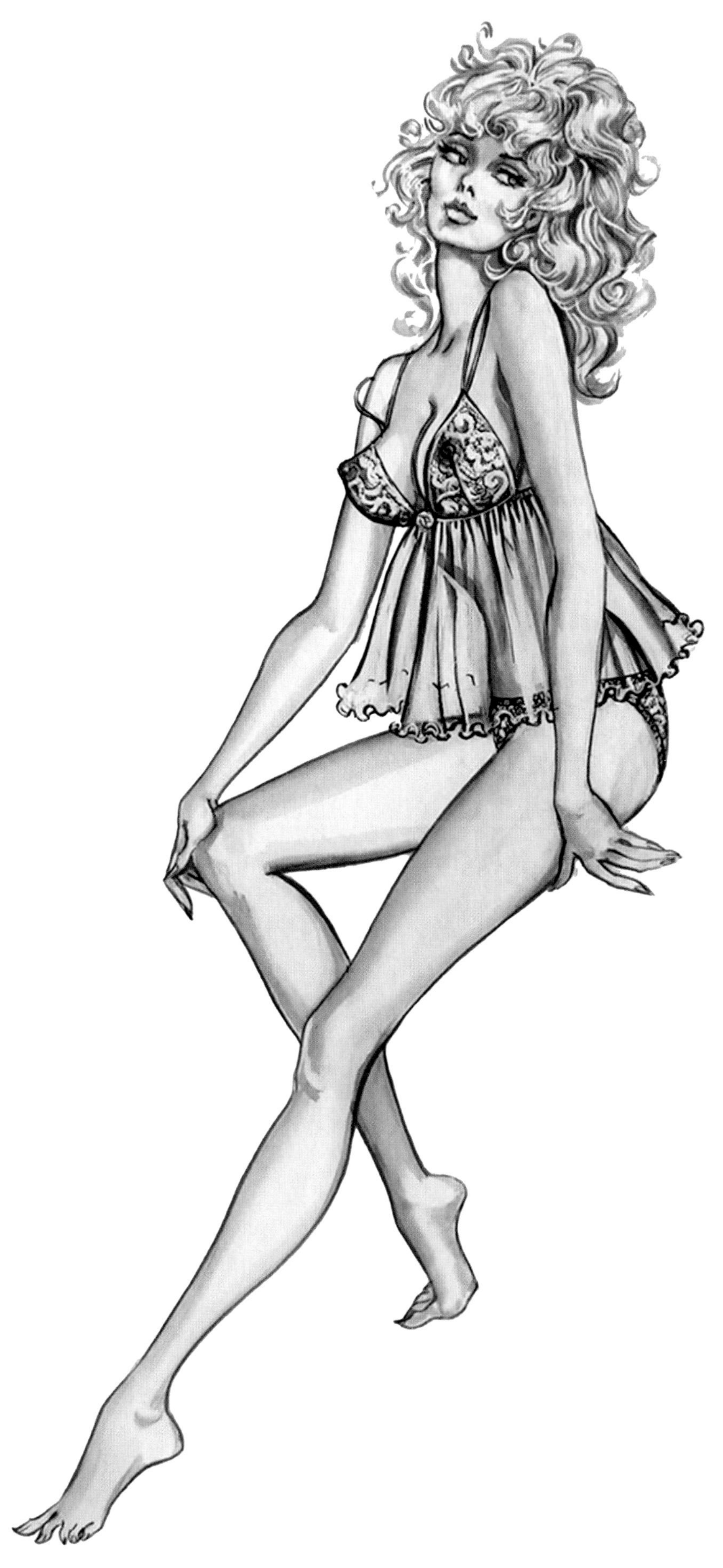

TINA

This piece flirts with full coverage while still serving serious tease. The ruched bodice adds playful texture, while the sheer bloomer-style bottoms bring a cheeky twist. A cinched waist and ruffled trim complete the look with coquette charm.

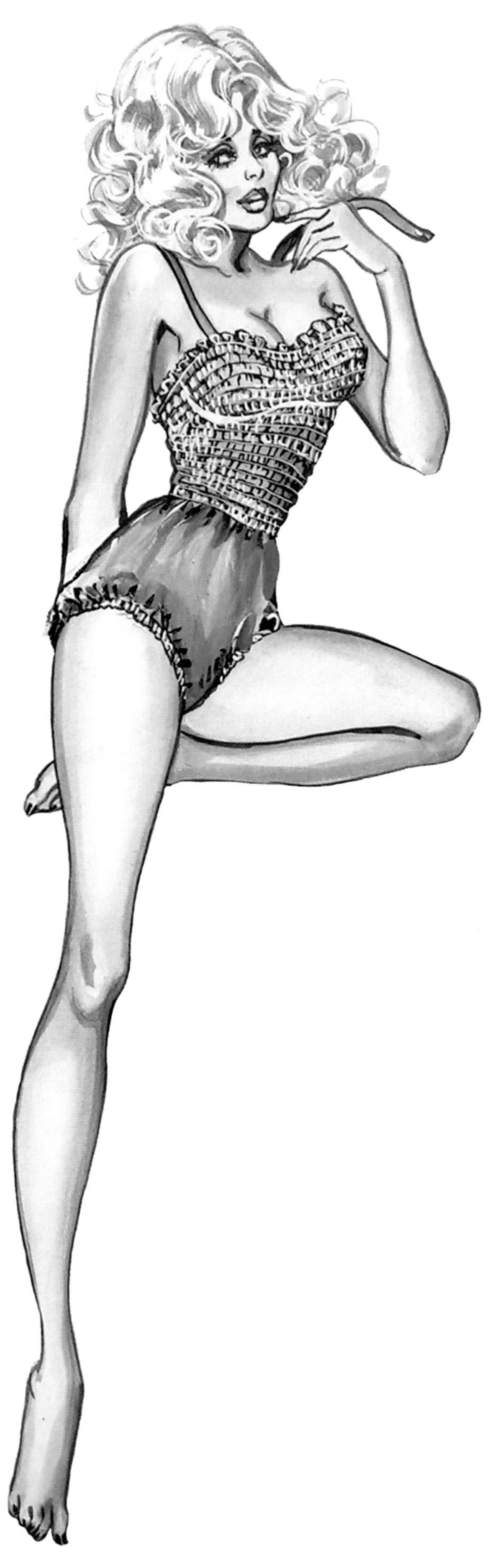

SABRINA

This two-piece fringed set was made for movement and mischief. With layers of playful fringe that bounce with every step, it's equal parts sass and swing. The halter-style top offers just enough coverage to tease, while the matching high-waisted bottoms give a cheeky peek beneath the flutter. Whether she's dancing the night away or just striking a pose, this look was born to shimmy.

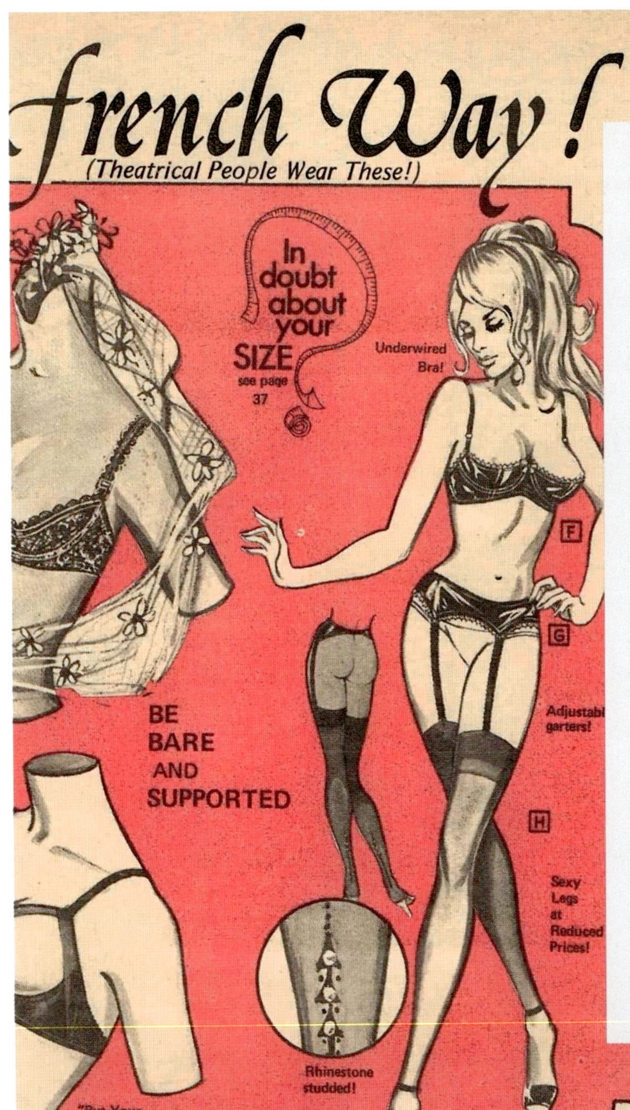

FRENCH DRESSING
Find the allure of oo-la-la dressing in an underwired half-bra and garter belt of SEXY "WET-LOOK" CIRE. Shelf bra undercups the breasts, leaving the nipples bare. Beautifully revealing.
Black only.
Order Half-Bra in sizes 32-34-36-38.
No cup sizes needed.
#4-5205 $8

SEXY LEGS
in sexy stockings! Flat-knit Nylon points up nifty ankles with arrows at the heeltops. Drops of rhinestones sparkle. Seamless, sheer sleek in Sun Tan or Off-Black. Sizes 8 1/2 to 11.
#3-4252 $3.99 Each Pair
2 Pairs for $6.99

Shown here is "Sabrina" adorned in a sultry lingerie ensemble.

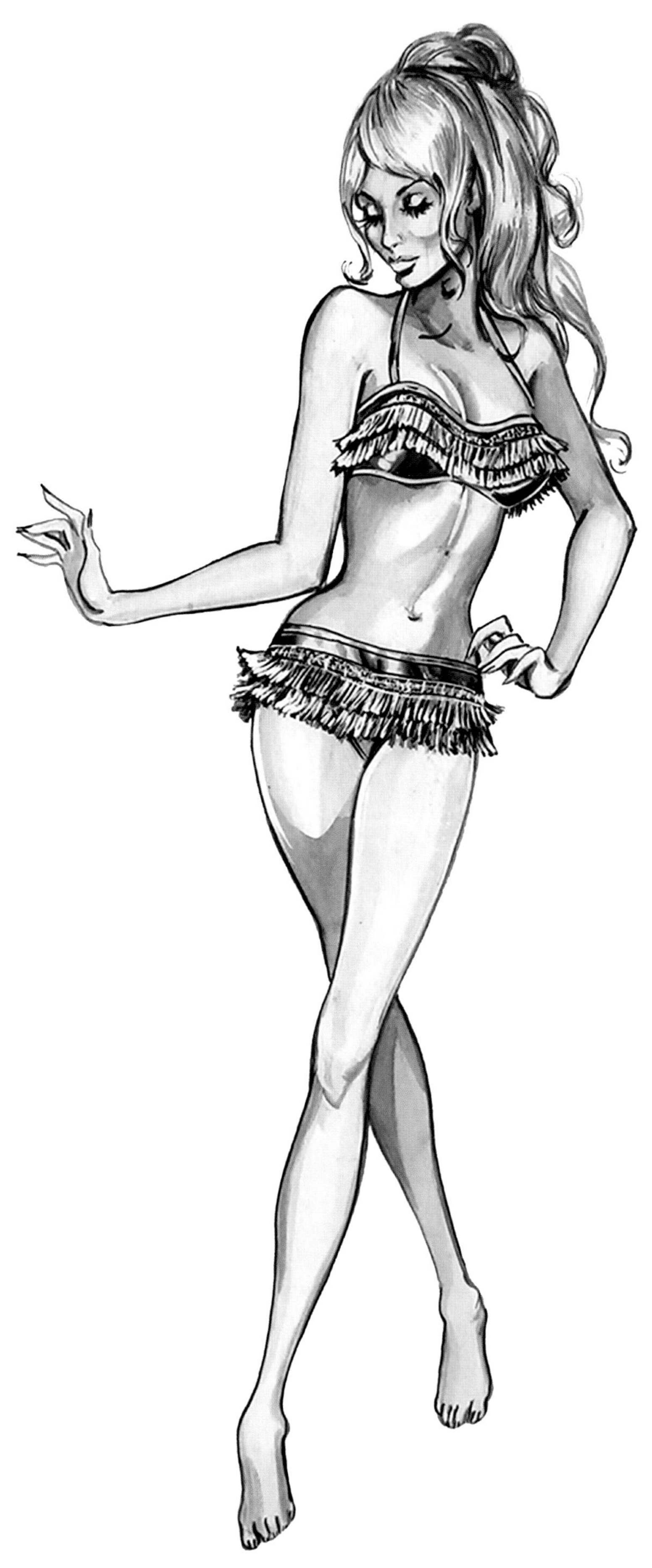

ELLEN

This two-piece sheer baby-doll set is flirtation in fabric. The plunging halter neckline and embroidered cups frame the bust beautifully, while the flowy mesh skirt hints at the matching bottoms underneath. A look that says "come hither" with every swish, this piece is the definition of bedroom glamour.

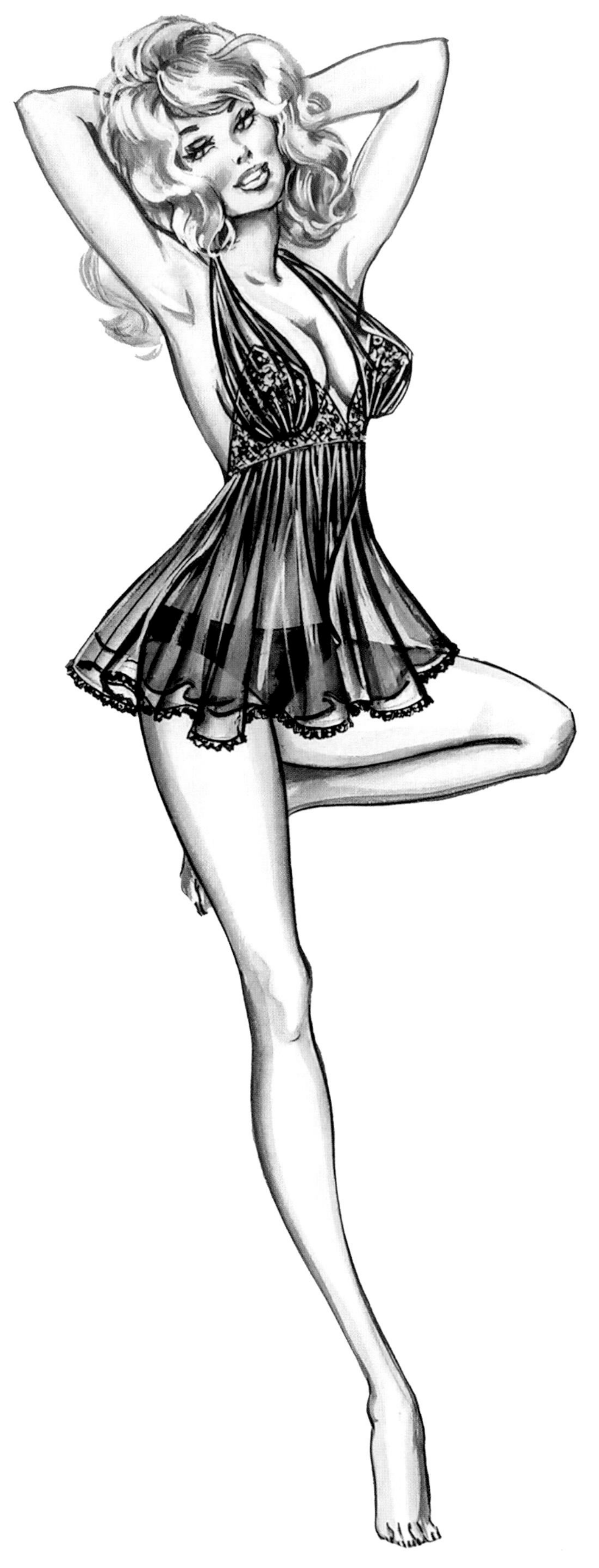

LAURIE

Serving goddess energy in this dramatic two-piece set. The ruched bust with ribbon detailing draws the eye, while the sweeping sheer robe adds an air of elegance and allure. Paired with coordinating lace-trimmed panties, this look was made for someone who knows how to make an entrance—and an even more unforgettable exit.

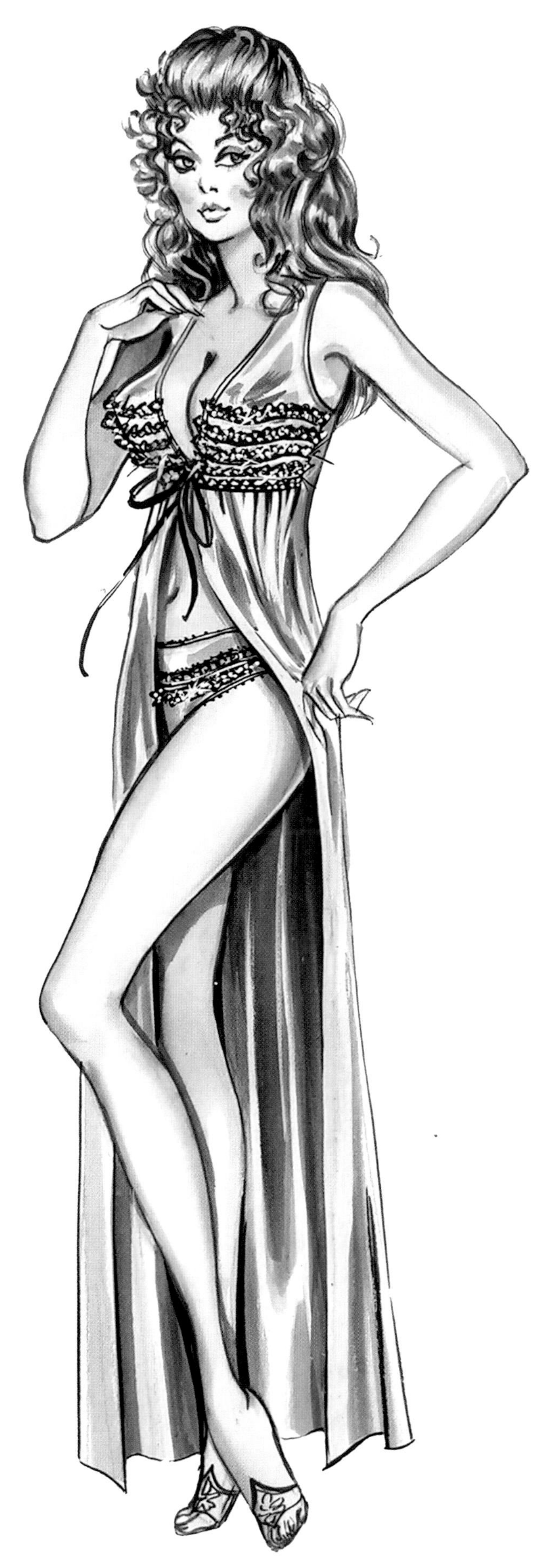

MARIE

A bold peek at a printed bra that's anything but basic. Playful motifs meet structured support, proving that lingerie can be fun and flattering.

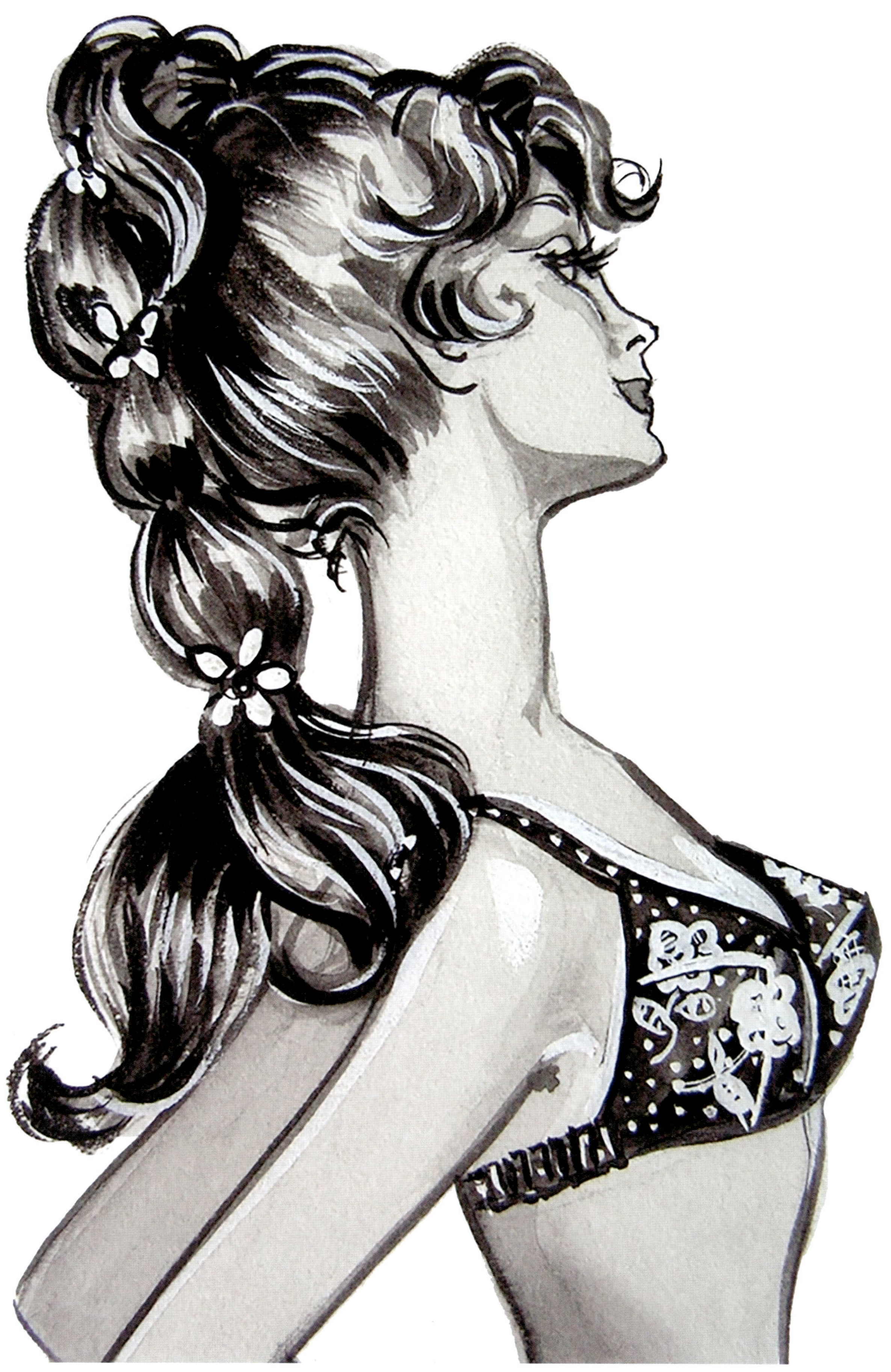

CHERYL

Effortless beauty in the basics. This timeless bra and high-waisted brief set delivers classic structure with a soft, feminine edge. Delicate trim and tiny bow details add just the right amount of charm—proof that sometimes simple really is stunning.

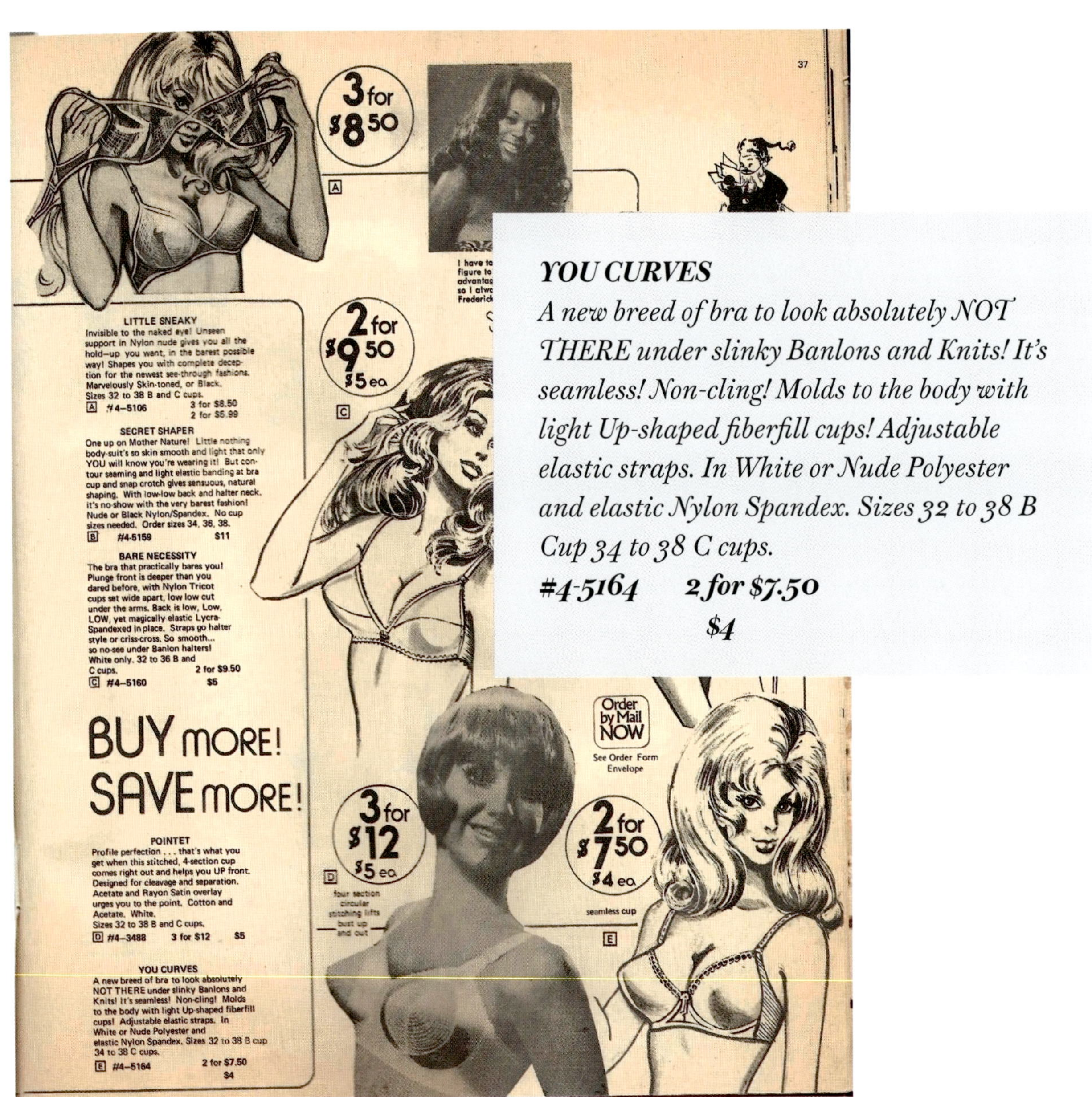

YOU CURVES
A new breed of bra to look absolutely NOT THERE under slinky Banlons and Knits! It's seamless! Non-cling! Molds to the body with light Up-shaped fiberfill cups! Adjustable elastic straps. In White or Nude Polyester and elastic Nylon Spandex. Sizes 32 to 38 B Cup 34 to 38 C cups.
#4-5164 2 for $7.50
$4

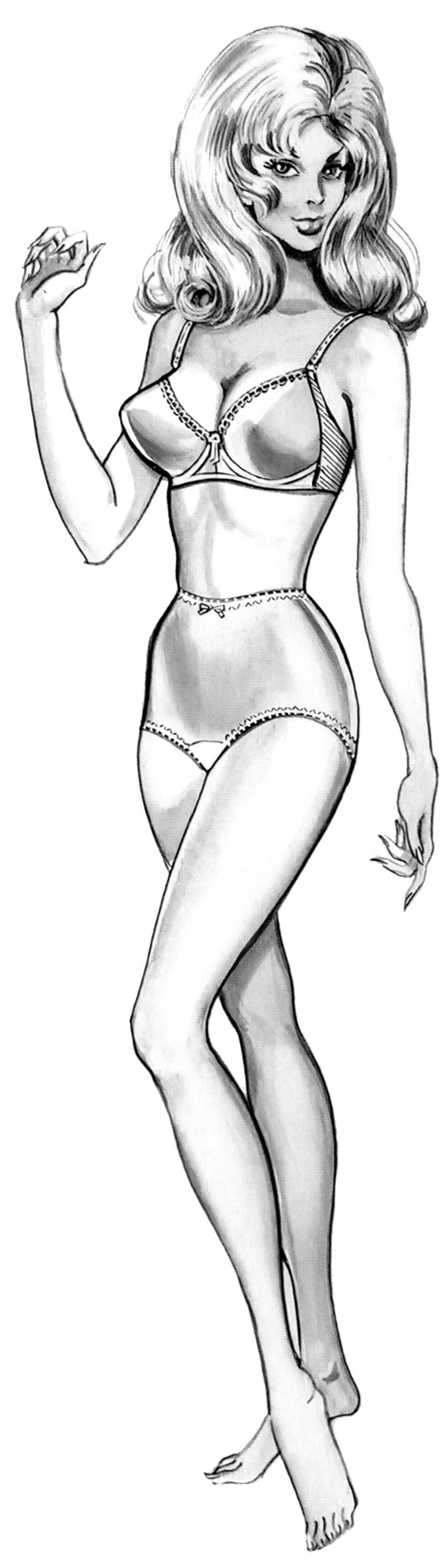

BRIANNA

This dazzling two-piece is made to turn heads. With rhinestone-studded cups, fringe that sways with every step, and a barely there silhouette, this look is equal parts showstopper and seductress. It's the kind of set you wear when you're not afraid to sparkle—and be seen.

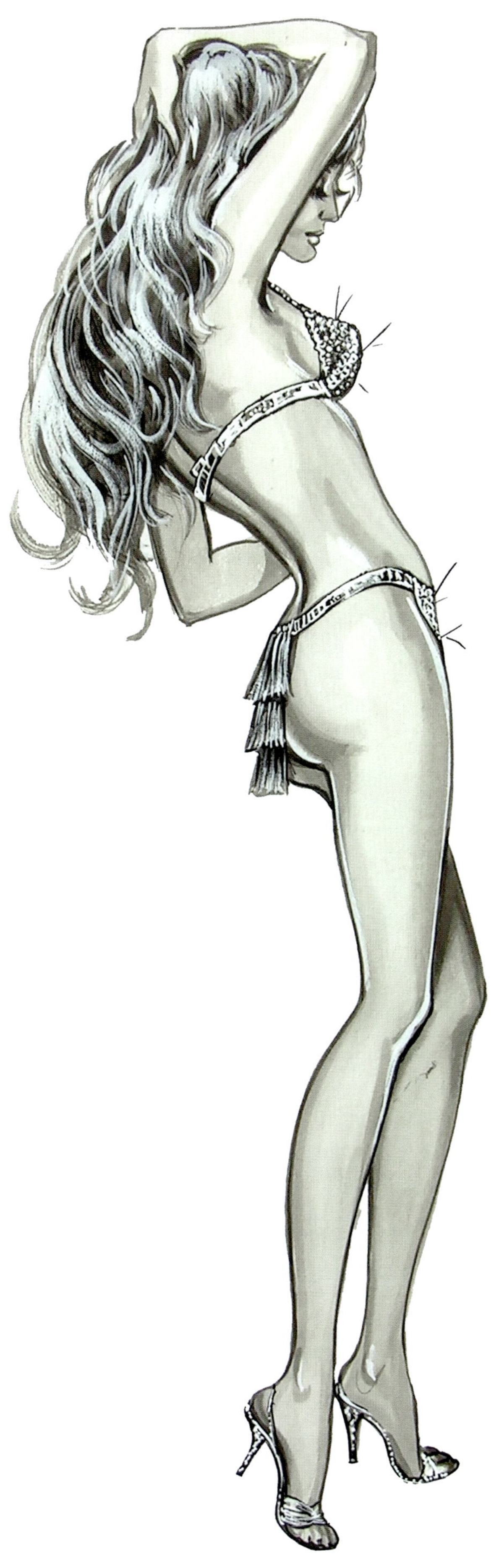

CAROLYN

Lounge, but make it luxe. This satin-look robe brings sophistication to your off-duty hours with its dramatic sheen, flowing bell sleeves, and flirtatiously short hemline. Cinched at the waist with a matching tie, it's the perfect wrap for glamorous mornings, sultry evenings, or anything in between.

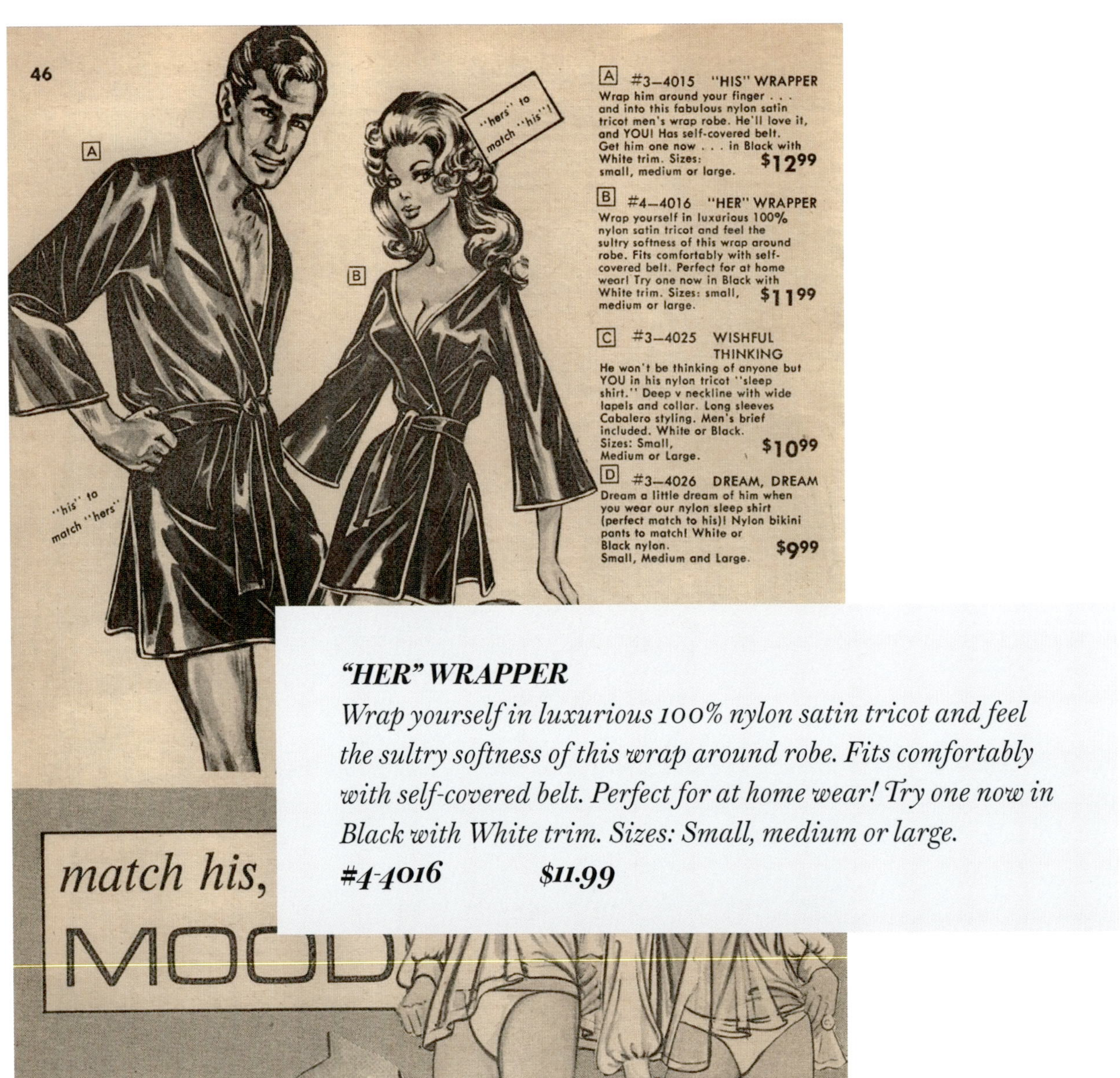

"HER" WRAPPER

Wrap yourself in luxurious 100% nylon satin tricot and feel the sultry softness of this wrap around robe. Fits comfortably with self-covered belt. Perfect for at home wear! Try one now in Black with White trim. Sizes: Small, medium or large.

#4-4016 ***$11.99***

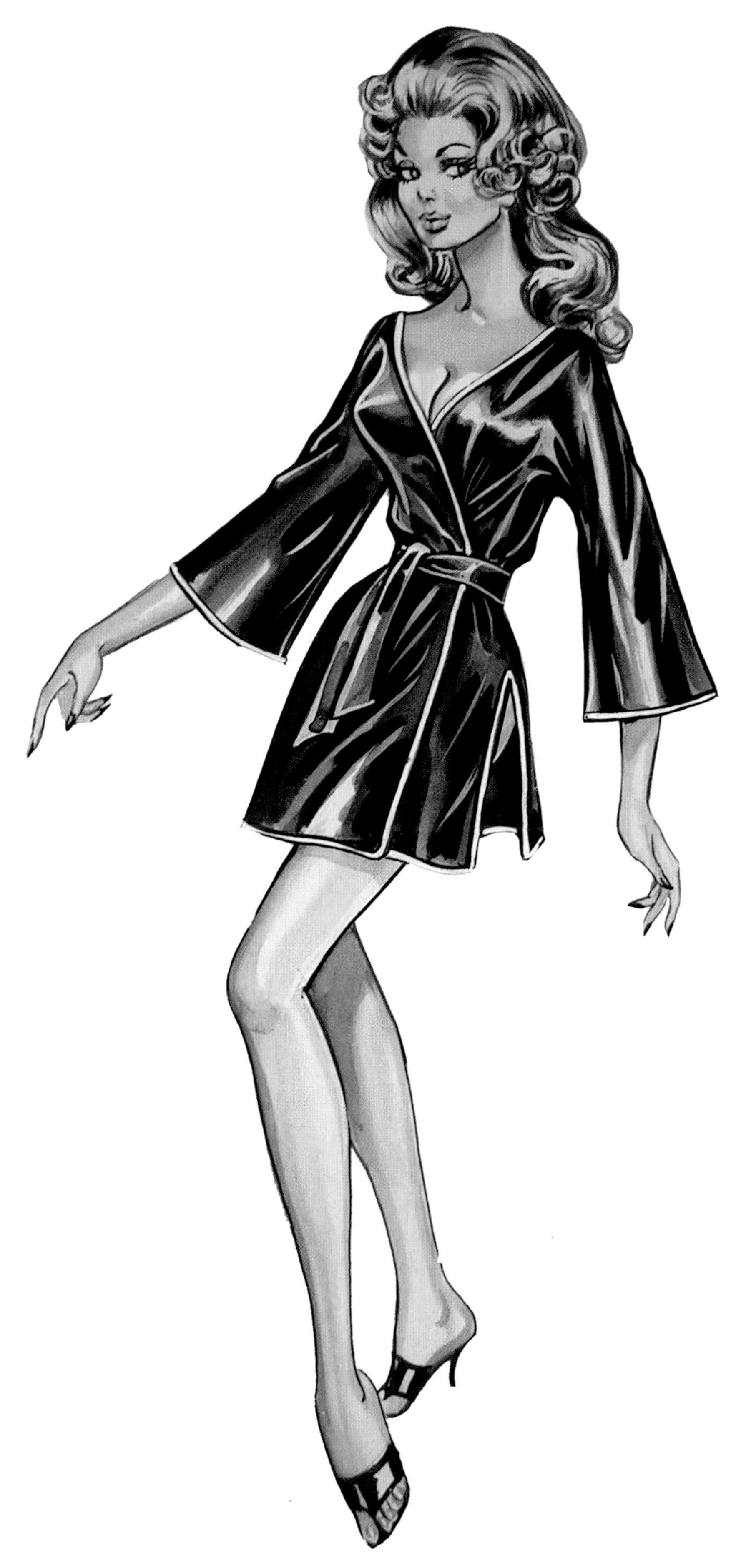

LYNDA

This two-piece swimsuit features a vibrant, retro print that adds personality without going over the top. The underwire top offers subtle support, while the mid-rise bottoms with side tie details provide a flattering fit. Perfect for lounging poolside or enjoying a sunny day with a little flair.

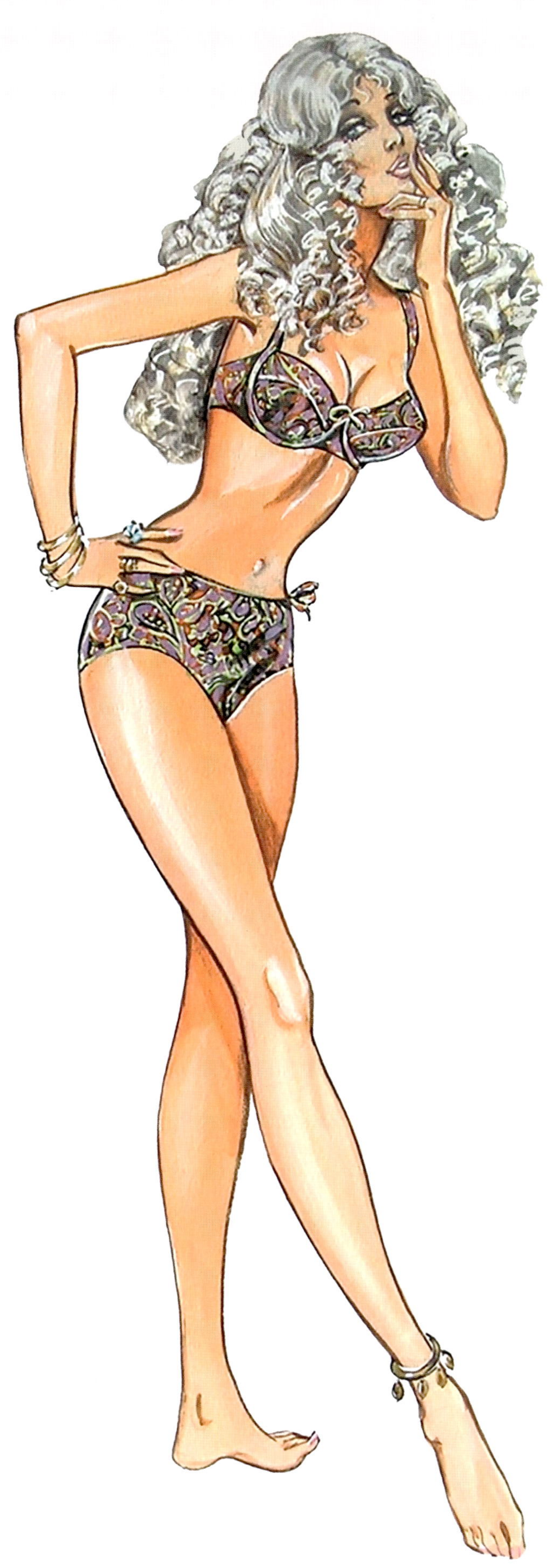

RAQUEL

This vibrant two-piece '60s-style swimsuit features a bold tropical print that captures the era's love of color and flair. The structured underwire top offers classic support, while the mid-rise bottoms are accented with a playful side tie. A perfect example of retro swimwear with standout style.

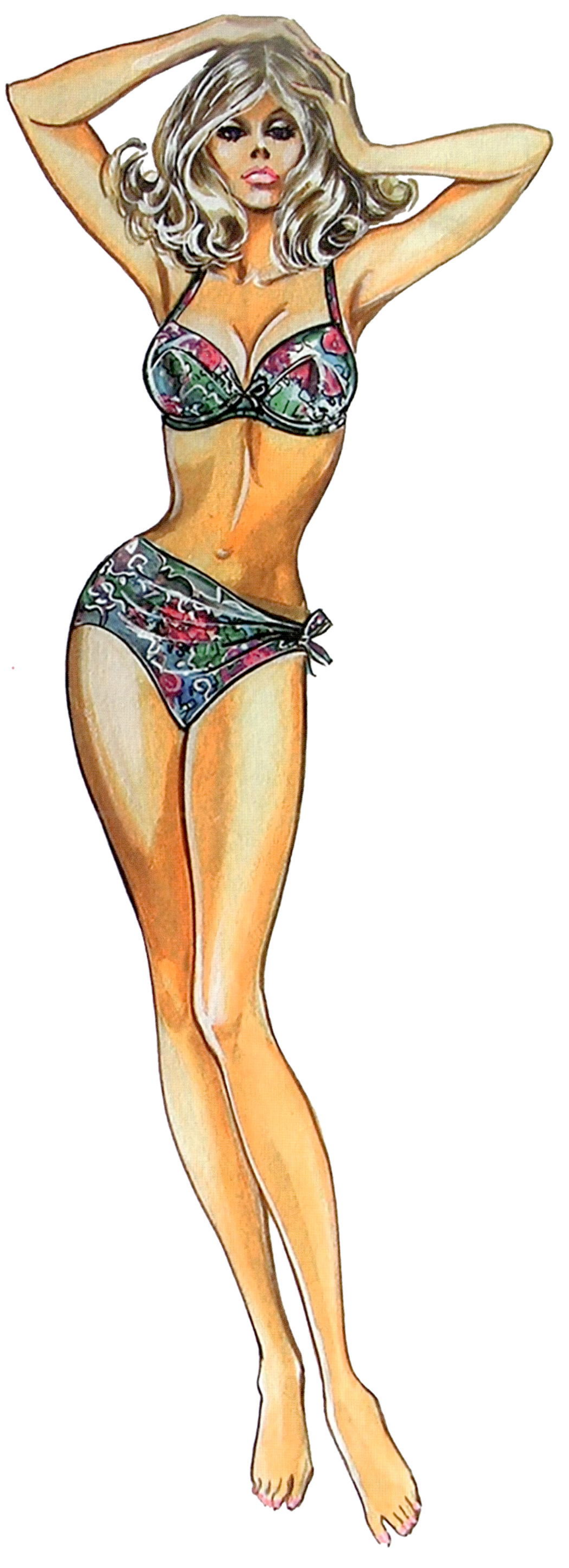

ROCHELLE

This black-and-white-striped bikini is a timeless classic. With its bold contrast and minimal design, it highlights the beauty of simplicity while perfectly showcasing her curves. A forever-stylish look that's just as striking now as it was in the '70s.

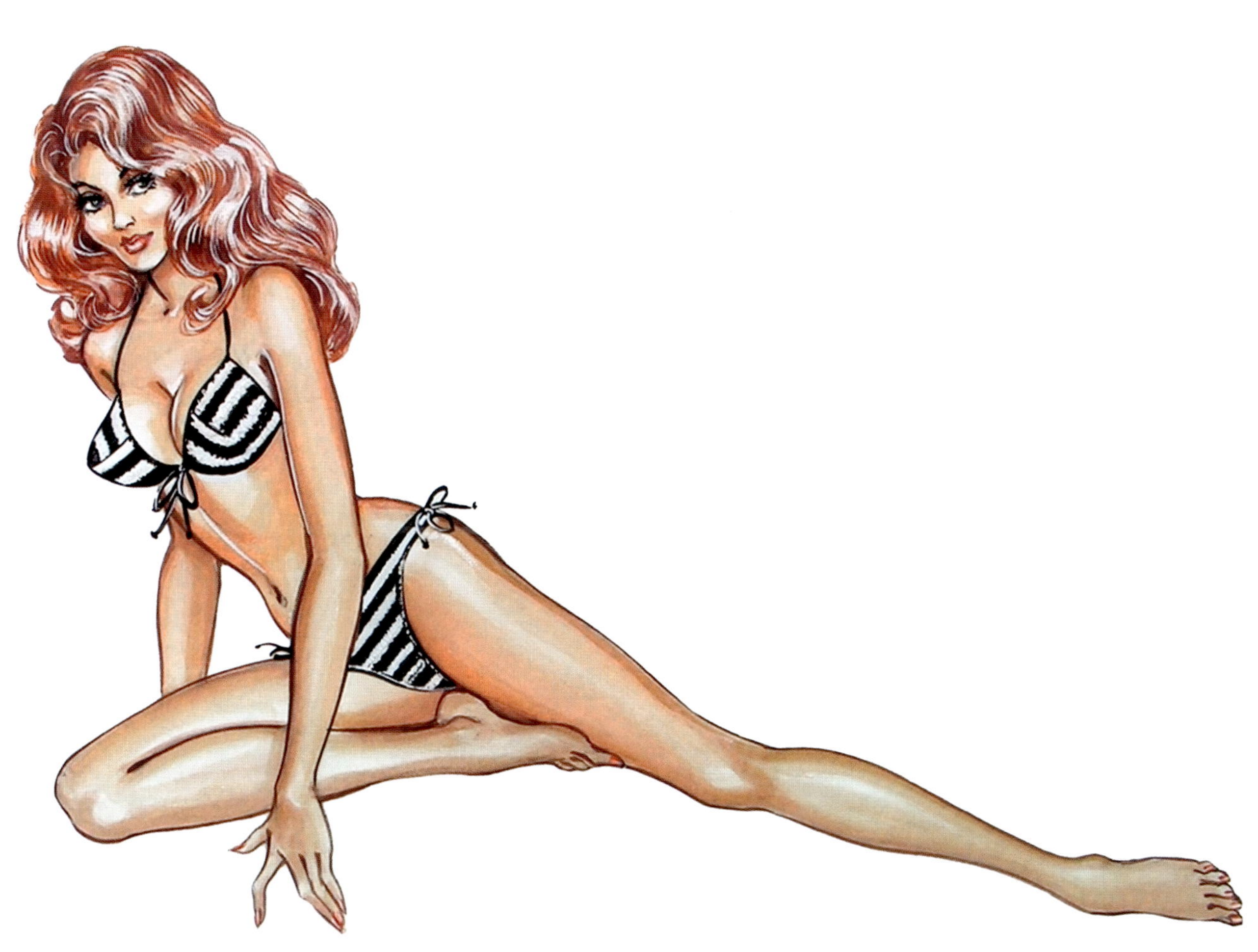

GWEN

Effortless summer glamour with a playful edge. Reclining in a confident pose, this chic model figure wears a bold, hot-pink bikini featuring metallic ring accents at the bust and hips–adding a modern, flirty touch to the minimal silhouette. Her oversized straw sunhat, trimmed with a ribbon, not only shields her eyes but enhances the sense of leisurely elegance.

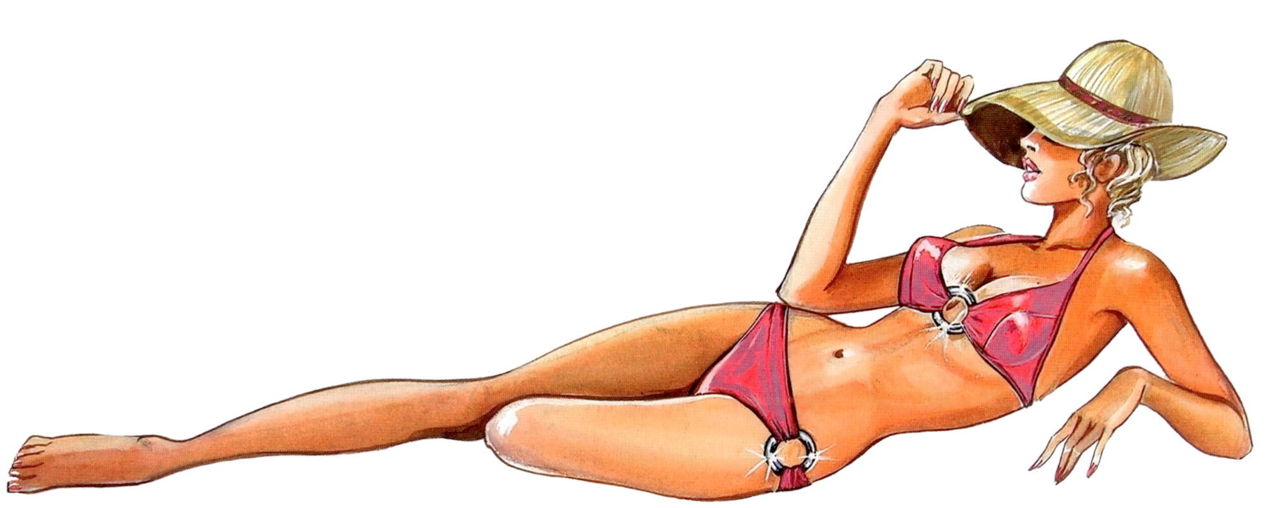

ANN

This playful little bikini brings the sass with its bold "Yes" and "No" script—because why not keep them guessing? With its minimal cut and flirtatious print, it's a '70s-style wink that says just enough without saying too much.

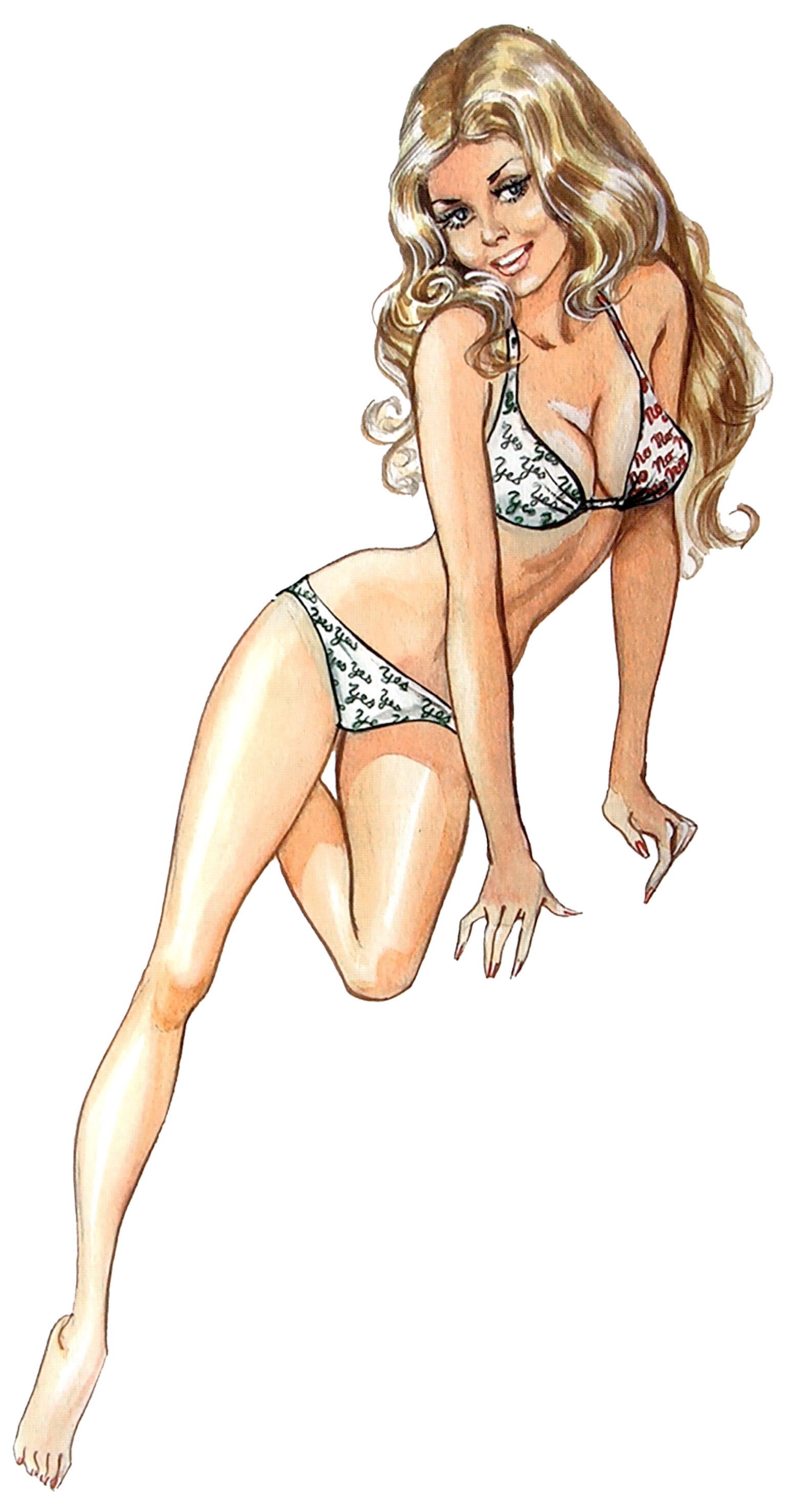

CASSANDRA

This one-piece swimsuit is elegant, sleek, and polished to perfection. Her look is proof that you don't need to bare it all to turn heads. The bold color blocking adds a vibrant, eye-catching twist to the timeless silhouette, making this a classy, quietly powerful statement.

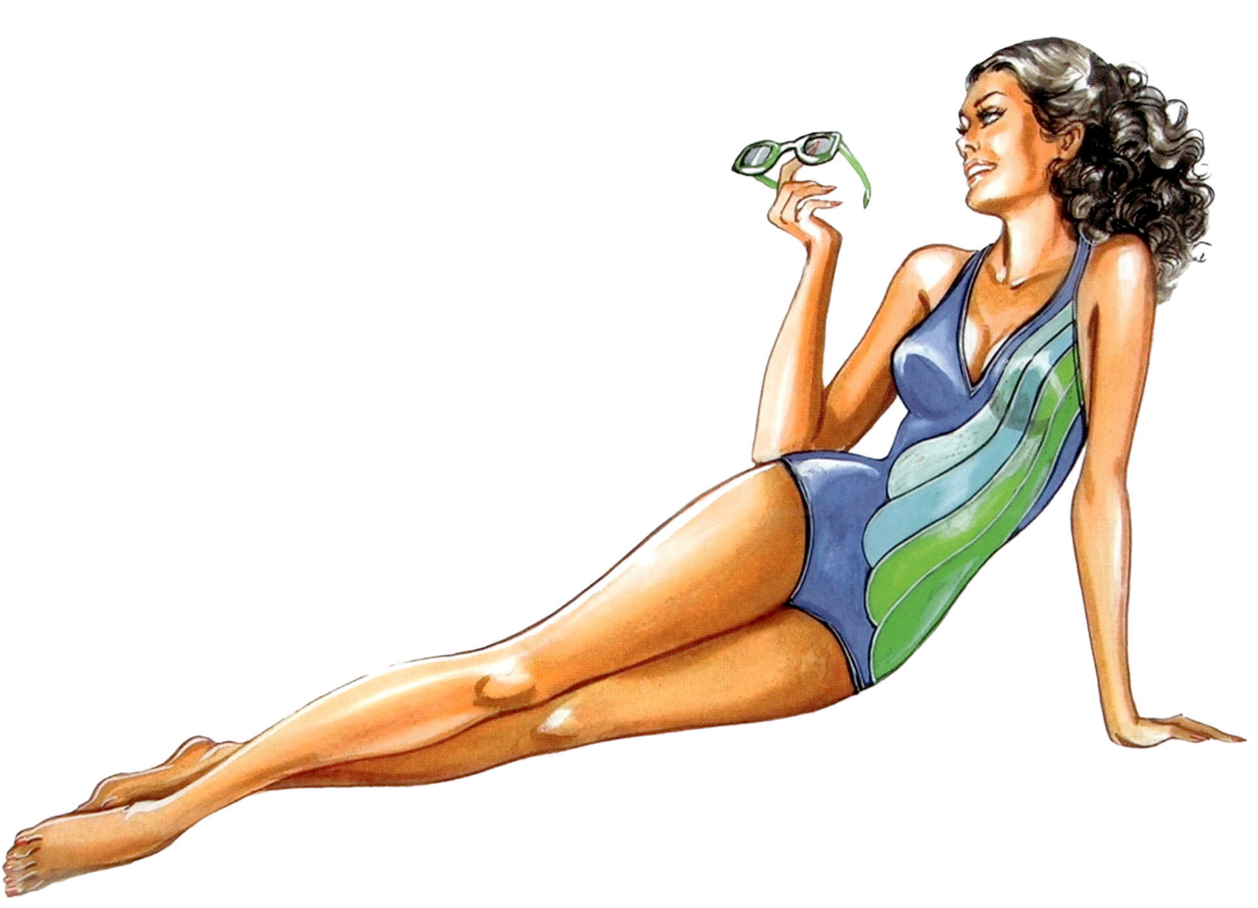

YVONNE

This suit is all about bold confidence. With a seductive gaze and effortless allure, she owns the moment in a barely there bikini detailed with shimmering metal ring accents. The textured pattern adds depth while the classic triangle cut keeps things daring and timeless.

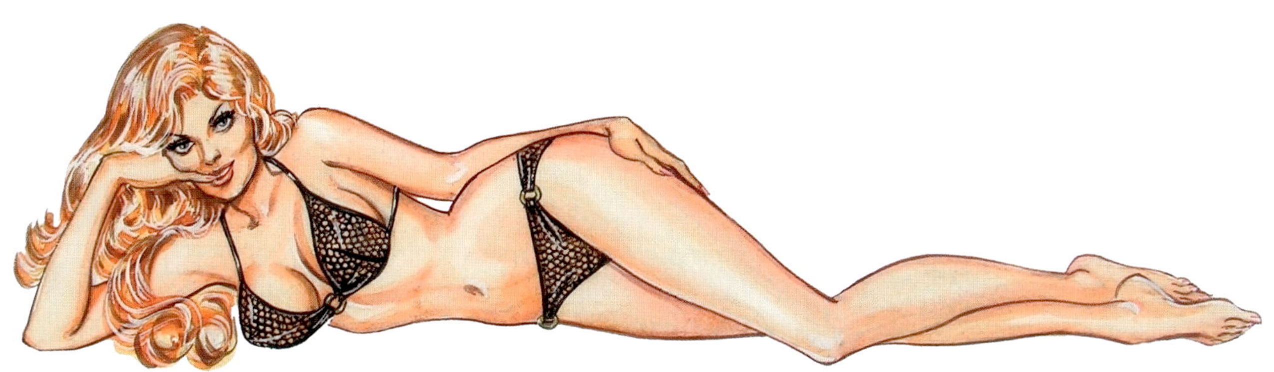

KATELYN

This look is playful perfection with a timeless twist. The retro bikini features a sweet polka-dot trim and a bold central ring detail, adding just the right amount of charm. Her flirty pose and vibrant confidence give this classic style a fun and fresh attitude.

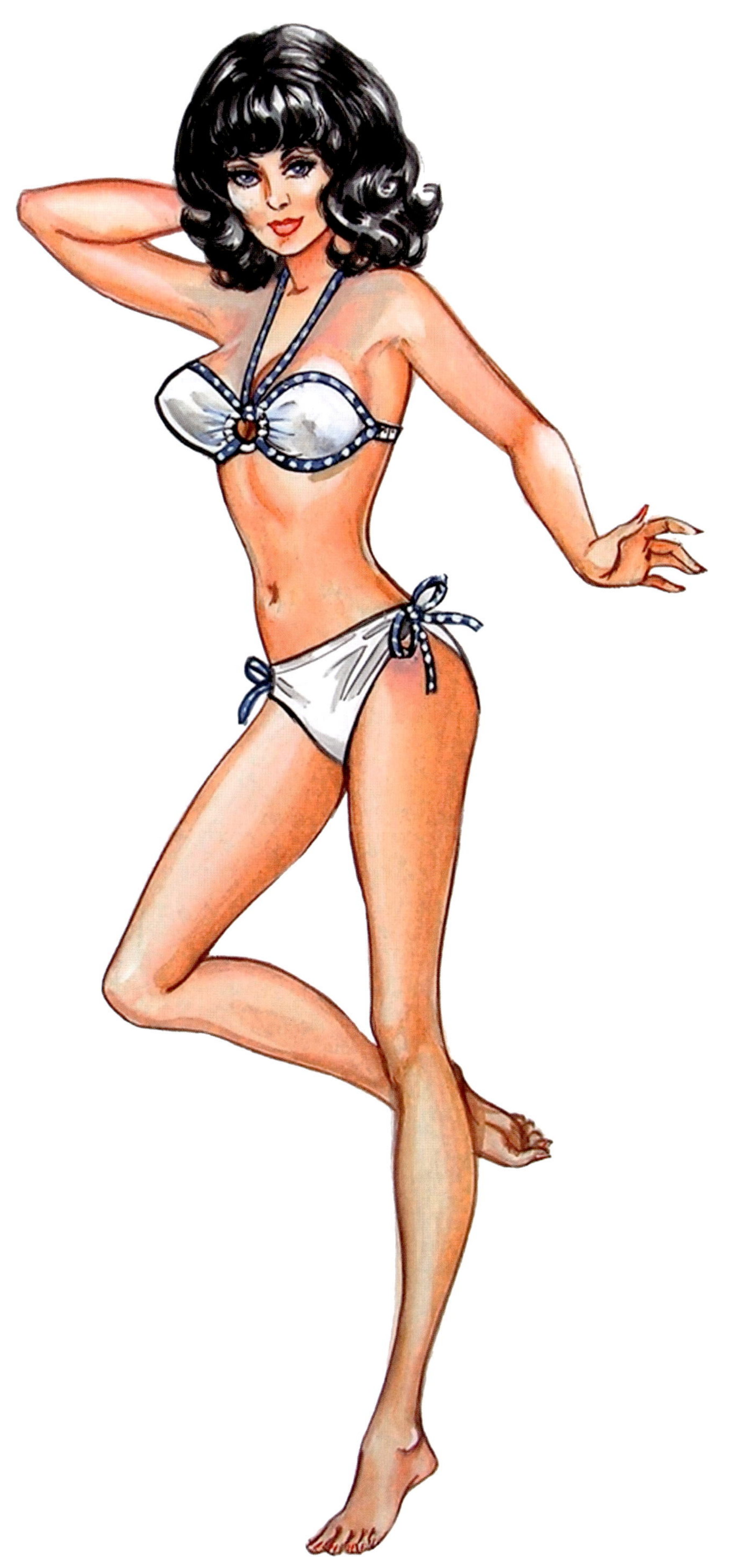

RACHEL

This swimsuit features a bold red-and-white-stripe pattern that's both playful and timeless. The knotted front and sweetheart neckline give it a flirty, feminine touch, while her pose and cascading waves bring out that classic mid-century pin-up appeal.

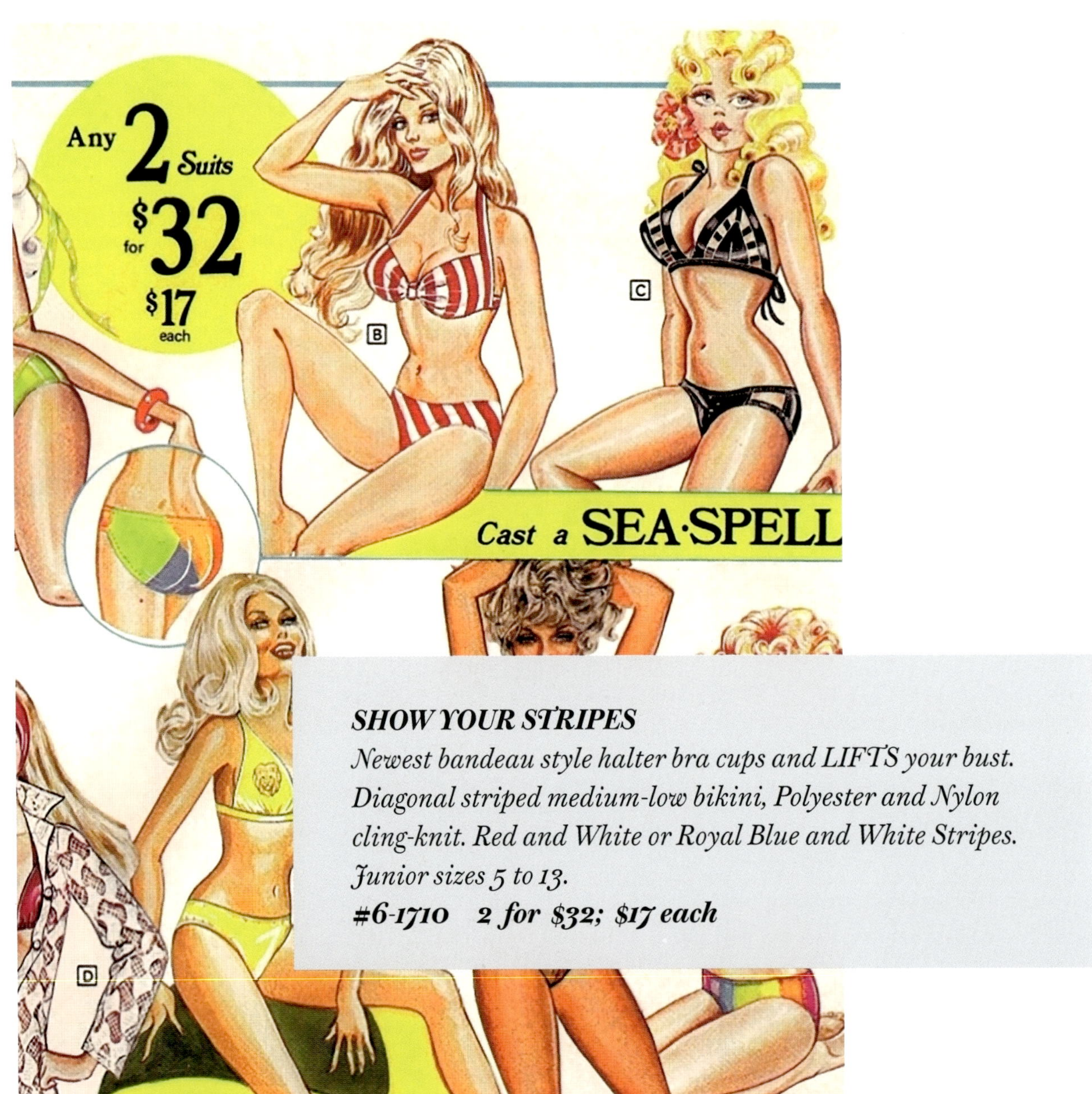

SHOW YOUR STRIPES
Newest bandeau style halter bra cups and LIFTS your bust. Diagonal striped medium-low bikini, Polyester and Nylon cling-knit. Red and White or Royal Blue and White Stripes. Junior sizes 5 to 13.
#6-1710 2 for $32; $17 each

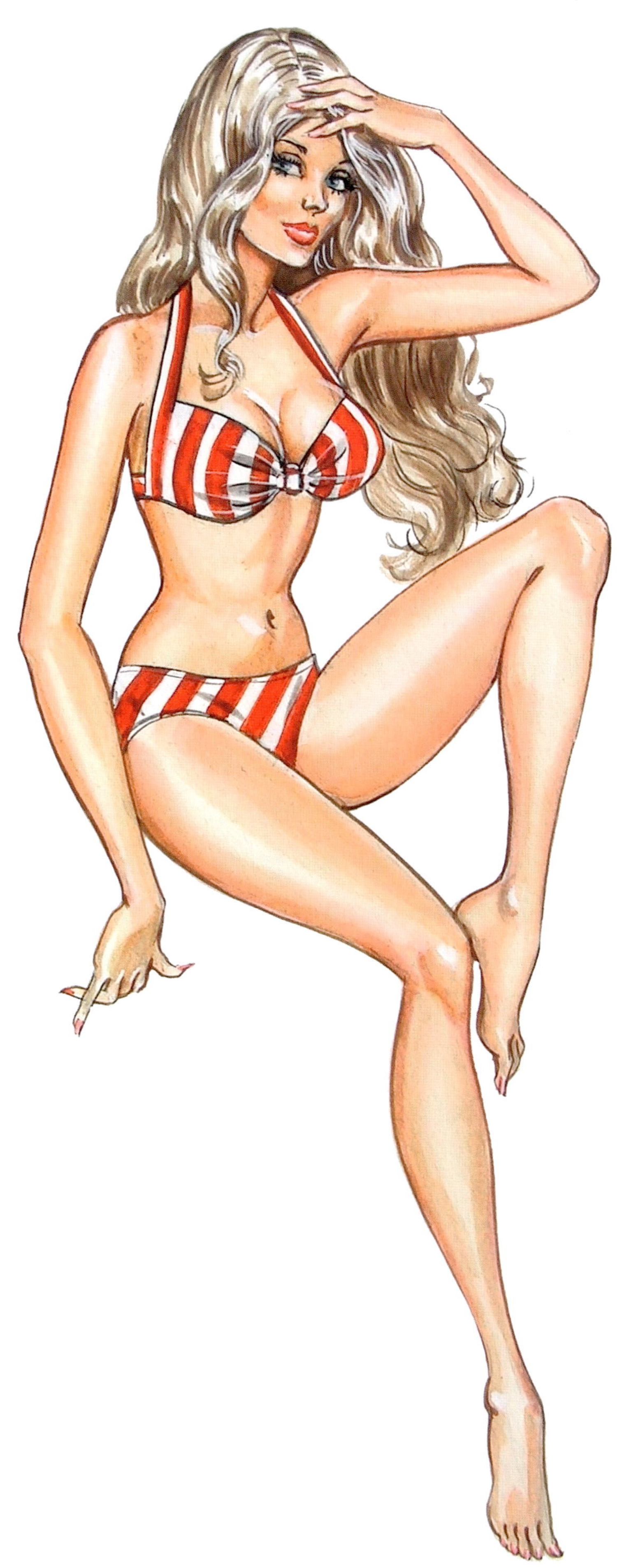

JOSIE

Can you say wow?! This look is a vibrant celebration of color. The bright rainbow palette makes her stand out in the boldest way. Her voluminous curls and big smile give off pure retro fun—she is playful, punchy, and made to be noticed.

RAINBOW RHUMBA
Bitsy bikini vertically striped with all the colors of the RAINBOW. Halter top ties with a large BOW between the breasts. Petite pull-on pants. Silky sleek Nylon in Junior sizes 7 to 13.
#6-1756 2 for $32; $17 each

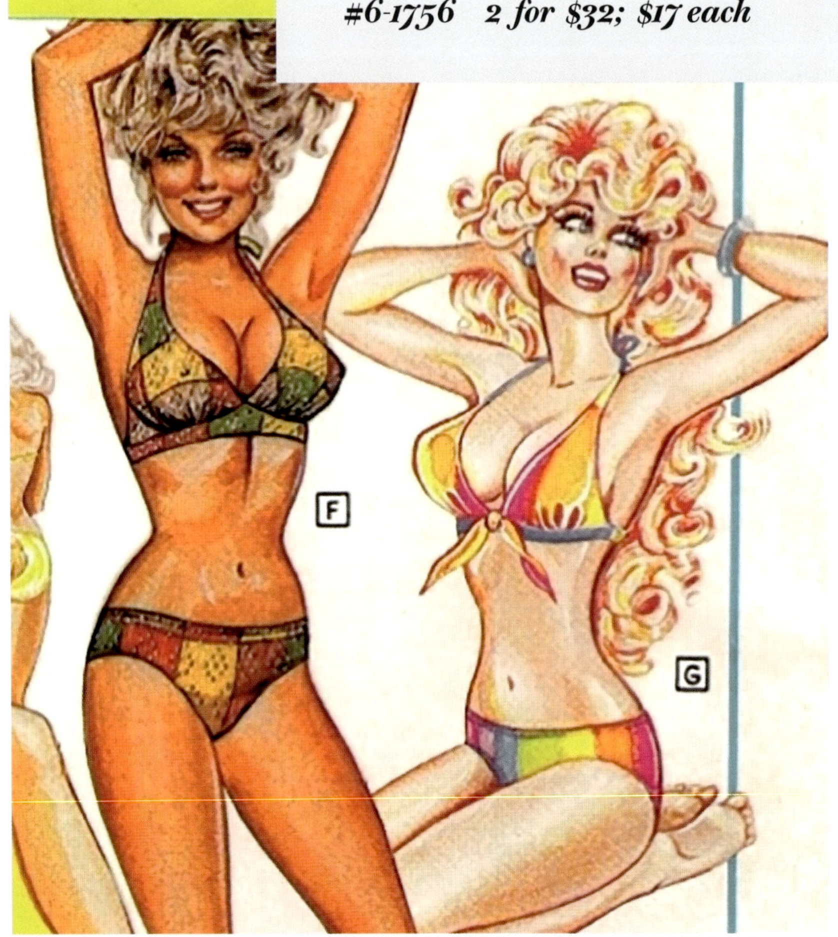

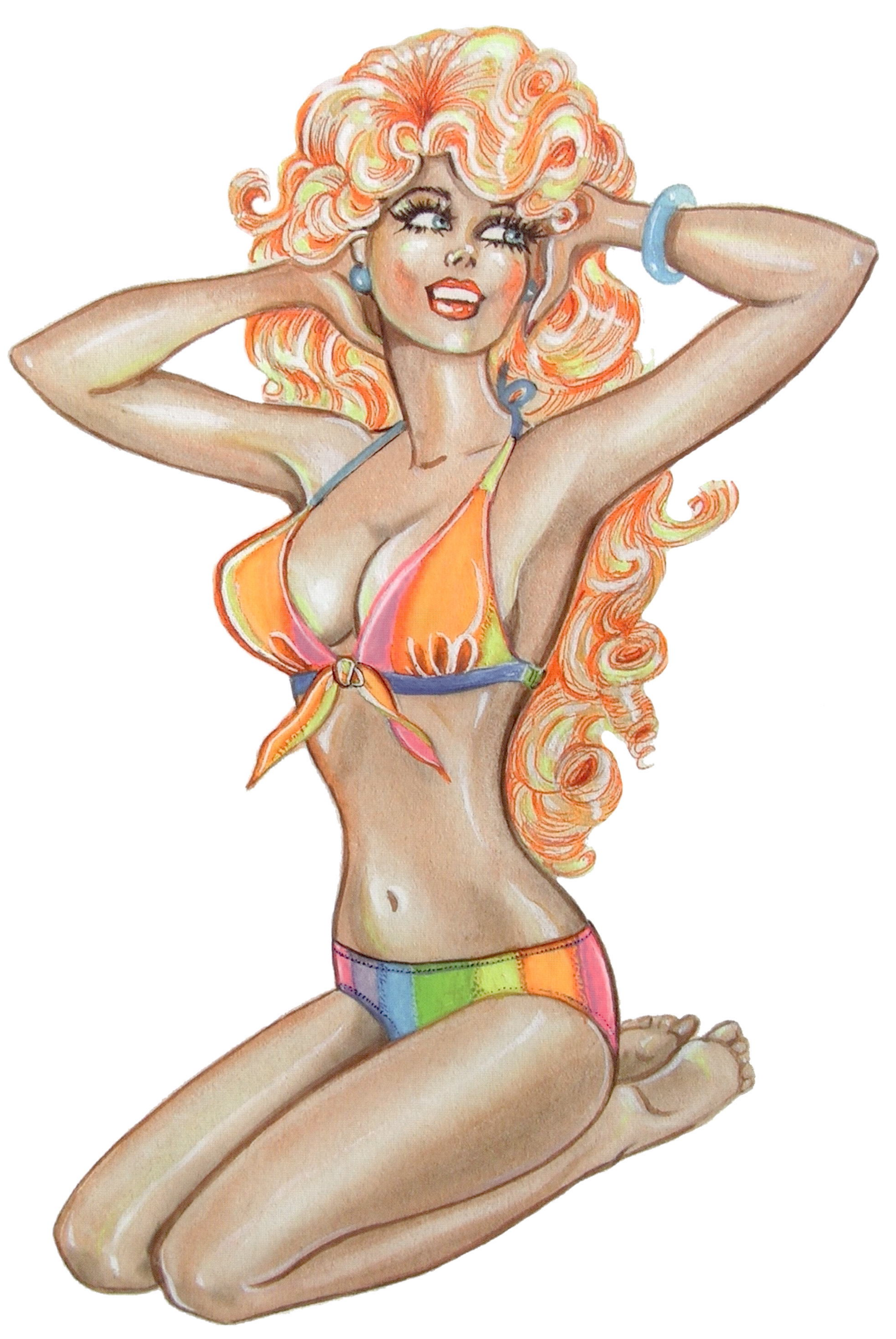

MARIANNE

This model captures that sweet, classic "girl next door" charm effortlessly. The playful polka-dot print, scalloped trim, and modest high-rise bottoms give the set a retro feel that's both nostalgic and fun. Paired with her soft, demure pose and voluminous hair, the whole look whispers vintage innocence–with just a touch of flirt.

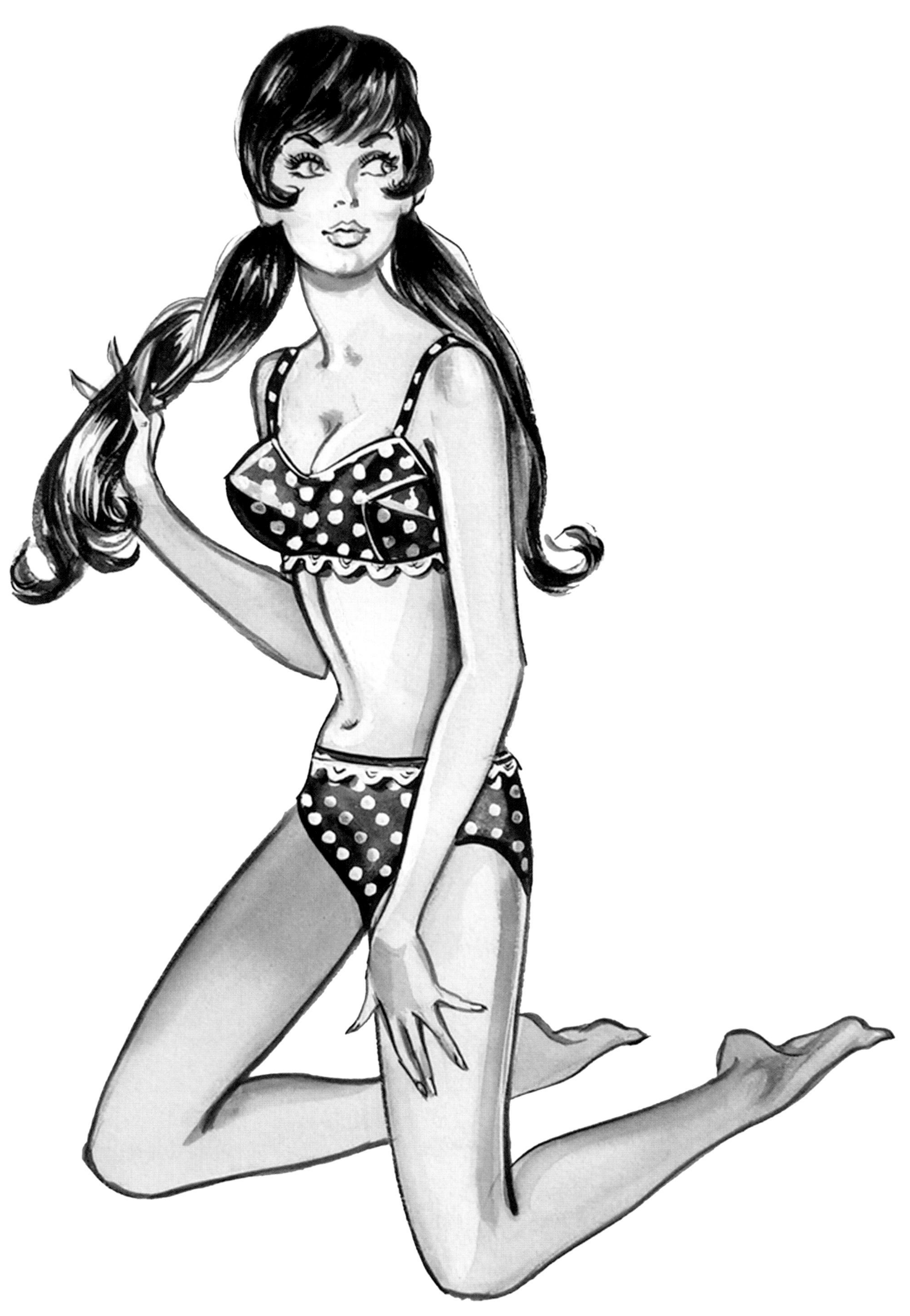

COURTNEY

This look is effortlessly sleek with a dash of drama. The high-neck halter top and bold keyhole cutout add structure and a touch of daring, while the minimal silhouette keeps it refined. Her confident stance and voluminous curls elevate the whole vibe—sophisticated, statuesque, and totally striking.

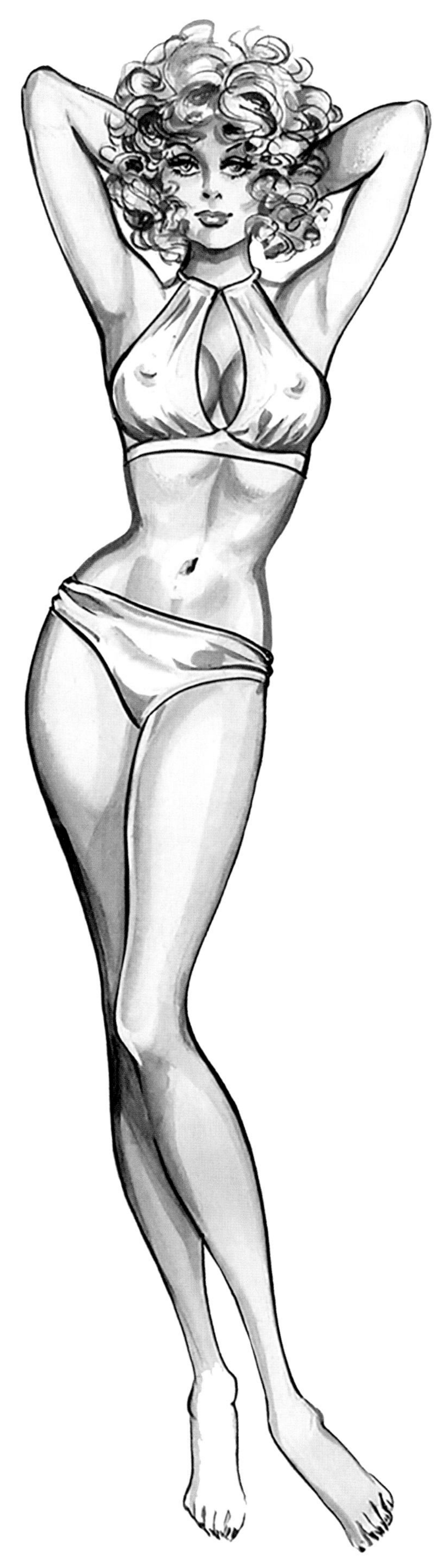

TIFFANY

This bold blue bikini is both simple and striking–a classic color that really pops. With the subtle knot detail on the top and her relaxed, confident pose, this look is all about timeless beauty with a playful edge.

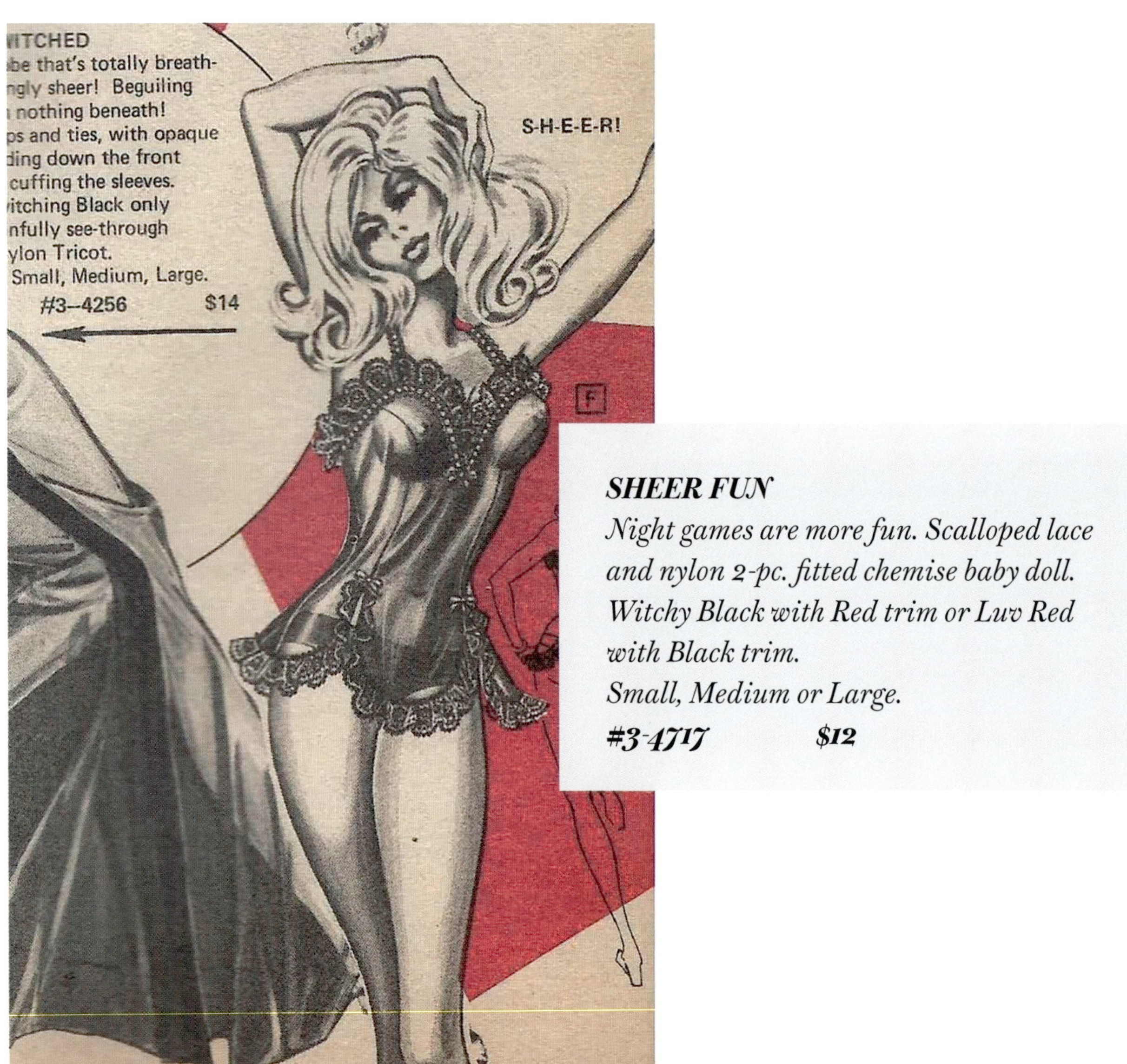

Shown here is a variation of "Tiffany" wearing a revealing baby-doll set.

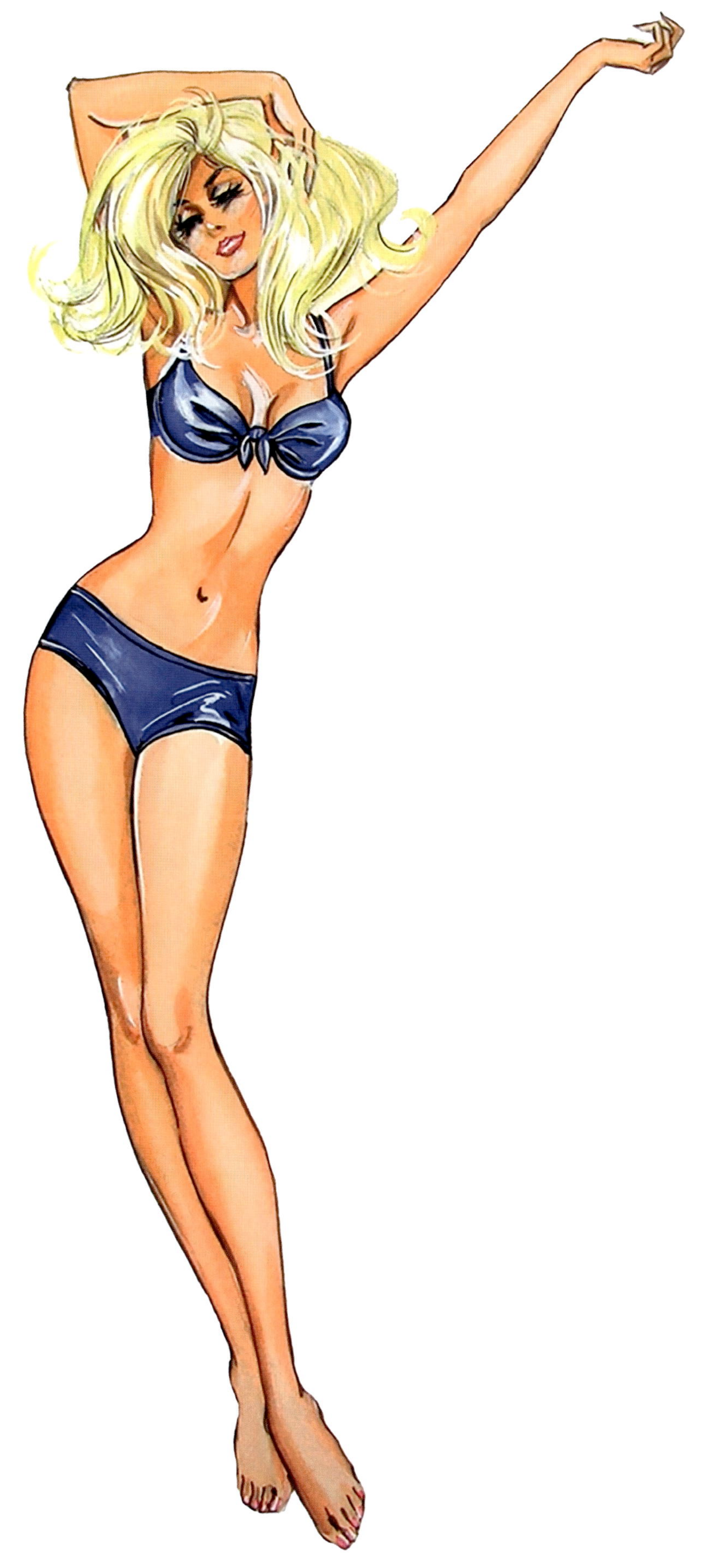

LESLIE

A bold and daring swimsuit design, with sleek black fabric and strategically placed cutouts that create a dramatic silhouette. The top features a plunging neckline, with wide straps that meet at the shoulders and connect to silver ring accents. Thin straps crisscross the midriff, linking to the bottoms with matching metal rings, giving the whole look a structured, strappy edge.

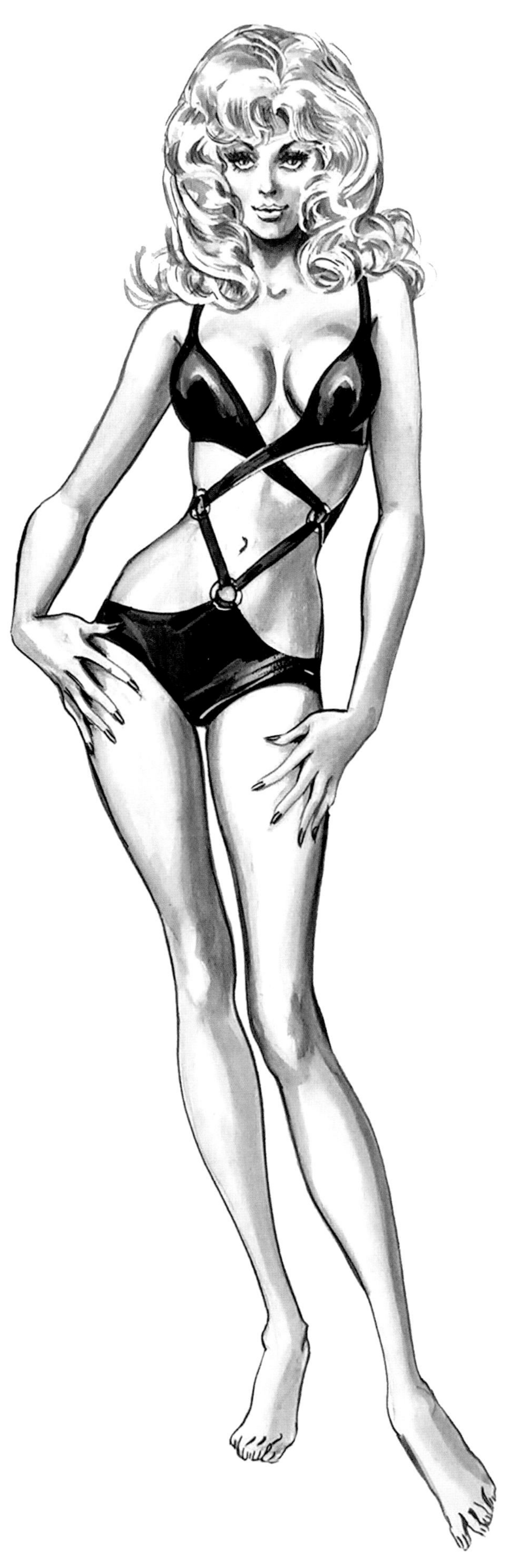

DAVID

We didn't forget about the gentlemen! In the 1970s, Frederick's of Hollywood expanded its catalog to include menswear, bringing the same flair and boldness to men's fashion that defined the brand's women's collections.

This illustration is a striking example of that era's adventurous style. The outfit features a sharply tailored two-piece set in a dramatic black-and-white color-block design. The top boasts an asymmetrical front closure, oversized collar, and wide lapels—classic hallmarks of 1970s fashion.

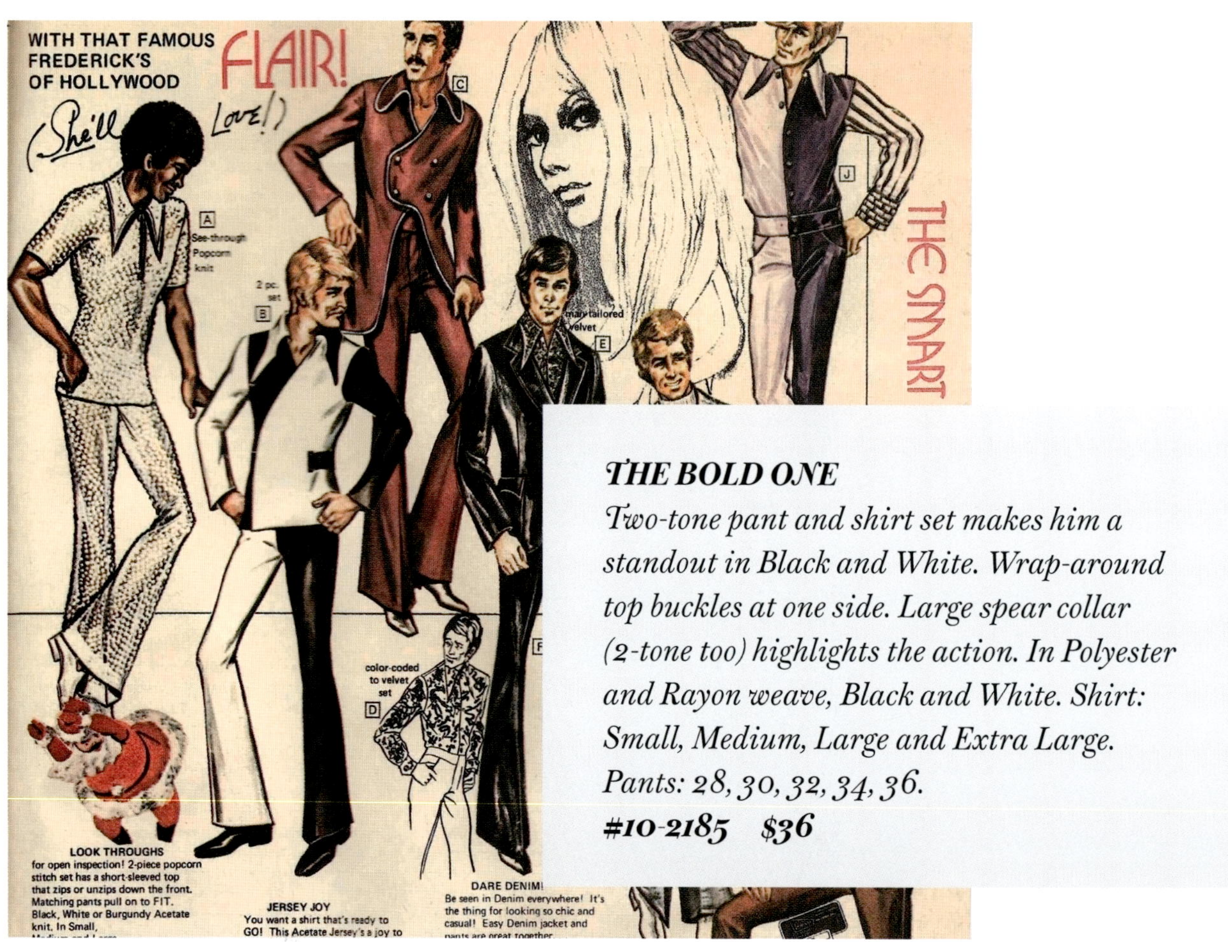

THE BOLD ONE
Two-tone pant and shirt set makes him a standout in Black and White. Wrap-around top buckles at one side. Large spear collar (2-tone too) highlights the action. In Polyester and Rayon weave, Black and White. Shirt: Small, Medium, Large and Extra Large. Pants: 28, 30, 32, 34, 36.
#10-2185 $36

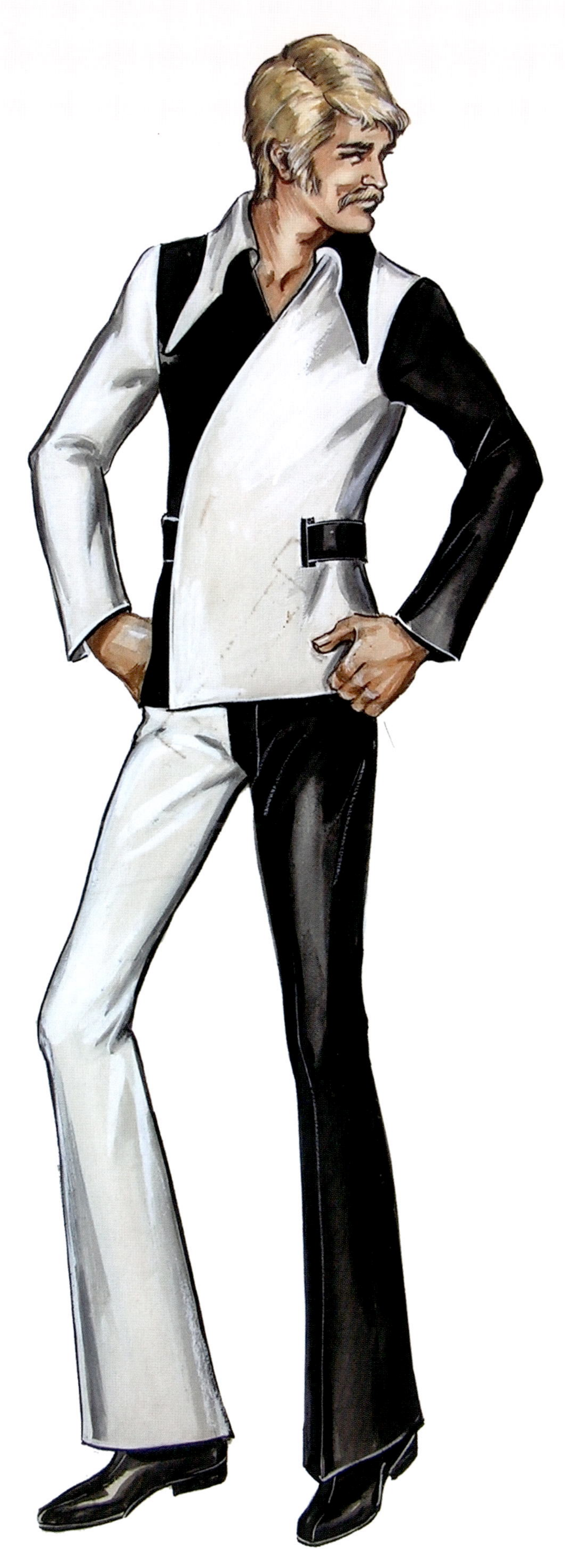

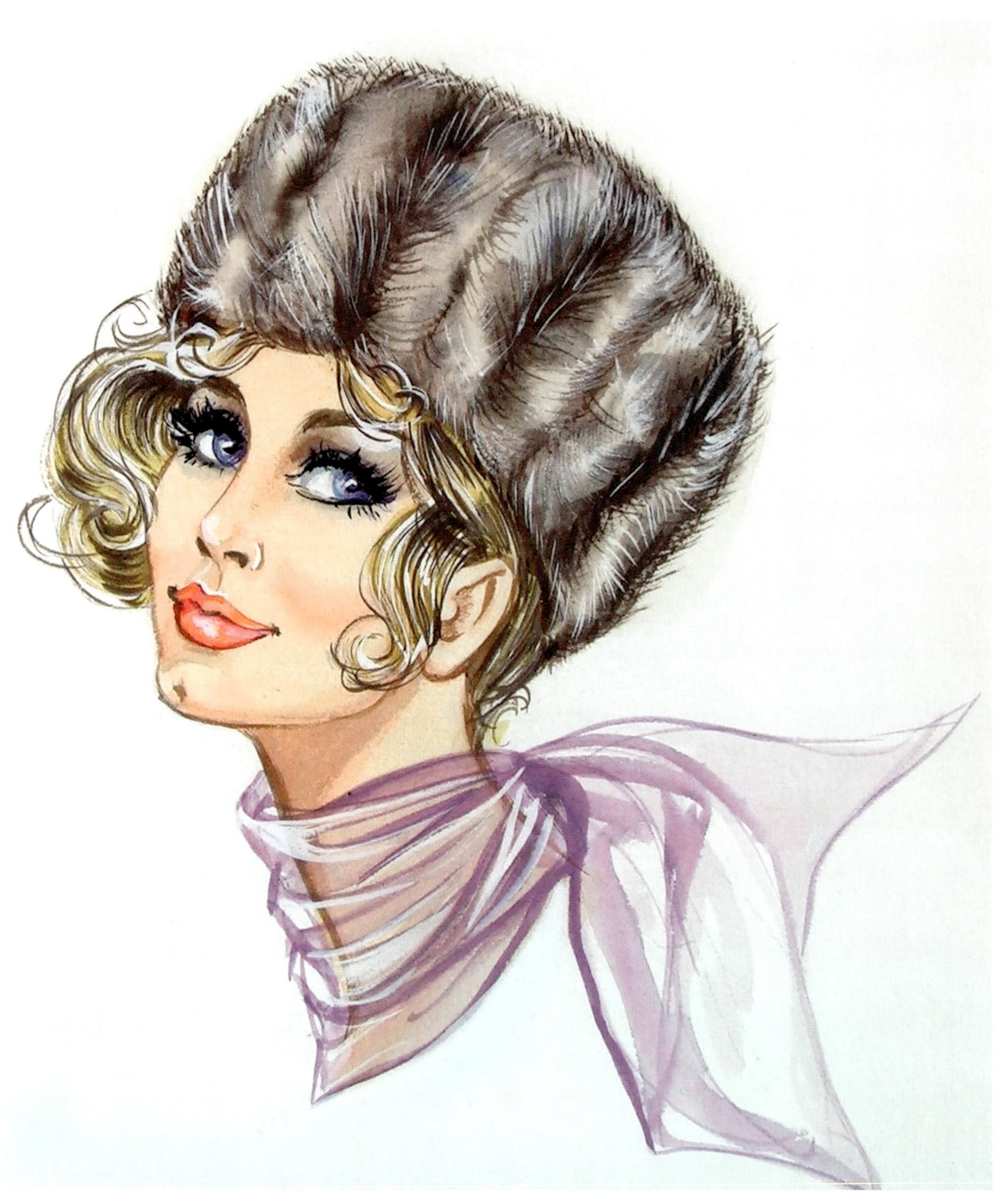

Dorothy's illustrations also included a variety of hats, accessories, and wigs.

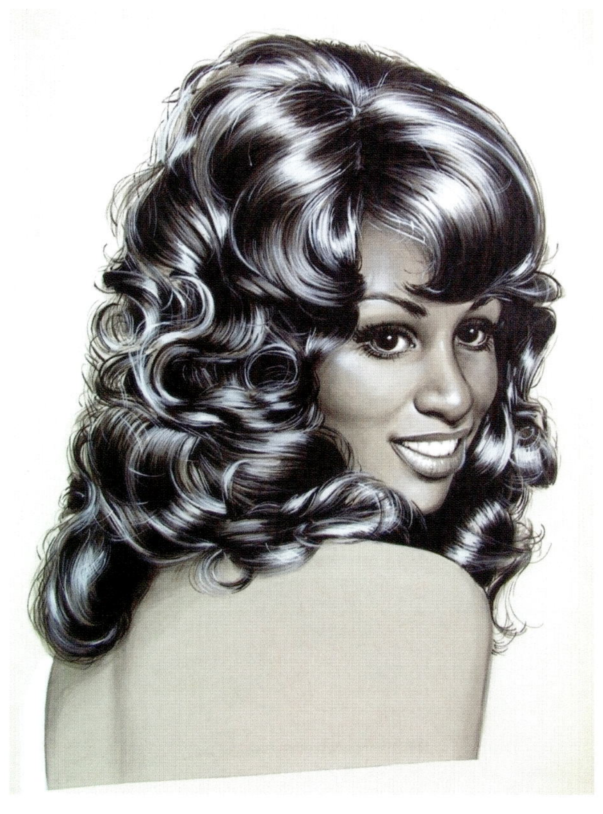

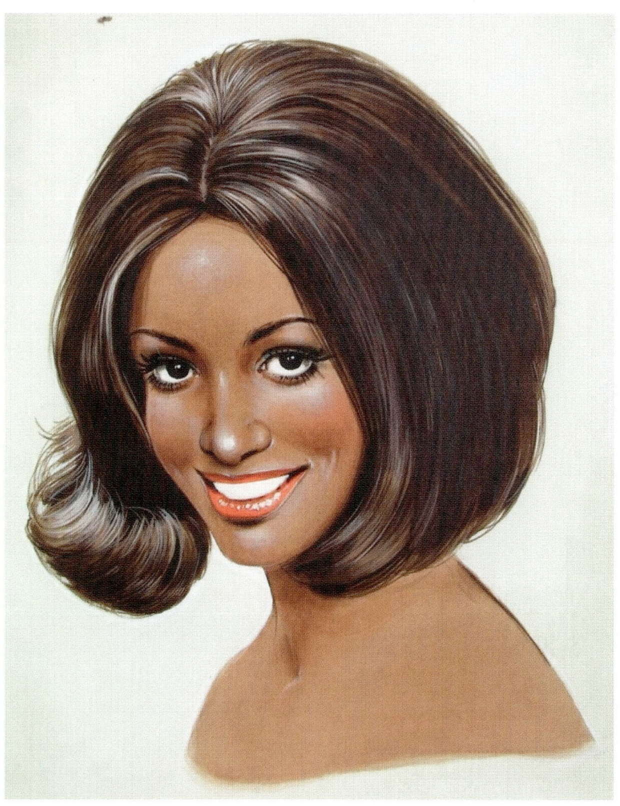

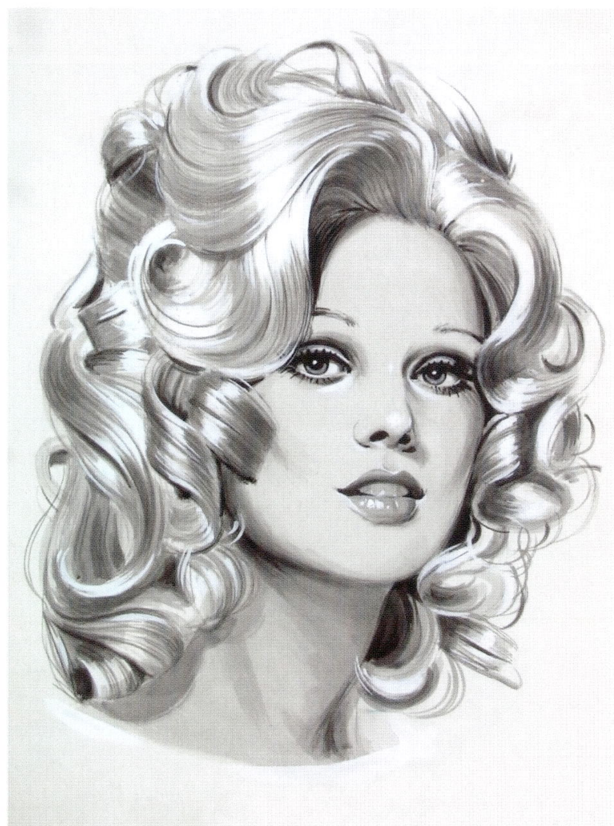

About the Author

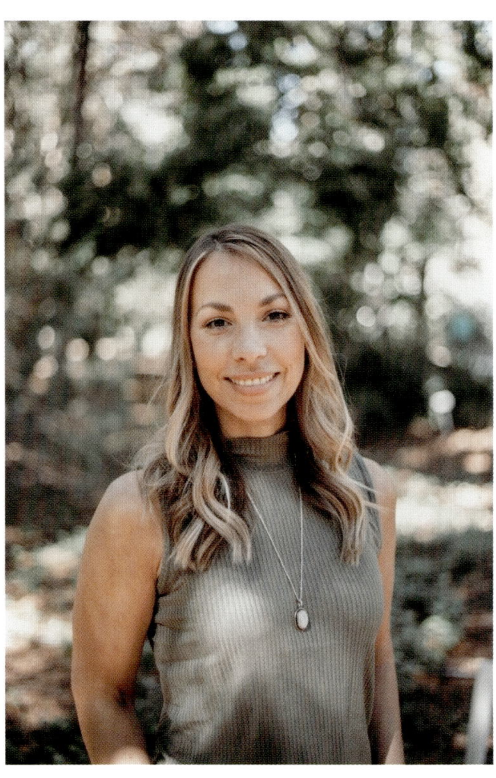

BARBARA WILSON, granddaughter and archivist of Dorothy Kahn, brings a unique personal and professional perspective to *Dorothy's Girls.* With nearly twenty years of experience in graphic design, publishing, and marketing, she expertly curated and designed this comprehensive collection of her grandmother's iconic pin-up illustrations. Based in Reno, Nevada, Barbara combines her passion for preserving art history with a clear appreciation of the significance and cultural impact of Dorothy's collection. Her goal is to honor Dorothy's legacy while introducing these timeless images to new audiences of collectors, artists, and enthusiasts worldwide.

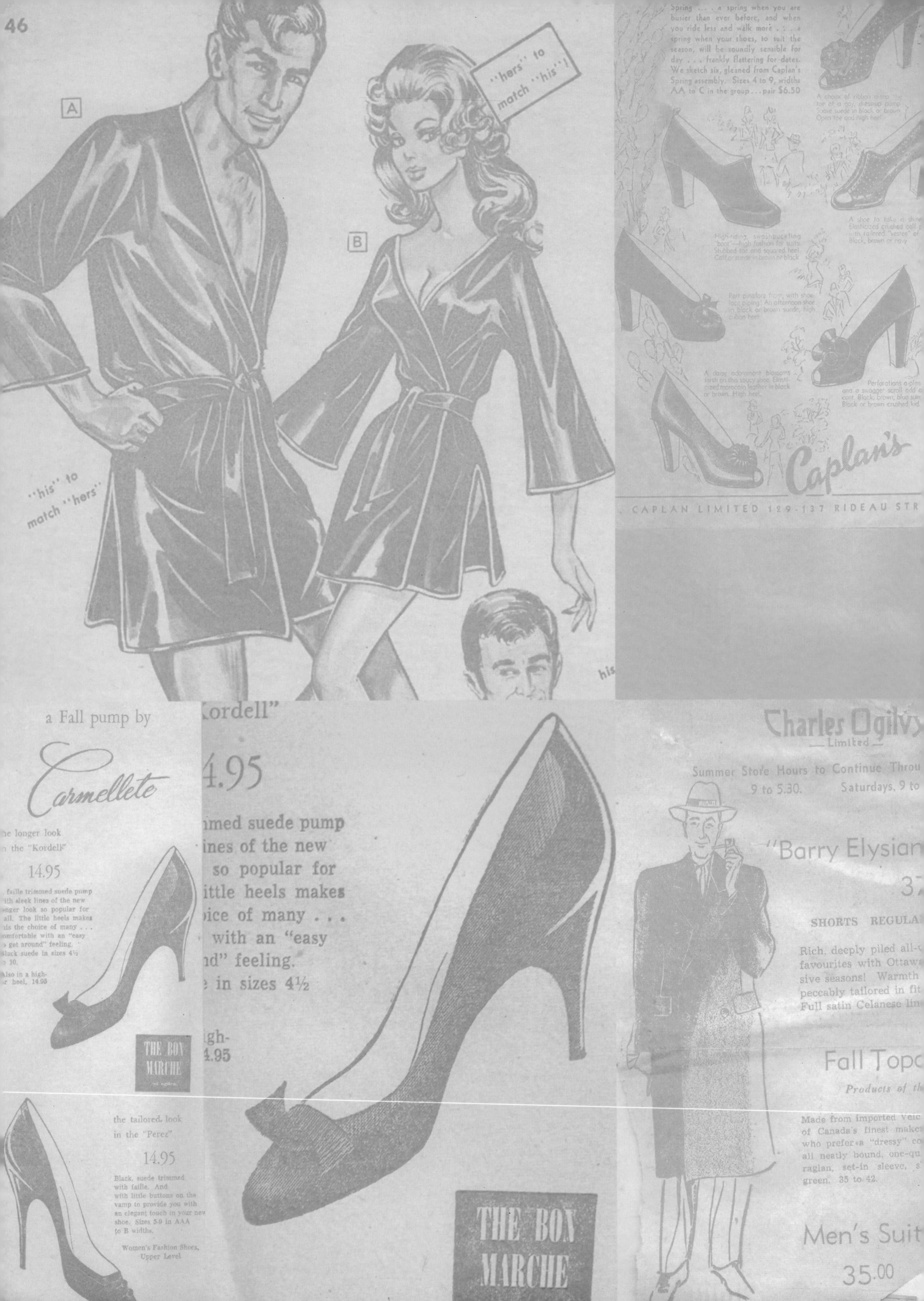
A
"hers" to match "his"!
B
"his" to match "hers"
his
Spring . . . a spring when you are busier than ever before, and when you ride less and walk more . . . a spring when your shoes, to suit the season, will be soundly sensible for day . . . frankly flattering for dates. We sketch six, gleaned from Caplan's Spring assembly. Sizes 4 to 9, widths AA to C in the group . . . pair $6.50
Caplan's
CAPLAN LIMITED 129-137 RIDEAU STR
a Fall pump by
Carmellete
the longer look
in the "Kordell"
14.95
Also in a high-
heel, 14.95
THE BON MARCHE
the tailored look
in the "Perez"
14.95
Black, suede trimmed with faille. And with little buttons on the vamp to provide you with an elegant touch in your new shoe. Sizes 5-9 in AAA to B widths.
Women's Fashion Shoes, Upper Level
Kordell"
4.95
mmed suede pump
ines of the new
so popular for
ittle heels makes
oice of many . . .
with an "easy
nd" feeling.
in sizes 4½
igh-
4.95
THE BON MARCHE
Charles Ogilvy
Limited
Summer Store Hours to Continue Throu
9 to 5.30. Saturdays, 9 to
"Barry Elysian
37
SHORTS REGULA
Rich, deeply piled all-
favourites with Ottaw
sive seasons! Warmth
peccably tailored in fit
Full satin Celanese lin
Fall Topc
Products of th
Made from imported
of Canada's finest make
who prefer a "dressy" co
all neatly bound, one-qu
raglan, set-in sleeve,
green. 35 to 42.
Men's Suit
35.00